Peter Lalor is an award-winning author and journalist. Now a senior writer with *The Australian*, he has contributed articles to *The Weekend Australian Magazine*, *Rolling Stone*, *Black + White Magazine*, *Luxury Travel*, *The Best Australian Sports Writing* and a number of books and international publications. He studied history at the University of Melbourne before moving into journalism in Melbourne in 1985. In his two decades as a journalist he has covered major stories including the Bali bombings, the Hoddle St massacre, the *Tampa* crisis, the Sydney and Athens Olympics and the Australian cricket team's 2004 tour of India. In 2002 his first book, *Blood Stain*, was published by Allen & Unwin. It became an instant bestseller and won the 2003 Ned Kelly Award for Best True Crime Writing and is the subject of a Discovery Channel documentary.

Sue Lalor is a graphic designer who took on the role of picture editor for *The Bridge*. Peter and Sue have two children, Lucy and Harry, and live in Marrickville, Sydney.

The Bridge

*The epic story of an Australian icon
— the Sydney Harbour Bridge*

PETER LALOR

Picture Editor
SUE LALOR

ALLEN&UNWIN

This paperback edition published in 2006
First published in 2005

Allen & Unwin
83 Alexander Street
Crows Nest NSW 2065
Australia
Phone: (61 2) 8425 0100
Fax: (61 2) 9906 2218
Email: info@allenandunwin.com
Web: www.allenandunwin.com

National Library of Australia
Cataloguing-in-Publication entry:

Lalor, Peter, 1963– .
The bridge : the epic story of an Australian icon : the Sydney Harbour Bridge.

1st pbk. ed.
Bibliography.
Includes index.
ISBN 978 1 74175 027 0 (pbk.).

ISBN 1 74175 027 X (pbk.).

1. Sydney Harbour Bridge (Sydney, N.S.W.) – Social aspects.
2. Sydney Harbour Bridge (Sydney, N.S.W.) – Design and construction. 3. Sydney (N.S.W.) – History – 1922–1929. I. Title.

388.132099441

Edited by Karen Ward
Text design by Phil Campbell
Typesetting by Kate Vandestadt
Index by Fay Donlevy
Printed and bound in Australia by Griffin Press

10 9 8 7 6 5 4 3 2 1

This project has been assisted by the Australian Government through the Australia Council, its arts funding and advisory body.

For Richard Raxworthy (1932–2003)

A historian with the foresight to record the stories of the men who built the bridge and the generosity to share his research and knowledge. Richard shared his invaluable primary source material and photographs with the author and was acting as a consultant on the book before his untimely death.

'You've never heard the bridge talking to itself … before the traffic was on we were doing stress measurements and she was so quiet at midnight there, you'd stand on the deck and you'd hear it muttering to itself … it had to be dead quiet and you could hear her talking.'

Design engineer Gordon Stuckey

CONTENTS

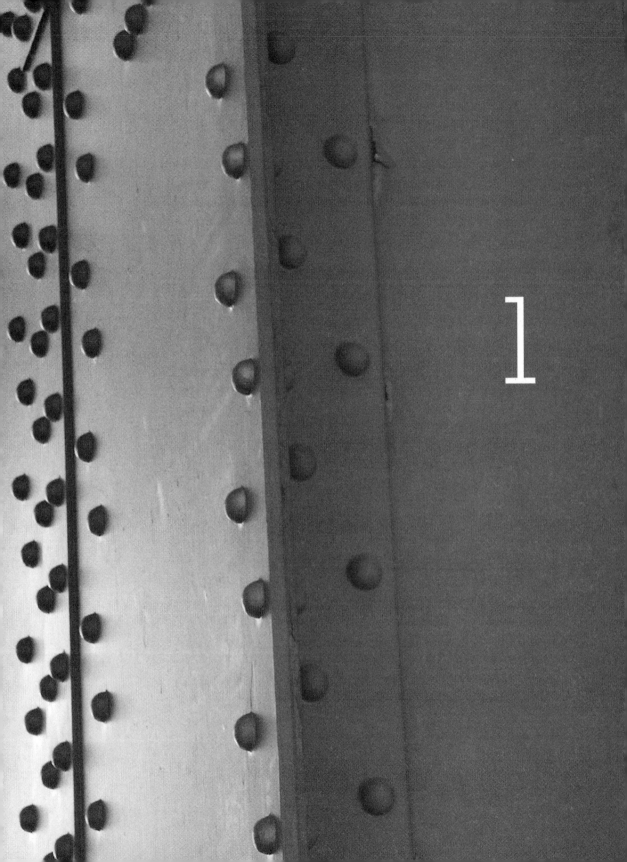

CLOSING THE ARCH

In which an Englishman walks the plank and in doing so becomes the first man to cross the harbour by bridge; below a whale hunt distracts from the closing of the arch and a terrible gale almost causes an unthinkable disaster.

Thursday 7 August 1930

She's almost home. An anxious metre separates her reaching steel arms. The great divide between the city of Sydney and the northern suburbs is about to be breached. They're so close now a riveter working on the north side could lean out, cup his hands against the ever-present wind and light a cigarette for a bloke on the south side, careful, of course, not to drop his matches lest they fall 120-odd metres into the waters below.

There are 28 panels in the sweeping arch of the Sydney Harbour Bridge, and today a barge has made its way from the workshops that stand on the future site of Luna Park and the workers have raised the lower triangle of the fourteenth northern panel. The boilermakers scramble along her length, using their long spanners to fix the nuts and bolt her into place. One short metre away the corresponding member from the fourteenth southern panel side has been waiting for this moment of symmetry.

As the men fire up the rivet furnaces somebody moves toward the gap and places two pieces of timber connecting the half arches. For the first time in history Sydney is, temporarily, united.

A large man in a three-piece suit, hat and round glasses stands on the city side of the arch. His clothing is out of place but it is clear

he is as comfortable up here as any of the tin hares, boilermakers and riggers. He knows them all by name and they call him Mr Ennis. The boss.

Lawrence Ennis, the Scottish-born director of construction for Dorman, Long & Co., the bridge builders, is about to step into history. Walking with confident steps he strides out on the narrow plank and pauses in the middle to take in the views. He is 123 metres above the water, on the bottom chord of the arch. The roadway will be hung later. Ennis takes his time before stepping off the plank onto the northern side where erection superintendent Clarence Hipwell is waiting. Hipwell then becomes the first man to walk in the opposite direction.

Later, Ennis climbs down, adjusts his spectacles, grips his lapels and describes the experience to reporters:

> A slight breeze was blowing from the north-west and the Blue Mountains shimmered in the morning haze. I have never seen

She's Almost Home: The bridge is at its most vulnerable as the two half arches reach over Sydney Harbour. The engineers' hardest task lies ahead. 1930.

anything so beautiful. I could see the smoke of a steamer right out on the horizon, towards New Zealand.

It was a great moment. The thought flashed through my mind 'Thank goodness that is done' then I walked over to congratulate Hipwell my construction superintendent.

On the Job: Public Works engineers Gordon Stuckey (with pipe), Bill Lush and Frank Litchfield oversee the closure with an unidentified worker. August 1930.

Hipwell had guided the two half arches, but has plenty more to do for she is not done. Science and brawn had raised these two 250-metre long, 15,000-tonne half arches to within a friendly gesture: bridging the last centimetres may prove more difficult than any of the work so far.

The two arms are designed to rest against each other and spread their massive weight into the sandstone on either side of the harbour, but at the moment they are held back, straining like a pair of rearing dogs on short leashes. In addition to their own weight each half arch carries two 575-tonne creeper cranes that have inched

THE BRIDGE

their way tentatively along the arch, panel by panel, and now sit either side of the void. The half arches are restrained by thick steel cables which loop from her end posts and deep into the earth on either side of the harbour. Each of the 128 cables carries 110 tonnes of tension and is tuned like a giant violin to ensure each bears the correct load. The total weight on each set of cables is almost 28,000 tonnes. Each of the four pins at the base of the pylons bears almost 18,000 tonnes. The end posts of the bridge are drawn back 90 cm from their final vertical resting place. This is white-knuckle mathematics for the engineers: the stresses are phenomenal and for these next few weeks the structure is more vulnerable and fragile than anybody cares to admit out loud.

The workers on the arch feel the tension. George Evernden works in the three-man riveting squad. It's his job to rivet the thick steel plates together after the riggers have lifted them from the pontoons and the boilermakers have locked them into position with bolts. As a holder-upper he has the worst end of the job, crawling inside the long coffin-shaped chords to fix one end of the rivet while another member of the crew works a pneumatic machine on the outside. Evernden is in his early twenties, and hangs on by his toes, pushing his back against the steel to gain purchase. He cooks in the summer and freezes in the winter and is burnt by the hot scalings no matter what the weather is like. His crew and a handful of others will have forced around six million rivets into the steel by the time the bridge is finished. The rivets alone add over three thousand tonnes to the weight of the bridge and by the time they have reached the fourteenth panel the men are anxious about the strength of the structure, which moves in the wind and shakes when the cranes move. Evernden feels her sway and vibrate. The bosses reassured the anxious worker.

Stan London, who works one of the long spanners to fix the plates before Evernden's crew rivets them, remembers that there has been a lot of talk by men worried the cables will one day spring out of the sandstone, sending the half arches and workers crashing into the harbour.

The engineers have done the calculations that tell them everything should be all right, but they are eager to lock the structures as soon as possible. The plan is to ease the cables out on either side until the bottom chords of the half arch are locked together. Engineers are crunching numbers, working out compression, tension, temperature and strain, working 24-hour shifts in a frenzy of effort and science. Bridging the last 100 cm is the most crucial and complicated part of the job. In the following weeks the bridge will change from a cantilever structure to a three-hinged arch (when the bottom chords meet) and finally a two-hinged arch. Each stage shifts the stresses on different parts of the arch and requires a bookful of complex mathematical equations. Nothing can be left to chance.

There are other strains too. The day Ennis and Hipwell walk the plank the English are enjoying the moment on their own. The Australians have faded into the background. The father of the bridge, Dr John Job Crew Bradfield, is nowhere to be seen. A quarrel has broken out between Bradfield — the local chief engineer — and the precociously talented Englishman Ralph Freeman, consulting engineer for Dorman, Long & Co., the English company contracted to construct the bridge. Newspapers and drawing rooms are thick with the battle.

Freeman has made a bold bid to be recognised as the bridge's sole and original designer and is backed by the *Sydney Morning Herald* in his proclamations. Bradfield, who has nurtured the work for the past three decades, is seething with indignation. The two sides have exchanged bitter words that have pitted the English company, which naturally backs Freeman, against its Australian employees. Ennis, as Dorman, Long's most senior representative in Sydney, has tried to keep out of it, with little success.

On the same day that the English clamber over the bridge's incomplete arch, the Director of Public Works intervenes.

'My view is that Dr Bradfield is the designer of the harbour bridge,' Mr Mitchell tells the *Sun*. 'My opinion is that Mr Freeman's claim will not stand against Dr Bradfield's. I don't want to enter into any controversy but when the time is ripe we will throw our cards on the table.'

THE BRIDGE

The English seethe quietly and enjoy the anticipation of triumph above the harbour alone.

Or do they? Bradfield, in his report to the Public Works Department at the end of the next financial year, gives a different version of events.

> On 7th August, 1930, the bottom chord of the fourteenth panel of the northern half-arch was erected and a short plank gave access across the harbour for the first time. Mr Holt, of this branch, was the first person to cross from shore to shore; Mr Ennis, Director of Construction for the Contractors, was the first person to walk across the gap at the centre of the arch.

Holt, one of the Australian supervising engineers, is never mentioned by Ennis in his version of events, but has apparently staked his claim for a historical first by making a longer crossing.

Sydney has watched its two half arches rise up above the roofs, eclipsing every other man-made object in sight. The city has never known such a momentous project and everybody shares in the excitement. Those who grew up with a metropolis perched on either side of the glistening, broad harbour must have strained their imaginations to picture the enormous arch. Even with the evidence before their eyes some strain to believe it.

The last inches of construction have the city holding its breath. For four years now ferry commuters have gazed up and wondered what it will be like to commute from one side to the other high above the water. They have marked her progress as she crawled up from the foreshores of Milsons and Dawes Point and then leaped out in a great arc above the water. Her construction has been recorded in endless newspaper photographs and articles. The bridge can be seen from many distant suburbs. The children at Ferncourt Primary School in Marrickville have a good a view from their inner suburban playground 7 km from the harbour. International visitors pulling into the harbour on ocean liners have looked up in wonder at the steel arch reaching for a point in space and wondered at the marvels of engineering and science. Is there nothing man cannot achieve?

All eyes are on that patch of blue sky but five days after Ennis's walk, on Tuesday 12 August, the crowds around the harbour are distracted by another sight.

Today there's a show in town, a commotion on the water that's more fun than bringing home the world's greatest arch bridge.

Like every day on the harbour, the water is choppy with peak-hour traffic as ferries, tugs, punts, cargo ships and fishermen jostle for clear passage on the crowded waves. And now, to add to the traffic, a 14-metre humpback whale has diverted from its annual migration, turning through the Heads into Sydney Harbour and announcing itself with a noisy spout of water and a great slap of its tail.

Word spreads around town and soon the shores at Kirribilli, Milsons Point, Blues Point and on the city side are crowded with onlookers who enjoy the spectacle of the humpback whale in the water and the closing humpback arch above it. Newspapers dispatch photographers and reporters to record the occasion.

Few whales make their way into the harbour these days and this one is about to find out why.

The Messenger brothers of Double Bay are fishermen and they figure there is no difference between landing a whale or some lesser sea creature and if this humpback is cheeky enough to come and play off Kirribilli Point then it is fair game. Late in the morning it surfaces in front of the bow of the Messengers' boat, which is cruising near the bridge. Charlie Messenger is ready. Rising to his full height, he raises his arm and launches a harpoon in its direction. It glances off the creature's skin and falls pathetically into the harbour. From 100 metres above, a wry cheer comes up from the workers who have been distracted from their work and have been directing the hunters toward the unfortunate whale.

Down in the water the whale senses that the Messengers' missile is a declaration of war and thrashes its tail at the small boat, smashing a window and parts of the hull. The would-be hunters hang on for dear life and wonder if this was such a good idea after all.

The brothers' distress has not discouraged others from pursuit and the whale is now leading a fleet of launches on a merry chase around the harbour, enthralling ferry passengers and the crowds on the shore. A photographer and reporter from the *Sydney Morning Herald* have hired a 'frail craft' to join the chase and almost find themselves the lead item in their own story when the whale rises beneath their boat, lifting it out of the water but causing only minor damage and no injuries.

Two other launches have joined in the hunt and a man on one lets off a rifle shot which again rouses a cheer from the bloodthirsty crowd in the stalls but little reaction from the great animal. Sensing an audience, the humpback swims beneath the bridge — the workers lean over the small gap between the arms and the mammal surfaces — and salutes the structure by spouting water up into the late winter air. Maybe it approves of the work above. Later, when the *Sun* photographer develops his pictures in a tank back at the office, he will notice that the animal's path out of the water describes a line similar to the bridge's arch.

Cliff Anning has been working on the north side of the arch. Like George Evernden, he is a holder-upper climbing inside the chords of the bridge and holding up one end of the hot rivets while the riveter fixes them from the outside. This morning he has come outside to watch the commotion. Half a century passes before somebody asks him what it looked like from up there.

I remember one day, a beautiful summer day, very clear and you could see under the water quite well. All of a sudden we saw a big form, it must have been twenty foot or thirty foot long I am sure, and it was a whale and he had barnacles on him. He couldn't get out of the harbour, I believe. I noticed a Stannards launch which used to take the workers over to the ships, they were following him with a photographer. Every time he came up he sort of spouted water, which whales do. Well, they lost him for a while, but we saw him. He came right under their launch and nearly tipped it up. That was the end of taking photos of the whale, they went for their lives.

Public works engineer Henry Peach works in the third-floor office of the Public Works Department with the draughtsmen planning the city's railways, but on this Tuesday he has come out on the bridge and climbed above the arch on the jib of the creeper crane. Later he recalls, 'I … went up just before the arches met. I remember climbing up on to the end of the creeper crane and taking photographs down to the water. It so happened there was a whale underneath there. As I was taking my photo, so the whale swam under the bridge.'

Having been harpooned and shot, the whale now heads off toward Bradleys Head on the harbour's north side with six launches, including the foolhardy Messengers, now in pursuit. Suddenly it changes course for Garden Island and then into Rose Bay before heading back toward Taronga Park Zoo where it utters 'a noise combining the elements of a grunt and a groan' according to one newspaper report.

On the shores the people delight at the hilarious, sometimes frightening, scenes. What a day it is. And the weather so perfect that you can feel the cloak of winter falling away and the first whispers of summer. A large high pressure system is settled over New South Wales but a cold front is moving across the Great Australian Bight and toward Sydney.

The clashing weather patterns create chaos in the heavens. Cold and hot air collide, creating a violent storm that produces rain, hail and even snow. It could not come at a worse time for the bridge. She has never been more vulnerable, there has never been more weight straining on each arm. When that last metre is bridged she will be strong enough to weather anything time or tempest can produce, but right now she is hanging on by her fingernails.

By Tuesday evening the whale has found shelter in a small bay and its hunters have gone home to tell tales of the one that got away. The temperature has begun to drop dramatically across the state. Down on the Victorian border a blizzard hits Mount Kosciuszko, dumping a thick blanket of snow on the surrounding countryside. Just after dark a terrific electrical storm hits Wagga Wagga to the south of Sydney, enormous hailstones beat down and the gutters flood with rain. Rivers, already swollen with water from snow melt, threaten to overflow their banks. Out in the west of the state, around Wilcannia, dust storms shroud the farmlands, adding grit to the evening meals. Immediately to the west of Sydney, the Blue Mountains which Ennis had viewed so clearly a week before are also covered with snow. In the swirling skies, the *Southern Cloud*, a mail plane, catches a hair-raising ride on the wind. Flying blind for most of the journey, because of snow gathered on its windscreen over Kosciuszko, the plane makes the trip from Melbourne to Sydney in a record three hours and three minutes.

By the time the front reaches Sydney it is loaded with frigid venom. At 9.05 pm the wind speed reaches 38 km/h, five minutes later it is gusting at 57 km/h and by 9.15 it is 110 km/h, already stronger than the Easter cyclone of 1927. The wind starts to hit 130 km/h at the headlands and even the boats moored in Watsons Bay, sheltered by the bulk of South Head, are lashed with large waves. One vessel breaks its moorings and is battered against the jetty. Large whitecaps play havoc with shipping on the harbour and fishermen at sea scurry back hoping for shelter. At Yarra Bay, near Botany Bay, a sand dredge begins to fill with water, then, caught by the wind, is lifted off the waves, capsizes and sinks, forcing its solo crewman, a Captain Summers, to swim for safety. Two wet fishermen are rescued from the stricken launch *My Elsie* off North Head.

In Bridge Street, Glebe, a brick wall falls and shatters across the street. Telegraph and telephone wires connecting Sydney and Melbourne are blown over; all communication with Wagga, Temora, Narrandera and everywhere south of Yass goes dead.

And nothing is more exposed than the incomplete arch of the Sydney Harbour Bridge.

As the temperature drops the steel members of the bridge and the cables holding her contract, and the half arches fall back, expanding the void Ennis had walked across. But it is the wind bang-

ing against the steel arms that really tests the structure.

The unsecured half arches begin to sway, the steel groans and the cables set up a terrifying noise. Almost 40,000 tonnes of steel complaining, pulling and grating against the sandstone bedrock of the city.

The wind blows through the door of a coke furnace the workers on the arch use to cook rivets, and the fire rouses itself. A swinging rope catches a flying ember and begins to burn like a wick. A nightwatchman notices the burning and worries that it might set fire to the wooden planks on the staging built around the arms. Foreman rigger Jack Harris answers the phone in his home at Salisbury Road, Willoughby, runs out to his car and is at the bridge in minutes.

Harris is dubbed the 'human fly' or Taffy; a little fellow, he is known to climb all over the bridge, squeezing himself into impossible corners. He has been brought out to Australia by Dorman, Long

The Right Pitch: The strains on the bridge's supporting cables were checked by engineers who measured the vibrations during construction and the delicate joining process. 1930.

because there are only a small number of men on Earth who can do the sort of work he does.

The rope is burning brightly and banging in the wind against the wooden planks as Harris begins the long, slow climb onto the swaying arm. The arch is wet, steep and slippery and the rigger takes his time, getting grip from the small round rivet heads. He crouches against the wind and climbs out to the centre of the bridge, leans out and grabs the rope, cutting it so that the burning end falls harmlessly into the choppy water, then puts out the fire in the rivet oven before returning carefully to the other side.

These are anxious moments for the men in suits with their slide rules and mathematical calculations, but it is not the fire they are worried about. The bridge is a house of cards with all the pieces in place but one. Ennis in his home hears the storm and comes to see what is happening. He recalls later, 'it was an impressive sight to stand on the forward end of one 825-ft arm and see the swaying end

So Close: The bottom chord of the arch, or Joint O, was closed, but sprung open again when the steel cooled overnight. August 1930.

of the other arm. Indicators, however, registered that the total movement between the two arms was barely 3 inches.'

The drama over, the engineers and workers return the next morning to continue lowering the two half arches. If the storm shook them a little, the fact that they have work to return to reassures them of the soundness of the structure.

In the past few weeks the engineers and builders have worked harder than at any other moment in the entire project. Easing the arches closed is a job that involves moving hundreds of tonnes of steel millimetres at a time. Enormous hydraulic jacks are used to take the weight off the cables so bolts at the end posts, by the pylons, can be eased out to lengthen the stays. For every 8 cm of extra cable let out from the sandstone banks the gap above the harbour closes by 30 cm. The job has to be done in a systematic and symmetrical order to ensure the steel does not twist and deform the arch. To further complicate matters, changes in temperature expand and contract the steel. The gap can shift from 53 cm during the heat of the day to 1.3 metres when the mercury drops. The heat of the sun on one side of the bridge is enough to make it longer than the shaded side. It's a nightmare for the engineers who constantly monitor the thermometers and strain gauges placed strategically in the half arches.

By the morning of 19 August the half arches are a few centimetres out of line because of the sun on the southern cables. By 11 am the gap dividing the two parts of the structure has closed to 11 cm on the eastern side, which is exposed to the rising sun, and a half centimetre more on the protected western side.

She is almost home.

At 4.15 pm the north and south half arches become one for the first time, but it is only a temporary state. The sun has already started to sink toward the west and the temperature is dropping. A few hours later the great steel arms are again separate, but the workers continue to jack the weight off the cables and ease them out. Sometime after 10 pm the bridge locks together on a central bearing pin 'as perfectly and truly as truth itself', according to Ennis, who is again standing at the top of the arch, but this time with the

Australian Bradfield and his nemesis, Ralph Freeman, who has travelled from England to witness the event. Hipwell, and Ennis's assistant, Alfred Martin, are also in the party high above the harbour.

The arms will not separate again as the temperature is already
as low as it will get overnight. When the sun rises in the morning,
heating the steel, the arms will lift each other up on the bearing pins.

Later, Ennis writes:

> There were only five men up there in the darkness when the
> actual closure took place ... when we realised what had just
> taken place we were so overawed with the mightiness of it all
> that we did not speak — I for one could not — and I think
> each was conscious of the feeling of the other. The silence to
> me was most impressive, and when I could trust myself to
> speak I broke the silence by saying 'Well, boys, that's that, and
> thank god she is home.'

The constructors have prearranged with the public that they will raise
the Union Jack and Australian flags on the jibs of the creeper cranes
when the bridge is joined. The engineers put off the ceremony until
the next morning when the harbour and foreshores are filled with
the very commuters and workers the bridge is being built for.

But Sydney has a hawk's eye for its bridge.

Neil Conran is one of the witnesses to history:

> I never forgot the night they joined the arch together. All the
> boats cockle-doodled and everyone got out of bed and we
> grabbed saucepans and spoons and things and went along the
> corner of our street because you could see the harbour from
> our street and banged ... all this noise because they put the
> arch together ... in the night time, because that was the best
> time to get the steel together.

The public is overjoyed and the engineers overwhelmed with relief.
Later, the erection superintendent, Hipwell, lets the workers know
just how anxious they all had been.

Stan London remembers the day:

I heard him say to another engineer 'We made it.' ... Hipwell often used to come and have a little chat with me. He was a pretty reticent type of bloke, conservative really, and he had every right to be, he was smart ... he said to me, 'That is a relief.' I knew it had something to do with the anchorage, the locking down of this mighty weight that was suspended in the air with 500 tons on each end of it. Commonsense told me because you could feel this movement and I always used to worry ... and not only me but everyone ... we would talk about it in the mess room, that we thought it could be possible for it to pull away from its anchorage. But ... after that testing it was impossible ...

Sydney Harbour's whale is, however, long gone. Having been sighted in Watsons Bay and chased for yet another day by various launches, it left the protected waters and headed out to sea.

2

A BRIDGE TOO FAR

A man drops a stone in a creek and becomes the first bridge builder, the melting ice caps flood an inland valley to create Sydney Harbour and the fine folk of the penal colony establish the geographical order for years to come as they ponder a town divided.

Before the Sydney Harbour Bridge there were two Sydneys. With it there was one, united by a monumental arch that rose above the water and the rooftops and wrote itself into the iconography and romance of the city and entire country. The bridge facilitated the greatest geographical change to the Sydney basin since the rising of the waters shifting the ocean to what would be the city's doorstep. The bridge brought together the 300,000 on the north side with the 600,000 to the south. It gave both access to land and facilities that had been prohibitively distant before, opening up the northern beaches and further afield.

Using a bridge is an instinct; building a bridge is an act of evolutionary progress. Faced with an expanse of water, a gentle stream or a raging river, the most primitive human looked for a way to cross via the shortest, driest route. In the desire to stay dry, early humans stepped from one stone to another, or took advantage of a tree that had created a crossing. The first bridge builders dropped stones in to create a path; if the water was deeper they dragged a tree trunk across the banks. A couple of trees balanced on stone piles was the first act of bridge engineering.

Bridges evolve from their situation. In the jungles of South America and the Himalayan mountains rope bridges were fashioned from vines, at first to swing across a chasm and later to support a path of planks. The Chinese created floating bridges with a walkway constructed across a series of canoes or sampans.

A bridge profoundly shapes the environment and the people's relationship with it. A bridge is a gateway to new land and opportunity, a carriageway for produce and a social link with the peoples of the other side. It is as much a leap of the imagination as a triumph over geographical division. As humankind became more skilled the engineering feats became more complex, employing the design strength of the arch, the simplicity of suspension or the technical skill of the cantilever.

The aesthetics of a well-designed bridge do not only catch the eye, they fire the emotion and the imagination, as the Sydney Harbour, the Golden Gate and scores of others prove.

The Sydney basin 230 million years earlier was a quiet wetland valley, fed by arctic rivers, hundreds of kilometres from the sea with absolutely no hint of the world-famous harbour and no need for a bridge of any significant scale. Even 15,000 years ago it was a land-locked river valley. A trip to the ocean from the Sydney Heads would have involved travelling 30 km east through native forest. In that period, at the valley's lowest point, a small catchment stream we know as the Parramatta River followed an east–west fissure; trickling down from the hills to the west it eroded a channel out toward the sea, etching a path, grain by sandstone grain, year by year.

When the ice caps melted, the Pacific came surging inland, pushing through the Heads and flooding into the valley until it formed what Captain Arthur Phillip described as 'the finest harbour in the world'. Phillip and his naval officers recognised it as a marine parking opportunity, a place 'in which a thousand sail of the line may ride in the most perfect security'. The millions of years of preparatory work done by the river created a harbour that was sheer and deep right up to its shores, and perfect for unloading ships, which could sail almost to the water's edge. Phillip's surgeon, John White, thought the area 'without exception, the finest and most extensive harbour in the Universe, and at the same time the most secure, being safe from all the winds that blow'.

For thousands of years the local Aboriginal people had fished in the harbour and crossed its waters in bark rafts held together by twine. The people to the north and south were content to be separated by the water, which created a convenient buffer, although they had occasional ceremonial contact. Things changed on 26 January 1788 when Phillip and his ragged convoy of eleven ships came up the Australian coast to Botany Bay. Captain Cook had reported fertile lands around the bay but when Phillip arrived the area was barren and dry so he decided to move a little further north. After a week at their first camp they pulled anchor and headed up the rugged coastline. Passing the narrow inlet at Long Bay and the beaches of Coogee and Tamarama, the convoy entered Port Jackson through Sydney Heads, sailing into the protected expanse of water with its apparently endless coves and estuaries.

That day the fleet anchored 8 km inside the harbour and the eleven ships began to unload, dumping 1000 ill-kept humans and

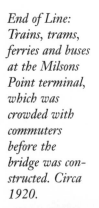

End of Line: Trains, trams, ferries and buses at the Milsons Point terminal, which was crowded with commuters before the bridge was constructed. Circa 1920.

THE BRIDGE

500 mangy animals onto the muddy shores of Sydney Cove. Even as they took in their new surrounds, some must have looked to the northern side of the harbour and wondered what opportunities lay on that shore. For the convicts it would have represented a place of escape, for the soldiers a chance to strip off a uniform and farm, for others just a place to be away from the crowd that flooded the hills of the cove in the coming decades.

Phillip's relocation was a canny real estate move. For the next two centuries Sydney's residents would follow his lead and jostle for a harbour frontage, view or glimpse.

Things changed rapidly in the 150 years before the arch of the bridge was etched on the city's skyline, but some things never changed. Migrants continued to sail through the Heads and disembark around Sydney Cove, almost every one of them captivated by the geographical beauty of the harbour and all but the lucky few settling for an address elsewhere. Over time millions found their way to the areas surrounding the small cove, sorting themselves out along geographical and social fault lines. Eventually a pecking order emerged, with the rich crowding around the water's edge and surrounds, the poor cramped into ever more distant locales. Today it costs millions to live in a waterside apartment little bigger than the rough shacks erected for the governor's men.

Sydney was always a town divided.

The first division was created by the Tank Stream which ran into the harbour at what is now Circular Quay. Its tree-lined waters provided the colony with fresh water but also a geographic line which separated the convicts and soldiers on the west from the Governor and his cronies to the east; to this day the seaside suburbs and eastern region remain the refuge of the town's wealthy and powerful. The stream also created the need for Australia's first constructed bridge — although there is little doubt Aboriginal people would have built simple structures to cross streams and rivers, none had the complexity of even this simple affair. Once settled, Phillip submitted a town plan for Sydney, which included 60-metre wide main roads and generous property frontages. He ordered his convict labourers to span the Tank Stream, and Judge Advocate David Collins recorded that 'A gang of convicts were employed in rolling timber together to form a bridge.' Bridge Street was born.

The colony's first major bridge was built up the Parramatta River at Parramatta six years later by Major Francis Grose, but was lost in a flood the next year. Other bridges were constructed along the river but while they united the north and south they were too far from the main game to be of any use to the bulk of Sydney's population.

The white settlers around Sydney Cove moved away from the water's edge and into the bushlands west and south with some reluctance. The fringe dwellers feared the loss of communication, services — no matter how rudimentary — and security, but the need for farming lands and the force of numbers compelled such migration.

Boats carried them up the Parramatta River and by 1791 the farming districts were connected by a crude 25 km stretch of track known as Parramatta Road. In 1855 a railway line further encouraged the spill westward. For a period around 1820 the population of Parramatta outnumbered Sydney's.

The division between the north shore and the city was an irritant for the early settlers and remained one until 1932. The north shore was less than 500 metres from the edge of Dawes Point as the crow flies, but it might as well have been 50 km. Indeed, for some time it was, for traffic, 50 km away. It was so close you could swim, but to travel by land in the earliest days meant rattling along the long road to Parramatta before crossing the bridge there and cutting back. Even a good horse took at least a day to take the visitor from one side of the harbour to the other as it journeyed 'around the Cape'.

Six years after the first settlers laid anchor at Sydney Cove attempts were made to settle the north shore in the hope of developing more farming land to feed the now starving colony. The soil was not good but some small settlements took hold.

In 1804 James Milson leased the land at what is know known as Milsons Point — where the Harbour Bridge begins its leap across the waters — from Robert Campbell for £8 a year and began to raise dairy cattle. The farm did a good trade with the ships anchored in the harbour. Sailors would get rum and sex at night from the Rocks district and milk in the mornings from the north shore, although the latter option was probably less utilised.

Later Milson built the Milk House cafe and while it was never a favourite drinking hole for the sailors, it became a popular destination for Saturday rowers. Unlike the city side, the north shore remained heavily wooded and sparsely populated.

The area became more accessible in 1816 when Jamaican-born Billy Blue, an emancipated convict, set up a ferry service to the north side. The colourful and popular character, often seen with a sack of oysters over his shoulder, was assigned the position of Water Bailiff and given a little stone house in the grounds of Government House before being granted a parcel of land on what is now called Blues Point.

Milsons Point began to expand in the 1840s when the first coal-powered steam punts, capable of carrying horses and carts, began to

Peak Hour: By the early 1890s five million people, 378,500 vehicles and 43,800 horsemen made their way by ferry between Circular Quay and the north shore.

operate. More people migrated to the north side and began to spread out with the building of a railway from Hornsby to St Leonards which was later extended to a station at Milsons Point, where it and a tramline connected to the elegant Milsons Point ferry wharf.

A telegraph cable was laid across the harbour in January 1875. The telephone exchange opened in May the following year and attracted three subscriptions: the Underwoods, Tamsets and Clarkes. Within two years seven subscribers, including the north shore cottage hospital, had phones and could be called between 8.30 am and 8 pm.

Despite a regular and reasonably reliable ferry service, the settlement to the north remained a long journey for anything larger than could be stored on a small boat and this inconvenience held back settlement. Over the years a host of bridges had been constructed along the harbour's chaos of coves and bays to the west but spanning the harbour was only ever dreamed of.

A City Divided: The view from Blues Point toward Dawes Point. Despite many proposals the bridge was still half a century away. Circa 1880.

THE BRIDGE

Eventually the land route from the city to the north shore became known as 'the five bridges'. By the 1880s, you could leave the city and travel across the Pyrmont, Glebe Island, Iron Cove, Gladesville and Fig Tree bridges, a journey that took 20 km off the old Parramatta Road route.

Naturally, ferries and punts were the preferred option and as the north shore grew, the small expanse of water became clogged with vessels plying their trade, filling the air with a thick black smoke and the piercing sound of foghorns. By 1890 the ferries carried 5 million passengers, 378,500 vehicles and 43,800 horsemen a year. Even if this traffic was spread equally over the seven days of the week, and it most certainly would not have been, it meant an average of 13,688 passengers, 1036 vehicles and 120 horsemen a day. The harbour was becoming chaotic and dangerous. Passenger liners and cargo ships navigated a precarious route through the frenetic ferries and pleasure crafts.

The problem grew with the population and a 1908 royal commission found that there were now 13 million passengers a year being shipped from one shore to another by five significant ferry companies. The boats lined up five deep at the wharves as up to 75 ferries jostled for position at Circular Quay every hour. Passengers complained of the danger, particularly on foggy mornings when the captains were guided blind across the harbour by the sound of brass bells at the wharves on the opposite side.

By the early 1920s Sydney had developed an intricate train, tram and road network but at its epicentre was a yawning gap. The city's greatest natural transport advantage, its harbour, was also a transport infrastructure disaster. Almost one million people lived in the town, but only a third of them lived in the open lands north of the harbour and most of those were at the mercy of the ferry fleet. The little boats stopped in fogs and storms and were subject to the whims of increasingly frequent industrial action.

Almost three decades after the royal commission, on the afternoon of 3 November 1927, as the approaches of the Sydney Harbour Bridge neared the harbour's edge, the worst fears of ferry passengers were realised. The Union Steamship mail boat, the *Tahiti*, had just left Darling Harbour with 300 passengers and crew bound for Wellington and San Francisco.

Around the same time the 4.14 pm ferry from Circular Quay to Watsons Bay, the *Greycliffe*, began its journey. The ferry, unofficially called 'the school boat' because of the number of children who caught it at the time, was struck on its port side and sank instantly. Forty passengers were killed and bodies were still being pulled from the harbour three weeks later.

Doug May, who was working on the bridge's approaches, remembers the incident.

> One night just before knocking off time, about a quarter to five ... the Tahiti had gone down — that was a ship going to America I think and it had gone down in the harbour. A little while later someone said it had hit a ferry and it was the Greycliffe. I remember the great activity there and the next week was very bad because they were bringing up all the bodies of these poor little schoolgirls that had got drowned there. It was a very gloomy week, that next week. I remember that very vividly.

A bridge could not come soon enough.

BRADFIELD'S BIG PLANS

A migrant railway worker's son tops his class in Ipswich, heads to Sydney to redesign the town and finds himself almost as famous as a racehorse and an opera singer. After 150 years of false prophets it appears the city has found the man to lead it to the water's edge, indeed, across it.

It is not generally known that the project to place a bridge across Sydney Harbour was in the air when Wellington & Blucher were defeating Napoleon at Waterloo.

The Age 16 March 1932

In the summer of 1886 the eighteen-year-old son of a migrant Ipswich railway worker stood on the deck of a small steamship making its way from the ocean into the waters behind Sydney Heads. The arrival of that young man, John Job Crew Bradfield, would have a bigger impact on Sydney Harbour than any one person since Governor Arthur Phillip arrived and established the convict camp there 98 years earlier. Bradfield would forever change the face of the harbour and city of Sydney in a way few, if any, could or have.

Even today, some might argue about who designed the Sydney Harbour Bridge but no single person can lay claim to the structure like Bradfield. He saw it and he built it. His will is in every rivet.

Bradfield had the dream and the drive. While some men look at the world and accept it for what it is, others strive to shape it, rearrange it, improve it. He was the only man who oversaw the bridge's conception, birth, growth and completion. He was its father, midwife, wet nurse and mentor. A man of incredible vision, he not only had the astute and extraordinary mind capable of the engineering, political, financial and public relations feats that would be involved in building a bridge across Sydney Harbour, he had the patience to pursue the project for 30 frustrating years as it was proposed and then deposed by government after successive government.

His fame during the 1920s and 1930s was extraordinary; politicians, poets and public lionised him as a national celebrity. Here was an engineer who was fêted like a sportsman or a soldier. Bradfield was elevated high into the national consciousness. For two decades he was the equal of the cricketer Donald Bradman and the racehorse Phar Lap. He was as heroic as General Monash, and as wonderful as the operatic star Nellie Melba. In the press they coined the phrase *Our Bradman, our Bradfield, our Bridge* — two out of three were Bradfield.

For this moment in history an engineer felt the bright lights of public acclaim on his large, balding head. Bradfield was almost a cult. He signed autographs, gave lengthy interviews, made speeches, posed for countless photographs and filled newspapers with his visions, but most importantly he built the Sydney Harbour Bridge.

John Job Crew Bradfield was an extraordinary man. Rising from humble beginnings as a temporary draughtsman, he led an undisciplined herd of politicians, engineers and ordinary citizens to the water's edge and over it.

At the end of the century the city's ad hoc road, tram and rail network needed somebody to connect the dots and weave the tangled strands together into a single, coherent thread. The north shore wanted a bridge, a tunnel; even a pontoon would do, anything, so long as it could be directly connected with the city. The transport network needed a visionary to see the system as a whole, to build a bridge that would carry the roads down from the north, spill them into the city and direct them off to suburbs. Somebody who could take the train lines, bring them over the harbour and unify them in an underground loop that would send them off again to the suburbs.

Somebody who could do the tramways too. Somebody who under-stood engineering and the jealousies of different government departments. A man who understood town planning, public service, public opinion and political weakness. Somebody who could stay up at night and check the effects of weather on steel in two states of stress then be up in the morning to watch that concrete was poured properly. Somebody who could lobby parliament and the public, the sort of speaker who could tell a council of church elders why they should let him pull down their House of God. A man who could, as the story was told, defy the 'howling storm' to climb high on the world's bridges in order to listen to them vibrate as a train passed below.

For those who lived on the north shore, Bradfield was some-thing of a saviour. There had been many prophets, but it was he who arrived to lead them from the wilderness. In 1924, eight years before the Sydney Harbour Bridge was finished and before construction work began, the councillors of the distant north side named a new suburb in honour of the man who they said 'will do something never before attempted and that will never be attempted again'.

While the Bradmans, Phar Laps, Monashes and Melbas are still celebrated to some extent, Bradfield's profile slipped after death, but his iconic engineering achievement is still crucial to the functions of the modern city. The Sydney Harbour Bridge is a symbol of Sydney and Australia, its image is used in a million forms and it says to the world: this is a place where nature and man coexist in rare harmony. Whether that is true or not is a moot point.

Poet Dame Mary Gilmore was a lifelong friend of Bradfield. In 1927 she gave him a copy of her book, *The Passionate Heart*, and ded-icated it with these words: 'To Dr Bradfield, who has drawn out a vision and made it in stone and steel. The Patriot speaks in deeds.'

Four years later, with the opening of the bridge just months away, she sent him another of her books, *The Rue Tree*, with this message: 'To Dr J. J. Bradfield "the bridge builder". Who are the great? They who bring unity to the separated, whether the bridging be done by word or steel.'

Engineers or their works are rarely fêted by the poets, but Bradfield was a rare engineer. In the 1930s he was praised across the country and beyond. He was, in the language of the time, an Australian who proved this outpost of Empire possessed men of talent the equal of anywhere in the world.

He was a steady and committed man who walked, spoke and triumphed slowly. He had the sort of patience you would expect from somebody whose second name was Job. He never swore or shouted; he saw what was possible and set out to achieve it.

'Where there is no vision, the people perish,' he would say, quoting the lessons he had learned at church. At other times he was fond of quoting American city planner, Daniel H. Burnham, saying, 'Make big plans, for little plans have no magic to stir men's blood and in themselves may never be realised.'

Bradfield was a visionary and a man capable of stirring the blood with his vision.

Top End of Town: Dr J. J. C. Bradfield, centre, on the deck with powerful local identities Judge Backhouse, left, and Sir Mungo MacCallum, right. March 1931.

At first he worked anonymously, computing and planning behind the scenes, checking others' designs and integrating them with the evolving public transport system. Eventually his work became more public and finally he was elevated onto the shoulders of the city and celebrated like few others.

To understand why, you have to understand the pride the Sydney Harbour Bridge project gave the city and most of the nation. Brave in conception, it seemed to be the only light that continued to burn in the smothering darkness of the Depression. In a country with an inferiority complex it was something people could boast was the biggest and the best in the world.

Building the bridge was a project that obsessed Bradfield for over three decades. It consumed Sydney for a considerably longer period.

Over the years the chief engineer committed himself body and soul to the project. It meant enormous personal sacrifices.

Bradfield was a consummate politician and eventually got his bridge. Perhaps it was the combination of mathematical and bureaucratic skills combined with an artist's passion which meant he was the man who succeeded when others had failed.

In Cologne in 1922, while on a bridge fact-finding mission, he came across a piece of wisdom from artist-philosopher, John Ruskin, which took his fancy.

Life without industry is guilt
Industry without art is brutality

Bradfield understood poetry and the practicalities of life in a growing city. His attention to detail was limitless. In Europe and America he discussed bridge design with the world's leading engineers, visited large steelworks to inspect the latest in manufacturing developments and even took time out to order the right coloured tiles for the train stations on the city loop. Museum station features a special antique tile he chose while abroad.

To some extent the idea of bridging the water must have

seemed almost fanciful to Sydneysiders of the time, particularly when you try to imagine 39,000 tonnes of steel suspended in one single dolphin leap. A bridge that is larger, stronger and more ambitious than any previously contemplated or completed is hard to conceive. The world's greatest engineering triumph right here in this little colony at the butt end of the civilised world was a long time coming. Australia's early history was peopled by many who imagined, and the odd dozen or two who designed a bridge over Sydney Harbour or a tunnel under it, but it took a long time to isolate the railway worker's son from the madding crowd.

BRADFIELD'S PREDECESSORS

The first to imagine a bridge across the harbour was a Dr Erasmus Darwin, grandfather of the naturalist Charles.

Erasmus was a member of the futurist school. Like science fiction writers, futurists imagined the developments of coming decades and centuries, but Dr Darwin chose to record his predictions in rhyme, not paperback.

After a visit to Sydney in 1791, when the city was little more than a collection of tents and squalid shanties, Dr Darwin wrote 'Visit of Hope to Sydney-Cove, near Botany Bay'.

> *There shall broad streets their stately walls extend,*
> *The circus widen, and the crescent bend;*
> *There, ray'd from cities o'er cultur'd land,*
> *Shall bright canals, and solid roads expand.*
> *There the proud arch, Colossus-like bestride*
> *Yon glittering streams, and bound the chafing tide;*
> *Embellish'd villas crown the landscape-scene,*
> *Farms wave with gold, and orchards blush between.*
> *There shall tall spires, and dome-capt towers ascend*

Darwin's latter-day readers were surprised to find that, Nostradamus-like, he had apparently predicted the building of a 'proud arch, Colossus-like bestride' long before such a thing was possible.

The arch had been employed in adobe structures of the Sumerians 6000 years before and the Egyptians mastered the use of the true arch to span distance and scale height 4500 years ago, but it would take all of the intervening period for the engineering skills and developments in steel production to even contemplate crossing the harbour in a single leap.

It wasn't until 1914 that Gustav Lindenthal designed the Hell Gate Bridge in New York, the first steel arch to span 1000 feet or 300 metres. Ten years later, in the Southern Hemisphere, a local engineer watched as the first piers were built for an enormous bridge, which would span 500 metres and bear the weight of twin tram and train tracks, a pedestrian crossing and a broad expanse of road for motor vehicles.

Sydney's bridge was not only 66 per cent longer than the Hell Gate Bridge, it had to give clearance for tall sailing ships, which still frequented the harbour, and it had to have the necessary capacity and strength to link two separated cities — Sydney and North Sydney — for centuries to come.

Even in 1788 the skill existed to build a structure from Dawes to Milsons Point, but it would have been a low-level bridge with broad supporting columns in the water, which would have been an unmitigated disaster for ships. 'Piers in the fairway,' Bradfield would say, referring to the navigational menace posed by such construction.

In the intervening years there were many plans for many bridges and it was fortuitous that no other was ever attempted, for none approached the utility or monumental magnificence of the one that eventually was. The time spent in reconnaissance was often frustrating but inevitably well spent.

While Darwin imagined a bridge, it was emancipated convict and government architect Francis Greenway who first proposed a harbour bridge to Governor Macquarie in a report dated 1815. Ten years later he was still advocating the scheme, writing to the *Australian* in April 1825:

Thus in the event of the Bridge being thrown across from Dawes Battery to the North Shore, a town would be built on that shore, and would have formed with these buildings a grand whole, that would have indeed surprised anyone entering the harbour; and would have given an idea of strength and magnificence that would have reflected credit and glory on the colony and the Mother Country.

Greenway was a century or more ahead of his time, but while he presented the idea of a bridge his work never progressed beyond the written word.

Half a century later a bridge was given rudimentary life in sketch form when, in 1857, English-trained engineer Peter Henderson drew the first recognised plans for a crossing. Henderson had worked in the workshops of George Stephenson, the inventor of the locomotive engine, and had also worked with Isambard Brunel, celebrated railway engineer. Brunel, like Bradfield, was the complete engineer designing the tunnels, gauges, rolling stock, bridges and platforms for his railways. He was also responsible for the first transatlantic paddle steamer, large screw propeller and iron hull. The Englishman was also a consultant during the development of Victoria's railways system.

In 1857 Henderson lived at Millers Point. His drawing is the oldest surviving practical plan for a bridge, but even a layman's knowledge of engineering would suggest the extended truss design from a single pylon on either side was completely impractical. Had it survived construction it would certainly have fallen into the harbour should the lightest vehicle attempt to cross it. Henderson was obviously something of a fraud; while he may have worked with Brunel and Stephenson it was more than likely he fetched their tea.

In the next half a century plans and promises rained down on the city like confetti. By 1920 some 76 plans had been submitted to the state government and bill after fanciful bill had been presented to the parliament. Some plans were even accepted, only to die of exposure to political reality.

Often there were pitched battles between those who favoured a subway or tunnel and bridge advocates.

The first politician to run hard with the idea was Sir Henry Parkes, who was the local member for the north shore electorate of St Leonards and realised that a harbour crossing was important to his voters. In the early 1880s he paraphrased Thomas Macaulay's Horatius, asking,

Now, who will stand at my right hand
And build the Bridge with me.

Nobody, it seemed, and one editorial following Parkes's inactive premiership noted, 'Someone must be standing on his right hand.'

On Friday evening, 2 June 1876, Benjamin Palmer, the Mayor of North Sydney, chaired a meeting at the St Leonards School of Art where it was resolved that 'the time has arrived when that portion of the county of Cumberland north of Port Jackson, and adjacent counties, should be connected with the city of Sydney by a high-level bridge at St Leonards'.

The north shore was beginning to organise and lobby.

In 1878 William C. Bennett, Commissioner for Roads and Bridges, was approached with the proposal to take the necessary surveys and borings to build a bridge. Bennett told the north shore that the best solution would be a pontoon from Dawes to Milsons Point, a floating bridge to carry cars, people and even a train, should it be necessary. This, he said, would 'be more acceptable to the interests of the inhabitants of the North shore than the costly and inevitably unsightly and monster bridge'.

In 1879 Colonel T. S. Parrot drew a seven-span bridge that was a more practical solution than Henderson's or Bennett's equally fantastic proposal, but posed the problem of being a shipping hazard. Anyway, the government was not interested in Parrott's idea as it had already begun to negotiate with J. E. Garbett to build a bridge. Parrot, like many others, rolled up his sketches and went home.

Garbett's plans advanced as far as the company lodging £5000 deposit with Sir Henry Parkes's government in 1881, but the money was returned the next year when the government changed and the idea abandoned.

As the north shore became more populated it also became more important to politicians and Parkes was approached with a proposal to mark the centenary of the colony in 1888 by building a bridge. It met with the usual fudging and prevarication and concluded with the first of a string of royal commissions on the subject. The commission was asked to investigate whether a bridge or a tunnel should be built and conveniently concluded that the best solution was neither, but if you really, really had to do it a high-level bridge was the best option.

In 1896 four bills were introduced to parliament regarding the bridge and four bills came to nothing. Two petitions, signed by over 100,000 people, also failed to move the politicians.

At the turn of the century, the People's Bridge League convinced Minister for Public Works E. W. O'Sullivan that a bridge or tunnel was necessary and he called for tenders on 4 January 1900. Tenders were received, an advisory board appointed to examine the tenders and a report was due in 1903, but by that time the government had changed and the project was abandoned, much to the annoyance of the tenderers, many of whom were overseas firms that had spent a lot of money getting their proposals together.

In 1906 the long-suffering people of the north shore formed the Sydney and North Shore Junction League with the prescient aim of connecting the shores by 'Bridge, or if preferred by a Tunnel, or by both'. In 1987 work was indeed begun on a tunnel to complement the existing high-level bridge, but back at the turn of the centuries the frustrated league published a manifesto that began with a plaintive cry.

'Everything comes to him who waits': so says the old adage. If this be so, the junction with North Shore should soon be an accomplished fact, for surely the people of New South Wales have waited long enough … Each day's delay is an additional reproach not merely to the city but to the State also, and to remove the stigma at the earliest possible moment is the fixed determination of the League.

Realists, they asked that 'in the event of the State timidly shrinking from the undertaking, to which various Governments in the past have been morally committed, no obstacle will be thrown in the path of private enterprise in carrying out the work'.

The league would have been well advised not to hold its breath waiting for a bridge, but the man who would build the bridge was now among them, although few knew it at the time.

Family Affair: Dr J. J. C. Bradfield with his family and the Model A Ford they drove in across the Sydney Harbour Bridge. March 1932.

THE MAN FOR THE JOB

John Job Crew Bradfield was the son of Englishman John Edward Bradfield, who in turn was the youngest of five brothers and the only to survive the Crimean War. John Edward married Maria Crew and migrated to Australia in 1857 with their three young children.

The family planned to disembark at Sydney Cove but Mrs Bradfield insisted they disembark at Moreton Bay after the unbroken

sea leg from China. Family lore says she refused to reboard when the ship was due to leave.

The family settled in working-class Ipswich and John Job Crew was born in Rainbow Street, Sandgate, on 26 December 1867, the ninth of ten children.

Bradfield's father served as an engineer in the Crimean War, but was described as a labourer on his marriage certificate. He went into a brick-making business with his wife's relatives, but the business collapsed four years after John Job Crew was born. At the age of 50 John Edward found a job as a fettler on the railways to support his large family. Bradfield senior had risen to the position of gardener by the time his most famous son was married in 1891.

Young John Bradfield looked a little strange. The boy was born with a large, almost bulbous, head. It was something that was often remarked on and phrenologists of the time may have produced their callipers and announced the measurements as indisputable proof of his incredible mental capacity. Big head equals big brain. Critics and enemies may have taken an alternative view, equating a big head with swollen ego.

Even in the backwoods of the North Ipswich State School the young man's extraordinary intelligence was recognised and fostered. His headmaster, George Harrap, would tell the students that there are two types of people in the world, donkeys and donkey drivers. Bradfield often cited the lesson and was clearly destined to be the latter. In 1880 at the age of twelve the brilliant youngster was able to attend Ipswich Grammar School after winning a scholarship to pay for his tuition.

Given the chance, the gardener's son shone brightly and the scholarship was extended so he could complete his schooling. 'He has the qualities of perseverance, thoroughness, steadiness, uprightness and loyalty to his masters and to the school,' headmaster Dr Donald Cameron wrote in a letter of reference for young John when he graduated.

Although Queensland had been named a separate colony in 1859, fortunately for Bradfield and Sydney, links with the southern state had not been totally broken. In 1885 he won Dux of School in his senior examination and was awarded one of three scholarships to study Engineering at Sydney University and live at St Andrews College. College fees and tuition took up every shilling, but Bradfield seemed to hold his own alongside the finest young minds of the wealthier colonials.

His arrival was timely.

It was the golden era of the city, the railway and the engineer. The frantic and frenzied gold rushes of the preceding decades now subsidised the infrastructure and education of the young nation. State-funded schools flourished and an egalitarian system of scholarships allowed even the lower classes to attend the finest university.

The ever-expanding railway system employed enormous teams of labourers, including the young scholar's father, to build new lines and open up the vast inland farming lands. While they laboured under the hot sun, engineers huddled over slide rules and rough maps as they drafted a series of suture lines that eventually joined almost every agricultural backblock with a coastal port. Their achievements were significant. The zigzag railway line through the almost impenetrable Blue Mountains to Sydney's west linked the rich western plains with Sydney Harbour and was considered one of the railway engineering feats of its time. The explorers may have discovered new lands, but it was the engineers who tamed them.

And, in 1889 the completion of a bridge across the Hawkesbury River to the north of Sydney meant a person could board a train in Adelaide and ride through Melbourne and Sydney to Brisbane, although the employment of different rail gauges by each of the states meant this could not be completed on the same train.

Sydney's transport infrastructure had grown as well, and with the population approaching 400,000, the city was, by population, one of the top 50 in the world, although at the time it ranked second to 'marvellous Melbourne', which was home to almost half a million.

Transport systems within the city grew at an incredible rate, but barely kept pace with the change. Sometimes the press of population retarded the services it so demanded. The train didn't stop at

Central station as the dead still rested peacefully at the Strawberry Hills cemetery (its eventual site) and business was wary of giving up a large part of the city to centralise railway services. The western part of the terminal opened in 1906, but the city platforms for electric services were not built until 1926. Development was often erratic and, even in Sydney itself, hamstrung by engineering challenges. For decades a horsedrawn tram took passengers from Redfern station to Circular Quay at the harbour's edge, but by the time Bradfield arrived in town it had been replaced with a steam tram.

Poet Banjo Paterson was a north shore resident who recalled with deadpan humour the frustration of getting from the city of North Sydney to the city of Sydney:

THE 10 pm tram from Ridge Street to Milsons Point on Monday night stopped where all North Shore trams stop, halfway up the hill called Alfred Street. The object of stopping halfway up the hill instead of going right down to the ferry boat is to give the passengers, especially the fat passengers of asthmatic tendencies, a chance to take some healthy exercise in running to catch the boat. It is a recognised rule of vehicular engineering in this enlightened country that the terminal point of any railway or tramline shall be as inconvenient as possible. I am inclined to think this is one of the causes of the declining birth rate. It is no wonder people object to being born in a country which always leaves the railway outside the town, same as New South Wales does. The city of Sydney is the only town of any considerable size on the earth's surface, which hasn't got a railway station in it. There is a railway station across the harbour in North Sydney, and there is one in the suburb of Redfern, but those are the nearest points by which the visitor may reach Sydney by train. Tramway terminal points are made similarly inconvenient, the object being, of course, to give the passengers plenty of exercise.

The Evening News 19 March 1904

The young Bradfield was drawn to the north side and would eventually live there when his studies were complete. Having to commute every day of his life for almost 40 years via a train and ferry no doubt drove his desire to build a bridge.

Soon after he arrived in Sydney, the student caught a steam-powered ferry across the harbour for what was a relatively big day in the history of the north shore. The tramways were testing Sydney's first cable car from the Milsons Point ferry terminal and the young engineering student was keen to see how it worked and keener still to take advantage of the fare-free trial.

The system was powered by a steam engine at the corner of Miller and Ridge streets, which pulled the dual-carriage tram up the hill from the ferry terminal to the centre of North Sydney on a cable. The trams could reach speeds of almost 13 km/h. It might have been slow, but at least it overcame the problem of conquering the steep incline and put an end to one of the irritations Paterson complained about.

Forty years later, standing outside Christ Church in Lavender Bay, Bradfield recalled that he was an 'irresponsible youth in my 'teens' when he made the free trip up the hill on the cable car.

There were only 300 students at Sydney University in 1886 and seventeen at St Andrews College when Bradfield began his studies, but surely the lowliest of all these colonial sons and daughters were the three who enrolled in the Engineering school. In their first year Bradfield and the other two were educated in sheds at the back of the main building. Their degree was not recognised by the government and the students were forced to clean the buildings themselves.

The engineers also suffered under a heavy workload and a harsh marking regime, but in March 1889 Bradfield graduated as a Bachelor of Engineering with First Class Honours and was awarded the Sulman Prize for Architecture and the University Gold Medal.

Bradfield had no intention of remaining in New South Wales when he finished his studies. A week before sitting his final exam, the 21-year-old revealed his nascent political skills, writing a letter to Ipswich parliamentarian and the Queensland Commissioner for Railways, George Thorne.

'If you could get me a position in Queensland, I would prefer it as I am a Queenslander,' he wrote. He pointed out that his fellow students in New South Wales could expect to start on £200; he was ready to accept half that on a trial basis.

He got the job.

He began as a draughtsman in the chief engineer's office, helping on the north coast railway which ran from Brisbane to Bundaberg and Gladstone. He was now sitting in an office in a suit and collar, working on the great spread of the railway system. Not so long before, his father had worked as a labourer on the railway tracks.

The job lasted little more than a year before an economic crisis hit and all public works were shut down. A Queenslander he might be, but Bradfield knew that the best prospects for further employment lay in New South Wales and applied for a job as a temporary draughtsman in the Engineering Drawing Office. He was told to start in 1891 and would earn the grand total of 16/- a day or £250 a year. Before travelling to Sydney, Bradfield married Edith Jenkins at St Johns Anglican Cathedral, Brisbane. The happy couple celebrated the event and then climbed on an overnight train to Sydney.

They settled into their first home at North Sydney and had two children before moving three years later to Ashfield on the city side where they had another child. In September 1898 the family of five moved into a house across the harbour at Gordon while their new home was being built for the cost of £387 at the corner of Park Avenue and Elizabeth Street, which is now known as Rosedale Road. Three sons were added to the family in the new Gordon home.

Some in the family said that even at this time he dreamed of a bridge. 'In 1893, as he walked the foreshore at Milsons Point he talked of his wish to build a bridge,' his daughter claimed 84 years later.

In the early years Bradfield's engineering work involved nothing so grand. He was involved in doing calculations for the Cataract and Burrinjuck dams, but most important to his future was the work

All Aboard: Dr Bradfield rides one of 96 locomotives used to test the strength of the bridge one month before its opening. February 1932.

he did checking calculations for the bridges branch, which included work on the Pyrmont and Glebe Island electric swing bridges and the Pyrmont Bridge.

He was then appointed to check the stresses of designs submitted in 1901 to build a bridge after successful lobbying by the People's Bridge League. It was probably one of the sorrier episodes in a very long, sorry history of government prevarication and duplicity when it came to the bridge, but it was a valuable lesson for Bradfield in both tendering and politics.

The young draughtsman was asked to give technical advice to the advisory board. The project was a farce. Twenty-four tenders were received, 24 displayed at the Queen Victoria Markets and 24 were rejected with most 'so incomplete and wanting in information, either as regards design, plans, or estimates, as to deserve but little consideration'.

Nonetheless, the government had promised that one design would be chosen and awarded a prize, and rules were rules. The board decided on a bridge designed by Norman Selfe, a local engineer.

Bradfield was not impressed. 'The bridge was located in the wrong place; it had two piers in the fairway, and would have been a menace to navigation,' he said later.

To add to the farcical nature of the project, the advising engineers, including Bradfield, advised that another bridge, with some modifications, might have been more viable. The competition was reconvened by the government. This time the call for tenders was more specific and the advisory board recommended all designs must allow a clearance of 51.8 metres above the water; the main span should be 365.6 metres and its complete length 913.9 metres. The board said the bridge should carry two railway lines, two 9-metre roadways, two tramlines and two footpaths. New tenders were to be submitted by June 1902.

The government told tenderers that this time it really 'meant business'.

Bradfield was left in charge of the drawing office when his boss and friend from university, Harvey Dare, took six months' leave. The tenderers, who had spent tens of thousands of pounds in the first round of the competition, were lured back for one more try. Plans were received again and all arch bridges duly rejected because arches were said to be too big, an eyesore and artistically objectionable.

Just to drag it out a bit further, another round of tenders was called in March 1903. The competition got down to three tenders, one for a suspension bridge and two for a cantilever design. Two of the bridges called for foundations sunk in clay beneath the harbour.

The government got as far as completing tests to see if the foundations would hold. When foundations were dug in the harbour one man died of the bends and the holes collapsed.

The advisory board eventually recommended an altered version of a cantilever plan submitted by J. W. Stewart & Co. and the MAN Company designed by Mr F. Bonny and Sydney engineer Norman Selfe.

The company representatives sailed to Australia to start negotiating with the government but when they arrived an election had intervened and the new Secretary for Public Works, Charles Lee, told them 'thanks but no thanks'. The bridge plans were shelved again.

Selfe, whose designs were twice accepted then rejected, was furious that so many companies had wasted their time and money on what he called the 'Sydney Bridge Guessing Competition'. In the long run, though, it was a good thing the bridge designed by Bonny and Selfe was never built, as a structure which allowed only two lanes of traffic would have been redundant in a matter of decades. The fact that its foundations were set in the water would have made it a navigation hazard for the life of the inadequate bridge. Unfortunately none of these far-sighted factors influenced the New South Wales politicians, who dropped the scheme because they had no will to continue.

It would be another two decades before the modern bridge was given the go-ahead; in that time developments in construction methods and materials advanced so much that the 500-metre leap across the water could be made in one clear jump. The twenty-year wait might have been a frustrating time for those who needed a bridge but it ensured that when the bridge was built it was the best bridge ever constructed and one which would serve the needs of the city for centuries to come.

While the north shore community and the companies, which wasted thousands of pounds on tenders, were frustrated to tears, Bradfield was accumulating knowledge and biding his time. However, the downside to the operation was that the next time anyone asked international firms to tender they would remember the waste of money involved in the 'guessing competition'.

DREAMS AND SCHEMES

Bridge building was always pressing the outer limits of engineering knowledge.

In 1854 the Wheeling Bridge, Ohio, the longest bridge in the world, literally blew over. In 1876 in Ashtabula, Ohio, a replaced section of the railway bridge collapsed under the weight of a train, killing 90 people. The bridge designer and the railway's chief engineer — who survived the crash — were both blamed in a coronial report before the latter killed himself.

In the following decade 200 bridges met a similar fate in the USA alone.

In 1878 the Tay Bridge in Scotland — the longest and biggest in the world — fell, killing 75 people when winds reached 160km/h as the mail train crossed. Engineer Sir Thomas Bouch, who had been knighted for his work, was blamed for the disaster and died soon after, ruined and bankrupt.

Bridges continued to fall and in 1907 the collapse of the Quebec Bridge in Canada, one of the cutting-edge steel cantilever bridges that had replaced the old-fashioned masonry arch and timber, or wrought iron, truss designs, proved engineers still had a lot to learn. The accident killed 85 men.

Bradfield, always abreast of developments in his field, was only too well aware of these disasters and the implications for engineers. Fortunately, he was a patient and careful man who was never hurried and never cut corners.

In 1906 Bradfield was asked to take charge of the railway and tramway designs, the biggest project being the 500 km North Coast Railway from West Maitland to South Grafton, which included 49 bridges and thirteen tunnels.

Engineering work was hands-on in those days and Bradfield later told his son Bill that he had gone into the forests around Kempsey to check the height of the ironbark trees to ensure he could get the best timber lengths to suit his plans before building the longest single-span timber bridge in the world. Two decades later the length of shippable steel members radically altered his original plans for the Sydney Harbour Bridge.

During this period Bradfield also designed the tramline, which ran from The Spit to Manly and included a ferry which transported the trams across Middle Harbour.

Living at Gordon he understood the needs of commuters. Bradfield had built the family an idyllic semi-rural retreat. The gardens reflected his Queensland origins and his own father's love of gardening. Bradfield's son Bill recalls:

> ... it was a solid, small double brick house built in the north eastern corner of the block. And he had left one third of the acre as natural bush, about another third he had a tennis court on it and the rest of the house and the garden, which was mainly filled with fruit trees ... he had an extraordinary number of different fruit trees and berries and all sorts of things. I tried to count them up one night ... we used to have about 30 different fruits and berries ... and it included things like plantain bananas, guava trees ... a macadamia nut tree that never had any nuts on it and oranges, lemons, cumquats. You name it it was there, quinces, pomegranates; he tried all sorts of things. He obviously tried a number of trees that he knew from Queensland because he planted amongst other things, a bunyip pine, it was 100 feet high and had to be cut down because of the danger, a beautiful tree.
>
> It was a wild garden, not a formal garden by any means, there were flowers all over the place, birds everywhere. He even had an olive tree.

The Bradfield jungle was a stark contrast to the next-door neighbour, Mr Pitt, who had a large rose garden and hothouses.

The emerging engineer loved to potter about in his garden on weekends or catch a train to Stanwell Park south of Sydney where the family had a small block of land where they would camp.

The family did not buy a car until 1928 when they invested in a Model A Ford. It would not only be the first car to cross the

Harbour Bridge; it would also set the first speed record across it. However, Australia's greatest engineer preferred public transport.

His son Bill recalls:

> He never drove the car, I'm sure he could drive, but he always went to work by public transport and by the time I came along in 1910 the train was from Hornsby to Milsons Point. To get to work he would go by train to Milsons Point, ferry across to Circular Quay and then walk it from Circular Quay to the Public Works Department Building in the northern part of Macquarie St, close to Circular Quay.
>
> He could see the harbour [from his office] … in those days everyone worked five days a week but also Saturday mornings and he used to take me into the office on Saturday mornings … It was a beautiful office, a beautiful seat, heavy wooden desk and furniture.

Following the Sydney Bridge Guessing Competition the government launched two royal commissions in 1908, one into the Improvement of the City and its Suburbs, the other into Communication between Sydney and North Sydney. Bradfield stayed back at night examining different proposals to tunnel under the harbour as well as schemes to improve the city itself.

For the next two years Bradfield and the public works draughtsmen prepared plans for railways, tunnels, bridges and streetscapes.

The commission for Communication decided that the city needed three tunnels, which would rest on the sea floor: one to be built immediately for trams, a second to be built when the railways were electrified and a commuter tunnel that could be postponed by introducing a new ferry service.

This plan was bitterly opposed by the railways who took the battle to the royal commission (Improvement), which was still taking evidence.

It was in this environment that Bradfield decided he had had enough of the public service circus and applied for the prestigious position of chair of the Queensland University Engineering Department, which had recently fallen vacant. Fortunately for Sydney and Bradfield he was rejected.

In 1911, he was appointed head of the Engineering Drawing Office, Plan Room and Ironwork Inspection and was caught up in another round of inquiries. Harassed by the long-suffering gentlemen of the North Shore Bridge League, who had again caught a ferry across the harbour to lobby, the Public Works Committee was asked to report on the possibility of a railway tunnel and separately on a bridge for road, pedestrian and tram traffic.

In January 1912 Bradfield dismissed the idea of a tunnel and presented a proposal for a road, pedestrian and tram bridge, but was asked to go away and include four railway lines in the design. He returned to the committee with two proposals for cantilever bridges, one of which was accepted. Part of the plan included four railway loops, which included the Hornsby, eastern, western and city lines. In October he presented these plans to the Public Works Committee.

Bradfield admitted his plans were not new. As Leone Yandell puts it in her thesis on his works:

> He did not plan anything new regarding the City Railway or the Bridge, but he linked up all the ideas as a complete unit and presented it in a workmanlike way to the State Government. It was his combination of ideas, which was unique.

Sensing they had found the man for the job, the government appointed Bradfield as Chief Engineer of Sydney Harbour Bridge and City Transit, later changing the title to Chief Engineer for Metropolitan Railway Construction and Sydney Harbour Bridge.

It was a canny move designed to cut through the chaos of commissions, reports and counter-reports and also delivered to Bradfield control of a project which would consume almost every waking minute of the next twenty years of his life.

Fortunately for Australia he was up to the task.

On 18 July 1913 his authority was recognised and his ambition to build a bridge almost within grasp when the Public Works Committee recommended:

> That in the opinion of the Committee, it is expedient to connect Sydney by means of a bridge and they recommend the adoption of the scheme submitted by Mr J. J. C. Bradfield, Chief Engineer, Metropolitan Railway Construction, for the construction of a cantilever bridge from Dawes Point to Milsons Point, carrying four lines of railway, one roadway 35 feet wide, one motor roadway 17 feet 6 inches wide, and one footway 15 feet wide, at an estimated cost of £2,750,000.

A lot more work needed to be done to establish how an underground rail network that was yet to be built or even designed could be connected with the bridge, but its position was set and so was Bradfield's. The 1903 bridges had been planned to connect Dawes and McMahons Point; a decade later Dawes and Milsons Point had become the favoured landing position.

After thirteen years of committees and commissions, tenders and tantrums, Sydney at least knew where its bridge would be built and who would build it.

In March 1914 the engineer was sent abroad to study underground railways and long-span bridges. It was the year work started on Lindenthal's Hell Gate Bridge, the largest arch bridge of its kind.

Bradfield said later, 'In 1914, when visiting the American Bridge Company's Shops at Ambridge, I saw the two heaviest sections of the Hell Gate Arch Bridge being butted, subsequently this arch of 977 feet 6 inches span was successfully erected.' The chief engineer implied that a seed had been planted in his mind about the arch bridge, but this may not be completely true.

Still, the New York arch was to play a key role further down the track. Had Bradfield known how much further, he may well have broken down and wept, for although his beloved bridge project must have felt near at hand, the world and Australia had other matters to deal with.

After a quick visit to Germany, Bradfield arrived in England just in time to find the two countries at war. He knew immediately that his bridge and railway projects would be an early casualty and presented himself at an enlistment booth in London. He was 47 years old and was duly rejected.

Bradfield returned to Australia in September and by early 1915 presented his plan for the electrification of the railway system, which included the underground railway loop Sydney has today and a host of other initiatives, including a loop through Sydney's inner west and an eastern suburbs line to Bondi Junction (which was not completed until 1979). He lobbied hard and soon the City and Suburban Electric Railways Bill of 1915 was passed in the parliament by a government determined to find work for the unemployed in the city.

Bradfield was placed in charge of the project, but these were difficult financial times and the government entered into an unworkable contract with an English firm which was supposed to provide finance and supervision of the project. In 1917 the work was cancelled, all railway work was transferred from Public Works to the Railway Commissioners and people whose houses were resumed for demolition were given them back.

Despite his pet projects being shelved, Bradfield was almost ubiquitous during wartime. Men like him rise to the challenge and throw themselves into every project available. He was a committee member and key player in the establishment of the New South Wales State Aviation School, which obtained planes and instructors from England to teach Australian airmen to fly. The committee established an airbase at Richmond, on the plain west of Sydney, for the purpose. He became an executive member of the Patents Investigation Board (part of the war effort), was a founding member of the Town Planning Association, a member of the Board of Control of the Soldiers Garden Village at Matraville, a Fellow of the Senate of the University of Sydney, and he also began work on the ambitious Murrumbidgee Irrigation Scheme.

Selling the bridge

By 1917 Bradfield saw that the war was ending and that he needed to start lobbying to get public support to build his bridge and complete his railway systems. The chief engineer began writing papers for town planners and engineers, lecturing and lobbying anyone who would listen. He improved his sales pitch, telling the businessmen how real estate and population changes would help them. He told aldermen on the north shore about revenue from rates in the newly developed northern suburbs.

Letter writers to the papers suggested a bridge be built to employ the returned soldiers and to honour the dead. The national psyche needed distraction, even healing. Humankind had proved during World War I that its inventiveness could be harnessed for destruction and it was through the construction of a bridge that faith could be restored. Bradfield understood this and in an account he gave some years later during the construction of the bridge wrote:

> Due to our gallant soldiers, Australia has recently been acclaimed a nation. In the upbuilding of any nation the land slowly moulds the people, the people with patient toil alter the face of the landscape, clearing forests, draining swamps, tilling fields, constructing roads and railways, building factories and rearing cities; they humanise the landscape after their own ideals. Thus in the years to come will result the perfect land and people, body and soul, bound together by innumerable and subtle ties.
>
> Future generations will judge our part in the upbuilding of Australia by our works, and when designing the bridge and its pylons, mayhap the largest structure ever erected in Sydney, I have endeavoured as far as my limitations would allow, to blend utility and strength with beauty and simplicity so that the Bridge may in some degree typify the resourcefulness and idealism of this generation, for notwithstanding the materialism of today, we are not dominated by cold selfishness, Australia has an inner life, we still have our dreams of beauty, truth and justice.

Four years hence the Arch should be completed; it is unique in that at times of National rejoicing the Arch can be illuminated to represent the badge of the Australian Commonwealth Military Forces, the Rising Sun and Crown, a fitting tribute to Australia's gallant soldiers, sailors and nurses, who of their own free will, set such a standard of Honour, Duty, Patriotism, Sacrifice that each succeeding generation of Australians will find difficult to rival and almost impossible to excel.

Bradfield was capable of poetic flights and understood as well as the next politician the need to appeal to people on a level they understood. He prepared plans of the bridge with an Australian military badge illuminated on it. However, it wasn't until the 1990s that the bridge was used for such political purposes. In 1998 the new Glebe Island bridge was given the Anzac title.

In May 1920 he gave the presidential address to the Sydney University Engineering Society. It was a long, detailed speech, which took in advances in cement, aviation, copper and steel. Then Bradfield asked the audience to stand as he read the names of the 39 university students who had died in the war and to remain standing while he projected an image of King George V standing in front of the cannons of the *Queen Elizabeth*. He told them, 'The picture is symbolic of the dignity and strength of the great Empire to which we belong'.

His conclusion gives an insight into his patience, determination and idealistic notion of the engineer's role.

In ever-increasing numbers the engineer, trained in the art of directing the great sources of nature for the use and convenience of man, will be found in the forefront of the world's progress, and the men who will be the most successful will be those who, with self-reliance, have learned how to wait, and wait patiently, for the realisation of their applications.

In April 1920 John Storey took over as Premier of a new Labor government and the time was right for Bradfield to act. Storey had been a keen supporter of the project before the war and the chief engineer determined that the left-wing party would be keen on a major infrastructure project.

Bradfield knew that the north shore, which had begun to agitate again, had to be smarter than before and he convinced the local politicians to accept a tax on the unimproved value of lands in the city and northern suburbs to pay for a third of the bridge's cost. Previous bills had legislated for a tax initiated on completion of the bridge; this one proposed immediate imposition of the tax.

It was a brilliant move.

The northern politicians accepted the idea and took it to the new Labor Premier. Storey was delighted to find a group in his office proposing they be taxed more; he promised them a bridge.

At the same time one of the engineer's friends, John Sulman, had drawn plans for a transport scheme which proposed tunnels instead of bridges, and he ambushed Bradfield with the idea at an Institute of Architects function. Bradfield was furious. If these ideas got abroad again they would be back to square one and the public arena would be full of bridge-versus-tunnel debates, allowing weak-willed politicians to divide and delay. He threatened to resign from the Town Planning Association if his friend's ideas were allowed to distract from his plans — and won the day.

Bradfield had courted the *Sydney Mail* newspaper and called on it to promote his ideas. On 18 August 1920 its front page featured a Lloyd Rees painting of Bradfield's favoured cantilever design for the 'North Shore Bridge' and inside was a glowing four-page report based on his electric railway blueprint.

The hand of Bradfield was all over the publicity coup.

The paper began its story with a colour piece about ferries almost colliding with ocean liners in the fog. It told readers that Bradfield's plans for the railway system were hailed in America as 'One of the most complete reports of its kind' and 'one of the best text books on the subject so far published', editorialising that 'there can be no possible question as to the advantages of a bridge over a tunnel. In the report by the Standing Committee on Public Works Harbour Bridge signed in 1913 by Mr John Storey (now Premier of NSW) as chairman a list of these advantages was given ...'

Bradfield and his friends on the paper were taking no chances for anyone to back down and nobody did. He was instructed by the Premier to get to work preparing specifications so that tenders could be called. The Labor government announced it would build the bridge and tenders would be called in October the following year.

With wind in his sails Bradfield immediately set to work on drawing up the specifications.

By 1921 Bradfield was comparing 'M' braces to 'K' braces and discussing the use of granite in the piers. He began to hire engineers and draughtsmen who had returned from service and they set up offices to begin work on the bridge. His attention to detail was extraordinary and is obvious from the entries to his work diaries from that year. Bradfield wanted to control and understand every element of the project right down to the paint scheme. In an entry dated 24 June 1921 he wondered: 'Which is the best invisibility colour, a yellowish green or a light warm, purplish grey? Want to choose finishing colour so that the blue sky will camouflage the bridge and make it as far as possible blend with its surround.'

He was working around the clock to prepare the bridge specifications and the construction of the electric railways, but at times there was room for a little humour. In July he amused himself by telling the office about 'new carriages being designed for one legged veterans' so that 'ladies and other two legged humans could not sit in them'.

The chief engineer now demanded that he run the entire project and the Minister for Public Works was instructed that there would be no advisory boards overseeing the bridge. Bradfield was adamant that committees would only hamstring the project; nobody knew more about what was needed than him and working with others just increased the chance that he might not get his own way. He proposed that he travel to Europe in 1922 to meet with potential tenderers and also to investigate the new technologies that had developed since his trip eight years earlier.

Bradfield was anxious that the politicians do everything correctly. In October he submitted a number of recommendations to the government and revealed there was some historical mistrust of the Sydney bridge by international tenderers.

'The firms who went to considerable trouble and expense some 20 years ago in submitting tenders do not think they were fairly treated by New South Wales on that occasion and with reason,' he said. He was anxious also to head off a suggestion of payment by toll, an idea which had gained currency, as it meant the tenders would not be paid out of the government purse but could collect revenue in years to come when the bridge was finished.

Bradfield's bridge appeared to be approaching reality.

However, in public life there is always an ambush waiting around the corner. In August Bradfield wrote in his diary that the Premier had asked him to write 'articles in the country press pointing out that the people of Sydney would pay for the Bridge and that the country would not be taxed therefrom'. Already, country politicians were lobbying against the vast expenditure required to build a bridge that would only service the people of Sydney.

A month later he made a note about giving 'a paragraph to the press' regarding the 'Kearney subway proposal'.

Just when Bradfield thought he had seen off the last of the tunnellers, the Kearney High Speed Railway Company of England popped up with a patented tube system which they said would allow trains to be dropped from street level down a grade of one in seven and propelled to the other side of the harbour via a tunnel. Or that was the idea, which had been tested on models but no further. Had it worked, the High Speed Railway Tube would have eliminated the headache of steep gradients for trains faced with either a tunnel or bridge, but nobody except Kearney and his supporters were absolutely sure that it could work.

Bradfield stoically sucked air through his teeth and hoped it would go away but he should have known better. Later that month he had a visit from a Mr Williams of the *Sydney Morning Herald* and noted in his diary: 'He told me the Caucus were [sic] behind Kearney and it was possible he might be brought out.'

Bradfield continued to work on the bridge, ignoring the matter as best he could. And on Tuesday 4 October he received word that the minister would be giving notice to the parliament in the next few days regarding the Sydney Harbour Bridge Bill. He was almost there.

POLITICAL MANOEUVRES

On Wednesday 5 October there is a one-line note among Bradfield's diary entries: 'Mr Storey, Premier, died today'. It was the worst possible news; the Premier was his ally and champion and had been on the Public Works Committee, which had approved the bridge in 1913. With the caucus wobbling on all sorts of issues, including the possibility of Kearney's tube and the chance of asking tenderers to receive delayed payment via toll-collection, the project could be shelved again.

The following night he delivered a lecture to 600 people on the north shore regarding the bridge and in the morning a notice of tenders was published in the *Sydney Morning Herald* and the *Daily Telegraph*. On Monday a Mr Graveling of Dorman, Long & Co. called on Bradfield to discuss the matter. Storey's replacement, another Labor politician, James Dooley, had opposed the Bridge Bill before the war. However, the new Premier put the engineer's mind to rest about the bridge matter. He would support it, he said, but first he needed to know more about Kearney's newfangled tube railway.

Bradfield spent the following Monday writing a terse report on Kearney's tube, but it wasn't enough to convince the Labor caucus, who continued to waver. Then, in early November, Bradfield received some welcome good news: Caucus had approved the Bridge Bill. It would go before parliament.

However, before the month was out the Kearney tube was back. The Premier, Dooley, had bowed to party pressure and referred the Kearney proposal back to the Public Works Department. Bradfield was furious and told one of Dooley's political operators that if there were 'enough lunatics at large to waste their money on such a proposal', he had no objection. He had seen off other fools and he would see off this one.

Despite the distractions the Bridge Bill had its first reading in the New South Wales Parliament the following day and was passed 52 to 13.

On 8 December 1921, as the Bill was about to be read for the second time, the state plunged into a minor constitutional crisis and again Bradfield and his bridge were swept from the agenda. Both houses were adjourned as the parties argued about who should provide the speaker of the house.

Dooley and his cabinet resigned on 20 December when they lost a vote in the Legislative Assembly, and Sir George Fuller's Nationalist party was appointed by the Governor to run the state with members of the Progressive Party, but it also met a deadlock in the Legislative Assembly and asked that an election be called. The farce continued when the Governor reappointed Dooley as Premier, as the former leader still had a majority.

Bradfield watched the parliamentary circus and must have again realised that he had to get the bridge approved and completely removed from the foolish world of politics and politicians as soon as possible. He noted in his diary the next day:

Fuller government formed and lasted 6 hrs 33 mins.

The suns rim dips
the stars flash out
at one stride comes the dark
In office dealing with papers and plans

Bradfield was quoting Coleridge's *The Rime of the Ancient Mariner* and two weeks later he had turned to Latin after noting on Saturday 31 November, 'Bridge Bill not passed, no money available for construction Ne cedas matis.'

Christmas passed and still the Labor government caucus could not make up its mind.

Early in the new year the Cabinet decided that Bradfield should take his planned trip abroad as it was committed to the tender process.

The next Wednesday he received approval from the government for £361 to pay for his passage to England. The government approved a £1000 payment to Bradfield as a raise for his extra work in association with the bill, but still the Kearney tube had not gone away. The week before, some members had pushed for a joint report on the proposal and the company was receiving positive press after a director travelled out and gave a luncheon at the Hotel Australia for northern suburbs councillors and politicians. Kearney claimed 20,000 people an hour could be transported under the harbour by the invention.

Bradfield continued on regardless and turned his attention to the city railway project, which was also back on the agenda, and told the minister, Jack Lang, that he needed £50,000 to fund it to June. Lang set out to raise £1 million in London to fund the public works program.

In February 1922 the railways emerged from four and a half years of hibernation and Bradfield's team began work electrifying the Illawarra (southern) and Bankstown (south-western) lines. Teams of men soon dug up Hyde Park in the city, burrowing beneath the grass and trees to begin work on the tunnel for the city underground loop stations of St James and Museum. Construction methods were still primitive and a long line of horse and carts lined up to take away the soil while men dug with pick and shovel below the ground. You can see photographs of the construction at the Museum stop today. The project employed 300 men and put a lot of pressure on the state's budget.

Like the bridge, the railway loop was closely identified with the chief engineer and when the two stations opened in December 1926 the *Labor Daily* described them as Bradfield's 'Xmas box to the public'.

The other stations on Bradfield's underground loop — Wynyard and Town Hall — were due to open with the bridge.

Nothing could stop the bridge now — well, nothing short of an election and there was one due in March, which must have worried Bradfield, as the Bridge Act had still not passed the state parliament's upper house. Before he left Australia on his fact-finding European trip, he embarked on an unprecedented publicity campaign in professional journals and the popular press. The *Sydney Mail*, which had published Bradfield's cantilever design on its front page two years before, interviewed the chief bridge engineer and wrote a glowing profile which began:

> To know this great Australian engineer is to come into contact with a modest, unaffected, muscular little man of quiet disposition, and a youthfulness of mind that makes him the more fascinating as a companion when one ponders over his extraordinary mental capacity, and his achievements in his studies and in railway work. For six months before the specifications for the bridge were completed he worked 18 hours a day. No one else could do the work — no one else had a grasp of the immense job. His powers of endurance are beyond normal bounds. Few men could stand such a long period of hard work with so little sleep. He looked deadly tired for months, but kept on each night in his little den in his garden at home, bending over his plans and calculations, while most men on his social plane were dozing in easy chairs, or playing billiards or cards. The notion of 44 hours a week must make such a man smile.

On 17 March 1922 Bradfield left Sydney. His diary entries for the period reveal it was not an entirely pleasant experience.

THURSDAY 16 MARCH
Left Sydney at 11am. Cleared heads at 1.35pm. Sea sick and sick of the sea at 3pm.

FRIDAY 17 MARCH

Still sick of the sea

SATURDAY 18 MARCH

Getting better. Took sick again. Doctor doped me with morphia and nearly sent me to sleep for good.

SUNDAY 19 MARCH

Slept nearly all day. Sighted New Zealand at 3pm

TUESDAY 21 MARCH

Left Auckland at 5pm in the teeth of a gale. very rough sea at night.

WEDNESDAY 21 MARCH

Very rough day … two rows of deck chairs along deck, each occupied by a human male or female looking as seedy as a broody hen. Felt the seediest of the lot.

Eventually the chief engineer began to find his sea legs, but back in the chaotic world of 1920s New South Wales politics another storm was brewing which was bound to bring on further nausea. The elections saw the Labor government dumped and a Nationalist–Progressive coalition take over the state under leader George Fuller. Bradfield received the news as the ship crossed the equator en route from Suva to Hawaii. Because one side in politics must necessarily disagree with the other, the newly elected were opposed to the Bridge Act and to Bradfield's fact-finding mission, which they felt should not have been undertaken so close to an impending election.

The chief engineer had done some number-crunching of a political variety and suspected the numbers were enough to pass the Act. Even so, he was still on edge during the voyage. He worked out his frustrations by pacing a measured course around the ship. Each day he walked seven to eight miles and noted by the end of March that he had 'done 100 miles'. He disembarked at Vancouver and after examining the national railway system caught a train to the United States, crossing the snow covered Sierra Nevada Range, constantly calculating and assessing. His notes, which were mailed

home and typed up to be included in his diaries, include the observation that he had travelled 1110 miles at 26.5 m/h on the journey.

In Chicago, Bradfield met G. Lewis Taylor, chief engineer of the McClintic Marshall Company, Pittsburgh, who 'said he never saw such complete detail in a specification before and was very much impressed with the plans from every point of view'. Taylor and a flattered Bradfield discussed suspension and cantilever bridges when the topic of an arch was raised for the first time in almost twenty years. Bradfield's diary notes: 'Asked if would consider a steel arch of 1600 foot span to save weight of shore span; after discussion agreed it was not practicable.'

Building an arch would have saved a lot of bridgework over dry land, but Bradfield believed the structure would not give enough clearance to ships. However, the idea would not go away and the

The First Couple: J. J. C. Bradfield married Edith Jenkins in Brisbane in 1891 and she was by his side for the Sydney Harbour Bridge opening ceremony. 1932.

chief engineer had an open mind even at this late stage when everybody in Australia believed he was out shopping for a cantilever bridge.

As it was, McClintic Marshall were not themselves convinced about an arch and returned to Bradfield later with talk of a two-level suspension bridge but were again fobbed off as the chief engineer was not keen on this style.

Bradfield went back to Canada and visited Quebec where the bridge had fallen in 1907; the new bridge, built in 1918, was the world's longest cantilever span — the sort of bridge he thought would suit Sydney. Just to make sure the modern designs were up to scratch, Bradfield climbed to the top of the structure to feel the vibrations as a train crossed beneath him. He was only too aware of past disasters. His diary entry reads:

> WED MAY 3 QUEBEC
>
> Arrived at Quebec at 7.30 am, drove out and inspected the Quebec bridge.
>
> Walked across the bridge on the top chords on the footways, on the railway and saw the piers, bearings and expansion arrangements, walked from top of main post down to main shoes on piers in rivers; spent 5 hours on bridge.
>
> The bridge is simple and effective and the K bracing looks better when you see the bridge than it does in any picture. The Bridge is massive but the idea of massiveness is lost with the surroundings & with the SHBridge this will be more so.
>
> Have been complimented by everybody on the outline & design of the SHBridge.

Bradfield was told that when the original Quebec bridge fell in 1907 the engineers could not get the men back to work even after offering them a fourfold pay increase. Finally the firm got the local Catholic priest to come down and bless the new work and the labourers returned.

Bradfield returned to New York.

His sightseeing included a trip to 5th Avenue Grand Central Park where he watched 'two towers controlling traffic by switching lights green, red, yellow'. This labour-intensive system pre-dated the modern traffic light. The Australian spent the following day discussing the new silicon steel with the American Bridge Company.

Bradfield was never far from trouble, however, and received a message that Sir William Arrol & Co., one of England's leading bridge builders, would not tender for the Sydney Harbour Bridge. The company had tendered twenty years earlier during the infamous guessing competition and was furious at its treatment. It claimed to have heard rumours via the British Trade Commissioner that the new government would again pull out of the tendering process as had happened at the turn of the century.

Then, the new government decided to flex its muscles and put an end to the project it had originally objected to, telling the *Sydney Morning Herald* it was recalling Bradfield from abroad. A cable demanding he stay in New York until the matter was settled was sent from Australia; however, his reliable secretary and office manager, Kathleen Butler, had got wind of the plans and alerted him in advance of the government's intentions.

Bradfield played smart and left early for England. Like Nelson, he never saw the message. In the meantime, for reasons unknown, the government backed down and decided to let him continue, but not before it had flagged its damaging lack of commitment to the bridge. This was further confirmed after Bradfield set up an office in Westminster. 'Received cable from the premier stating the government would be prepared to consider alternative tenders on the toll basis. Spent some time considering the reply to be sent,' he noted.

Naturally, he advised against the idea, which was sure to further spook potential tenderers. But Bradfield himself would soon cable home to suggest changes to the tender process.

In early July, Mr Evely Carey told him 'the first tracing he ever made was in Batsen Fowlder's Office in 1880 for a Suspension Bridge across Sydney Harbour'. The following day he had meetings with

Dorman, Long & Co. and the Cleveland Bridge Company, who would become two key players in the history of the Sydney Harbour Bridge. On the same day he met Mr Needham from Armstrong Whitworth & Co. who again raised the idea of an arch bridge. Bradfield's diary notes, 'I pointed out that the headway was restricted at each side of the harbour and that the Public Works Committee had not approved of my similar design on account of this.' However, the idea was almost starting to appeal to the chief engineer who wrote: 'An arch bridge would require less steel than the cantilever bridge.'

Although still a long way from Australia, Bradfield was again playing politics, encouraging Australian agents in London to send cables home discouraging the government from pursuing a toll-based payment scheme to tenders and to pass the Bridge Act quickly. Bradfield also felt he needed more time to convince the sceptical European bridge builders and asked for an extension to the tender cut-off date so that nervous companies could be assured of the government's determination to proceed and would then have time to organise an appropriate tender. He even wrote speeches for north shore members in the upper house of the New South Wales Parliament along the same lines.

The government extended the time for tenders to September the following year, which gave him some breathing space in negotiations with the international firms. Kearney, however, continued to cause problems for Bradfield, who noted in his diary, 'Wrote to Mr Kearney pointing out that his statements were not only untrue but contemptible.' The following week he met the tube train inventor and watched a model built on a 50-foot long track successfully negotiate steep gradients, but was still not impressed. The following month they met again and the arguments became heated as the chief engineer insisted that a model was not proof of the system's viability. 'My candid opinion is that Kearney is obsessed with his patent and is suffering from softening of the brain.'

It was Bradfield, however, who was softening, as despite his repeated rejections, the arch bridge, like Kearney, would not go away.

On 9 August he received a copy of the American Society of Civil Engineers 1918 journal, which included a report on Lindenthal's groundbreaking Hell Gate arch, which he had seen during construction in 1914. The following day Mr Dixon, the chairman of the Cleveland Bridge Company, again met with Bradfield and brought from Paris G. C. Imbault, who had used the ingenious cable method to construct the arch at Victoria Falls twenty years earlier.

> Mr Imbault says the specifications as drafted is very satisfactory. When a tender is accepted the successful firm and myself would work out the design in detail. He prefers an arch design and has himself prepared a design for an arch span across the harbour.

Bradfield finally came around and cabled home his intention to include an arch bridge in the specifications for tenders and that the Bridge Act, should it ever be passed, should include such wording.

In mid-August he caught the SS *Diogenes* for Australia and despite difficult conditions on board worked day and night on specifications for an arch proposal; one month later he concluded that such a bridge would use less steel and would cost the State of New South Wales £400,000 less than a cantilever design.

Bradfield may have been stubborn and committed but he was intelligent enough to adapt when necessary. He left Australia a committed cantilever man and came home converted to the arch, which meant he had a lot more work to do.

The ship docked in Melbourne late in September and he caught a punt up the Yarra before boarding a train to Sydney. Despite spending seven months abroad, there was no time to waste, as his diary entry reveals.

> Arrived Central [station] 11.40pm [he means am]. Alan met me at train with Keith and Stanley. Got luggage and left Central about 12 pm in taxi, Alan and boys went home with luggage. Called in at office; saw Miss Butler, Mr Cooper and

Minister for Works Mr Ball, with whom I had an interview from 12.40 til 1.50 pm. Saw Mr Fox for a few minutes and caught the 2.10 pm boat arrived home at 3 pm. Left home at 8 am Thursday, March 16th and returned home Friday September 30th at 3 pm.

Bradfield's commitment was extraordinary, but the trip had worn him down and his meeting with Ball plunged him into despair. At home he made this entry into his diary:

> Do not think govt. are in earnest re Bridge Bill. They have introduced it in such a way as to ensure the defeat, if possible. However the work I have done will not be lost — it is one chapter in the romance of the Sydney Harbour Bridge, which some day I hope to write. Romance never dies; it is as beautiful as the line where the sea and sky meet beyond the boundless expanse of the oceans, as the seven seas themselves in their varying moods, as the melody of the mountains or the setting sun. In the annals of the past each silver lake, each brimming river, both mountain and valley have been shining strong to tell and so also in the lives of men have courage, unselfishness, endurance and patience won through and so it has been so it will be.
>
> I will see my Romance of the Bridge become a Reality.

Bradfield went to work the next day, a Saturday, and was back Monday despite the fact that it was a public holiday. True to his word he pushed on, meeting with the Crown Solicitor regarding the addition of the two words 'or arch' to the Bridge Bill and instructing his draughtsman William Lush to prepare elevations of an arch design.

Bradfield soon had Ball on side and the Bill was reintroduced to parliament in September 1922. The minister was a fan of the project and the chief engineer and told parliament:

Mr Bradfield is looked upon not only in Australia but in the engineering profession throughout the world as one of the most competent men associated with bridge work, and I do not know of any man who would be better qualified to advise the government in regard to the design of the bridge.

Bradfield intensified his efforts to keep the parliamentarians in line and he was such a common sight around Parliament House in Macquarie Street, the *Bulletin* observed: 'While the matter was before Parliament, Bradfield almost lived on the premises. The Minister (R. T. Ball) made a speech or two on the floor of the house; Bradfield made a hundred in the lobbies and the party rooms.' He was in the gallery when the minister told the house on 10 October 1922, 'Mr Bradfield … is the designer of the bridge and the man who has had all to do with the preparations of the plans and specifications,' before asking that the act be varied to allow for an arch or cantilever bridge.

That will give us an opportunity of considering tenders which Mr Bradfield says are likely to be received owing to the fact that there has been a development this year in the manufacture of steel unknown to builders a few years ago, but which it has now been proved can be applied to bridge building. It will enable a great reduction in the weight of steel used.

The Bill was put to the vote in the Legislative Assembly and the last objectors had their say. Dr J. B. Nash, the last speaker, had opposed the bridge and may have had a little tongue in cheek by closing his speech with: 'Ad gloriam Bradfieldii … Good luck to him!'

The Bill passed the lower house and then passed its last test in the Legislative Council by 41 votes to 13 on 24 November 1922.

Bradfield and his bridge had been given the green light and although he didn't know it, not a minute too soon. By the time the arch began to grow over the waters of the harbour the dark clouds of depression were hanging over Australia and by the time the bridge opened almost all other construction work had ground to a halt.

It was not the first bridge act to pass, but this one had a built-in guarantee that had been skilfully inserted by Bradfield, who was wary of the weasel ways of politicians and now one step ahead of them at all times. As Bradfield had agreed with the Labor Premier, Storey, back in 1920, the act called for the introduction of the land tax a year before tenders closed. Bradfield boasted later that should any government decide to shut him down now 'the fire and smoke from Sydney's greatest conflagration would have faded into insignificance with that raised by the taxpayers who had paid the tax for a year and still had no Bridge!'

The search was now on for a bridge builder who could meet Bradfield's exacting demands as spelt out in the tender process.

> The Bridge must be the best that engineering skill can devise. It must be of unquestionable strength and stability. It should have the maximum of rigidity vertically under the rolling load and laterally under wind pressure so that by its freedom from vibration it may have the reputation of being the strongest and most rigid in the world.

The Bridge should be simple to erect and safe at all stages of erection.

> NO untried material, or material of which there is the slightest doubt of quality, must be used in the Bridge.

Furthermore, the tender document insisted that all such materials should be sourced in New South Wales where possible.

THE FIRST SOD

In a muddy field somewhere in north Sydney a
politician plunges a ceremonial shovel into the earth
and proclaims the bridge project a goer. There are
many speeches and toasts and Bradfield is presented
with a lovely silver model of a bridge he has no
intention of constructing.

July 1923

Before 3 pm the elected and elevated steered their shuddering motor vehicles to the side of the road, peered up at the miserable skies and searched for their place on temporary staging at the corner of Miller and Blue streets, north Sydney, stepping gingerly through the water-soaked earth to the platform.

Above their appointed seats the flags of empire and state hung limp and wet. Looking through the bunting the dignitaries and their lady wives were greeted by a bouquet of umbrellas arranged against the persistent winter, protecting the crowd from the rain falling on this muddy paddock.

The unofficial guests had been filing onto the vacant block for hours. The boy scouts were soaked to the skin but remained in a solemn formation near the foot of the stage. A small boy and girl in Sunday best escaped parental disapproval and the rain by climbing beneath the platform. By the time the Mayor of North Sydney, George Clarke, cleared his throat to welcome the dignitaries there were thousands pressing for a glimpse and late arrivals were forced to stand across the road.

The whole area was abuzz with the coming of the Sydney Harbour Bridge that was soon to be built. Along the street, residents had decorated their homes with flags in anticipatory celebration.

'It was unfortunate that the rain detracted from a good deal of the dignity of the proceedings. Even the Premier was much too wet to look magnificent,' reported the *Sydney Sun* after the event. At 3 pm the not-so-magnificent Premier, George Fuller; the Minister for Public Works and Railways, R. T. Ball; and the north shore's favourite son, J. J. C. Bradfield were standing either side of the local mayor as he began to speak. 'I have the honour of presiding at this celebration, which is a prelude to one of the greatest events about to take place in modern history,' Clarke informed the guests, whose vast presence on such an inclement day indicated they may have been of similar opinion. 'When completed, I venture to say, that our bridge will be classed alongside similar undertakings in the world. Mr Bradfield says the bridge, which is on the cantilever principle, will be the world's heaviest structure.'

The mayor was clearly not alerted to the fact that the structure might be an arch, not a cantilever, but nonetheless believed the bridge would tilt the whole of Australia on its axis and the neglected northern shore would benefit more than anywhere else by the shift.

> The direct route to Queensland, the northern towns and districts of New South Wales will be via the bridge, our northern shores will be requisitioned for shipping, then our manufactures and other commercial pursuits will follow, to say nothing of the opening up of large areas of residential lands, which are properly described as the highlands of Sydney. We, who reside on this, the northern side of the harbour; welcome our guests.

Clarke spoke of the sacrifice of the northern Sydney ratepayers 'nobly responding to the call to pay their portion of the cost' but ventilated a common local grievance by asking, 'why not the whole of the ratepayers of the metropolitan area and the people of the state — they will all benefit'.

Weather or Not: The north shore gathered on the corner of Miller and Blue streets for the Turning of the First Sod ceremony. July 1923.

Had any of the country members been present there would no doubt have been some consternation at the suggestion all should pay for Sydney's bridge. That said, this was no time to quibble, 'the Sydney Harbour Bridge, when completed will be one of the greatest undertakings ever achieved in Australia,' Clarke told them, his mayoral chains clinking with pride.

However, a hint of uncertainty coloured his closing remarks.

Ladies and gentlemen, I thank you for your attendance today, take a hopeful view of the future, do not look on the dark side of things. The immediate construction of the bridge is assured; the Ministry, a majority of members of Parliament, and the people are behind it, it must go on, the end crowns the work.

THE BRIDGE

The north shore knew very well that while the will was strong, no tender would be chosen for months and it had lived through many broken promises regarding the bridge.

The Premier, Sir George Fuller, had just returned from an overseas trip and was pleased to bathe in the north shore glow. 'Today the Harbour Bridge Act is a law of the land and you have a Ministry in power which is determined to have it carried out in the interests, not only of Sydney, but of New South Wales at large,' he said.

The Premier had also jumped on the Bradfield bandwagon. He was not only a great engineer; he was a fearless hero devoted to the cause. The Premier told the starry-eyed crowd that whilst in Quebec he had been told of how the little man had climbed to a great height on the local bridge, in a 'howling storm, in order to test the vibration made by a passing train'.

The Minister for Public Works and Railways reiterated to the crowd what a good job the politicians had done in passing the bill to build a bridge that would be one of the biggest public works ever contemplated in the Commonwealth. Not only that, it was 'designed by an Australian'.

With the rain still falling, Ball was handed a ceremonial silver shovel, complete with a ribbon on its shaft and a special inscription. Attuned to the demands of history and publicity, the minister waited until the press photographers had arranged themselves and then plunged the shovel into the muddy earth, which squelched with disagreement as he Turned the First Sod.

The crowd broke into spontaneous applause and the band struck up a rousing version of 'Advance Australia Fair'. Swept up in the magic of the moment, the crowd's voice rose as one.

It was indeed a historic occasion.

At 4 pm, with the token sod lying exposed to the rain, the 500 invited guests moved to St Thomas Memorial Hall in McLaren Street for a celebratory banquet, a series of toasts and a few additional speeches. The backslapping was nearly as loud as the construction work it was meant to celebrate.

Mayor Clarke proposed a toast to the King; the mayor of nearby Willoughby, Alderman E. M. Clark, proposed a toast to the ministry and parliament, saying the bridge undertaking had been one of 'broken hopes and hearts' until, of course, this great day. The Premier proposed another to mark the occasion and to chastise those who said he was ignoring country interests. Wasn't the government building four bridges across the Murray? he asked, then added cheekily that if all parties were now supporting the government on the bridge question they could support it on a few others, too. Councillor McIntosh proposed a toast to the distinguished guests.

The Honourable W. A. Holman took to the stage to be greeted by cheers and 'musical honours' and proposed they drink to the health of the designer of the bridge, John Job Crew Bradfield.

The King's Counsel praised Bradfield 'as one of three persons in this country who were the equals, or the superiors, of their confreres in any part of the world. Madame Melba and Victor Trumper contributed to the innocent gaiety of the nations, and General Monash was a great soldier' while Bradfield was a 'born genius', Holman told them, his 'skill was unchallengeable' and he 'pictured Sydney as Napoleon did a field of battle'. (It was not the only time that the little Australian was compared to the maniacal little Frenchman; Jack Lang wrote that 'Bradfield wanted to be the Napoleon III of Sydney. He wanted to pull down everything in the way of his grandiose schemes. He was always thinking of the future. He was probably the first man to plan for Sydney as a city of two million.')

Holman said Bradfield was in the front rank of the engineers of the world. His skill was unchallengeable; it had run the gauntlet of the world specialists, and had come out unimpaired after three months' close examination. Not even the Belgians could suggest an improvement on the Australian engineer's plans.

A sombre, but secretly delighted, Bradfield responded by explaining how the war's aftermath had affected tendering, but he expected eight international and one local firm to apply to build the bridge. When finished it could carry 100,000 people by rail and tram in an hour, he added. He explained to the crowd that the bridge would be the heaviest ever built and would set new construction records because its individual members would be the largest ever constructed, lifted or set into place.

The Mayor of North Sydney then presented Bradfield with a silver model of the bridge mounted on an oak stand and enclosed in a glass case. It would be an heirloom to hand down to his children, Clarke said.

Bradfield replied graciously but his smile would have been a little uneasy.

The silver model was a beautiful version of the cantilever bridge that was nothing like the one he now believed should be constructed across the harbour. Still, at this stage perception was everything and the ceremony was all part of the chief engineer's manipulation of politicians and public relations. Keen to relieve the anxiety of potential tenderers, Bradfield had written a note to the government encouraging them to act as if the bridge was a 'fait accompli' and convinced the minister that the construction of the northern railway approach should begin six months before tenders were due to close.

It didn't matter that tenders had not been received or accepted and that they wouldn't be opened until January in the following year. The bridge had finally gained momentum, regardless of who would build it or what shape it would eventually take.

In less than nine years those motor vehicles parked around Miller and Blue streets would be able to fly above the water between the city and the north shore on a path so high that on this day in 1923 it was obscured by cloud.

5

WORK STARTS

Or does it? Bradfield's ever-present secretary throws
a ceremonial switch and more speeches are made,
but who will build this celebrated bridge and what
will it look like when they do?

July 1923

Bradfield took his redundant model of the cantilever bridge home and placed it on the sideboard of his northern Sydney home that Sunday night. Early the next morning workers arrived on the vacant block at the corner of Miller and Blue streets. The rains had cleared and it was a perfect Sydney winter's day.

As one group began unloading tools to dismantle the stage where the mayors, Premier, minister and chief engineer had paraded two days before, others cast their eyes around the neighbourhood and began to go door to door, posting notices on homes and shops.

Almost every house in Blue Street was given the bad news. By the time the men had finished their work almost 500 buildings on the north shore alone had been earmarked for resumption and demolition. The bridge was not to be stopped by anything and that included family homes, corner shops, schools or even churches. All could be and were compulsorily acquired and demolished to make way for the great structure.

The Reverend Frank Cash ambled up from Christ Church down at Lavender Bay and watched with a mix of excitement and sorrow. 'A new and unsettled feeling had sprung up within ourselves,' he wrote. 'The work of the Sydney Harbour Bridge had begun.'

Before the week's end smaller crowds began to gather on street corners and the auctioneer's hammer fell.

That Monday a field office was opened in Bolwarra Flats at the corner of Walker and Blue streets to oversee the work; adjoining properties were resumed and hastily demolished. Heavy machinery, including a stone-crusher and air compressors, was installed.

Two months later, Bradfield and his secretary, Kath Butler, joined the relevant ministers and secretaries on the vacant land at Blue Street for a ceremony on the site where they had all gathered on that rain-sodden July day for the Turning of the First Sod. For the first months of work the railways had provided electricity but now the bridge builders had their own supply. The current was switched on and Miss Butler flicked the switch to start the large air compressor. Jackhammers started to attack the sandstone as the first holes were drilled and a charge laid. The Public Works minister, Mr

Dorman's Sheds: The massive bridge workshops where the steel pieces were cut, drilled and assembled were under construction at Milsons Point, where Luna Park now stands. Late 1923.

Ball, fired a charge to mark the First Act of Construction in the building of the bridge. The workers were now ready to blast into the rock beneath the Church of England Grammar School, tunnelling a route for the north Sydney rail line.

In the meantime, with little else to do but run the enormous railway construction project, Bradfield began work on a thesis for his PhD. On his fifty-seventh birthday he presented the paper, entitled The City and Suburban Electric Railways and the Sydney Harbour Bridge, an extraordinary document that even included illustrations of an ornamented park running from Lavender Bay to Milsons Point and a dramatic entrance way from the bridge to the city. Bradfield's grand plans knew no limits.

Aiming High: The first section of steel for the bottom chord of the approach spans is moved by small gauge rail through the falseworks. 1927.

A Clear Path: Homes and businesses once stood in this area of The Rocks between the Argyle Cut and the emerging bridge. 1930.

THE PRICE OF PROGRESS

In north and south Sydney the harsh realities of the project are driven home as the poor and powerless are driven from their homes. Women speak of suicide, old couples accept a few pounds in return for their life's work and politicians demand nobody be compensated for fear a precedent be set. All the while an eccentric priest photographs the strange happenings.

Old North Sydney

They're shifting old North Sydney—
Perhaps 'tis just as well—
They're carting off the houses
Where the old folks used to dwell.
Where only ghosts inhabit
They lay the old shops low;
But the Spirit of North Sydney,
It vanished long ago.

The Spirit of North Sydney,
The good old time and style,
It camped, maybe, at Crow's Nest,
But only for a while.
It left about the season,
Or at the time, perhaps,
When old Inspector Cotter
Transferred his jokes and traps.

A brand new crowd is thronging
The brand new streets aglow

Where the Spirit of North Sydney
Would gossip long ago.
They will not know to-morrow—
Tho' 'twere but yesterday—
Exactly how McMahon's Point
And its ferry used to lay.

The good old friendly spirit
Its sorrows would unfold,
When householders were neighbours
And shop-keeping was old;
But now we're busy strangers,
Our feelings we restrain—
The Spirit of North Sydney
Shall never come again!

Henry Lawson, 1904

There Goes the Neighbourhood: Princes Street was the heart of community life in The Rocks but its homes were resumed and demolished for the bridge. 1927.

The Sydney Harbour Bridge spans a void over the waters, but its long approaches cut a swathe through two communities on either side of the harbour. Its path drove out the families and tenants, corner stores and schools, playgrounds and parks, churches and pubs. The area became a war zone with people forced to pack their belongings on open carts and trudge out one end of the street as the invading army came in the other.

The government decreed in black legislative print that no obstacle should halt the advance of the great project and few dared challenge its great march. This was half a century before phrases or institutions developed to protect people and neighbourhoods from progress or development.

Shaking the shore

The sleepy north shore woke to a brutal new reality with the coming of the bridge. The earth shook with the subsonic rumble of progress, walls cracked as homes shifted on their foundations, others tumbled to make way for the bridgeworks, and the village calm was destroyed by the sound and activity of construction.

The Shore, as it was known, had been a quiet place away from the hustle of the city on the other side of the water; at night you still hear the lions at Taronga Park growling — but those days were coming to an end.

The thunderous first steps of the bridge shook the streets of North Sydney, crushing whole neighbourhoods, crumbling cliff faces and demolishing elegant hilltop mansions. Uprooting the trains and trams and ferries, its heavy pylons took root in the sandstone and permanently changed the ecology of life on the Shore.

In North Sydney, the tiny communities at Milsons Point and Kirribilli had huddled together on the headland since the farm lands were subdivided a century before.

The small businesses, boarding houses and even residents who had settled in the area believed the building of the bridge would bring prosperity and progress. Few imagined it might destroy their homes and livelihoods and even if they did there was little they could do about it. Even for those who kept their houses or shops the bridge meant disruptions and eventually a steady stream of traffic that careered over their heads toward the city or in the opposite direction toward the new suburbs of the ever-expanding north.

By the 1920s the fabric of this community was tightly woven, but the construction required that a whole panel of the fabric be unstitched and discarded.

The Shore, like the Rocks, which was also in the bridge's path, was one of Sydney's most unique areas, having developed with a sense of otherness or estrangement from the city. It was part frontier, part refuge from the higher prices and crowding that occurred around the Quay on the opposite shore.

For the 1920s commuter, the Milsons Point ferry terminal was a more popular and functional transport hub than the recently built Central station to the south. Once a sleepy stopping-off point for travellers, the ferry terminal had been shaded by a century-old Port Jackson fig whose surrounds were a local meeting point, although that changed in 1900 when residents awoke to find the giant toppled by an overnight gale. As the north shore grew, the terminal became a bustling commuter exchange where ferries spilled passengers onto the enclosed wharf and within a few metres they could connect with a train, tram, taxi or bus. Longtime resident Florence Innes remembers it well:

'It was a most beautiful place [Milsons Point arcade] … The trams came down inside the arcade and the shops there … you couldn't be beaten, they were so excellent. As you came off the ferry, off the wharf, there was the post office, also a wine shop, an exclusive cake shop and I think a dry cleaners, but there was an opening through from the post office where you got your cab.'

It was an energetic place: ferries lined up to drop off and pick up passengers, lines of drays and cars sometimes stretched over a kilometre up the hill as they patiently waited for a punt, trams careered down the Alfred Street hill and into the open terminus to unload before straining back up with another load. The trains avoided the incline, emerging from the Lavender Bay cutting and snaking around the foreshore. Inside the elegant building a fish and chip shop filled the air with the smell of hot oil and fish caught fresh that morning. The dry cleaners hissed steam and the daily traffic moved to its own rhythms; the labourers and shift workers early, in collarless shirts, wool trousers and serviceable shoes first, then the clerks and business types, secretaries and public servants in their pleated dresses, gaberdines and hats. Victor Wills can still picture the neighbourhood.

> If you commence at the waterfront which is now the point underneath the north pylon, there was Milsons Point wharf; on the eastern side of Milsons Point wharf was either the ferry dockyards where there were workshops, then there was a timber yard. There was also a vehicular punt ... I don't think it was at Jeffrey St, I think Jeffrey St came later. Moving up, going up the hill, we come into the populated areas ... the area was densely populated. Twenty-foot frontage would have been pretty common. There were many terraced houses and they were two storey. They lined Alfred St from Dind Street where Dind's Hotel was, where they had all the bohemian gatherings. From Dind Street ... virtually up to ... Junction Street were terrace houses on both sides of Alfred St. So that the cross streets like Pitt St, Fitzroy St, Burton St, were all lined with terraced houses ...
>
> There were shops from Milsons Point wharf right up till Fitzroy St, a wide variety of shops, fish shops and cooked shops — what we would now call take away food shops — there were so many houses cleared out of there. Somebody said there was 300, a thousand would be a closer estimate I think.

Wills was right about the Jeffrey Street ferry, it did not open until the bridge constructions began in 1925 and before then had been a timber yard.

In the early years many a grand home was built at Milsons Point, but by the 1920s many of these had been converted to boarding houses, which seem to have been run by war widows and other single women. The owners leased their properties to the women for a large 'goodwill fee' and they in turn sublet the bedrooms for a small profit. It was a respectable and convenient way for a single woman to support herself. The area was popular because rents were relatively cheap and the proximity to the ferries meant people could commute to work across the harbour.

Australian scientist Victor Trikojus was born in Darlinghurst to a Russian migrant father and recalled growing up in the area at this time.

> My father died in August 1911, leaving my mother with three children, two boys and a girl, and limited funds. We continued his hairdressing business for some 2–3 years at 150 William Street, then moved to 10 Campbell Street, Milsons Point, an area now occupied by the Sydney Harbour Bridge. Here we ran a small guest house. I managed to supplement the income by odd jobs during school vacations and from the age of 12 to 16 I [ran] a newspaper stall at the old Milson's Point railway station, after school and at weekends, for the New South Wales Bookstall Company.

Many of the shops in North Sydney were also leased to the businesses that occupied them. But by the 1920s most leases had expired and people were content to trust long-term arrangements.

Then work began on the bridge and the peace was shattered. Explosions sounded up on the hill to drive the railways tunnels under the grammar school, the cliff face at Lavender Bay was blasted back, brick walls began to tumble and a way of life was undone.

The coming of the bridge shifted the transport system on the Shore around like pieces on a puzzle board. Every move involved a counter-move. Changes were both permanent and temporary. Some streets were closed down for the best part of a decade. Some for good. In the meantime the quiet, secure world people knew was turned on its head.

It was the job of the successful tenderer — whoever that might be — to build the bridge and approaches alone. The preparatory work was left to the Railways and Public Works Department, who spent almost £20 million preparing the place for the bridge builders. In many ways the work undertaken by the Railways and Public Works Department, under Bradfield's guidance from 1923 was more involved and complicated than constructing the bridge itself, which was still some way off.

To place the critical jewel in the city's transport system a lot of the existing routes had to be either permanently or temporarily re-routed.

On the city side the underground link with Central station was started in 1922 and on the north side trains had to be diverted from Milsons Point to a new station at Lavender Bay, the ferry terminal needed to be moved at the same time, trams had to be re-routed, a new bus route introduced and a new car ferry built at Jeffrey Street dock with a new road run to it that would have to avoid the broad approaches to the bridge and still have room for the line of traffic that sometimes stretched over a kilometre back from the water's edge.

One of the last buildings to disappear was the old Ferry Arcade at Milsons Point. Once the busiest place on the north shore, it fell in a cloud of dust and was carted away like every other impediment to the future. This site would become ground zero for the bridge, the place where the approaches met the arch proper, where the pylons, the twin towers of the bridge, would rise, broad and high.

Sitting on the sandstone balcony of Christ Church, Lavender Bay, Rev. Frank Cash, the eccentric local priest, watched and documented the changes going on in his area. A former metallurgist with a metaphysical bent, he had a love of photography and writing and produced a valuable record of the building of the bridge.

Cash was given dress circle seats to the biggest show in Sydney's history when he was appointed rector at the church on the hill in 1922. The editorial in the *Parish Paper* soon moved away from pure biblical lessons to include reflections on God and man that were gleaned from his musings on the construction of a bridge.

Cash was an extraordinary figure, opinionated, argumentative and curious. The bridge became his obsession and in 1930 he published a book, *Parables of the Sydney Harbour Bridge*, which featured his photography and chapters with titles like 'The Parable of the Skewback', 'Everlasting Granite' and 'Timber Towers'. 'The Parable of the Rock' makes the observation: 'a surprising likeness exists between the main span of the Bridge, and the span of human life. Both are weighty matters, and both, if they are to be carried though with safety and stability, must be founded on a rock.' There were many similar lessons to be gained from the intrigue of bridge building, but a lot of the things recorded in his *Parish Paper* also document the changes to Lavender Bay and Milsons Point.

Cash explained in the introduction:

> The opportunity for making such a book, is the natural outcome of the circumstances, in which we find ourselves. It is obvious, that some privileges and qualifications were essential. The first is, that one must live on the spot. The photographer must be in the near vicinity when the houses are being demolished. A telephone call, that a fine wall was coming down in five minutes; or a demolisher coming soon after seven o'clock in the morning, with a hurried message 'come on, we are waiting', speak plainly of the privilege of living on the ground.

Cash was so close he could shoot the construction from the rectory veranda or window and then race upstairs to immediately develop the film.

The Cash and Bradfield families had been close and the chief engineer was called on to unveil the new gates at the church in 1925, but the pair fell out when the bridge builder denied the priest access to the works during construction. Cash was granted permission by the English contractors and felt he had been badly treated by Bradfield, but the latter had an agreement with builders that only official photographers be allowed near the structure. Perhaps that is why the chief engineer appears only once in *Parables of the Sydney Harbour Bridge* and the foreword was written by Dorman, Long's Lawrence Ennis, who stated, 'The Rev. Frank Cash can claim to be the only person, outside of those connected with the bridge, to have unlimited access to the work, and in the seeking of his information he has shown a complete disregard of personal risk.'

In 1927 the Rev. Mr Cash published a photograph of the site of the Milsons Bay ferry wharf, taken long before it had been constructed or demolished.

> Without fear of correction, it is safe to say that perhaps no part of New South Wales has undergone such far-reaching change within the last sixty years as Lavender Bay and Milsons Point ... How often have you looked upon this scene, when tram travelling to Milsons Point! Or how often, if you travel by the punt, paid your fare as you waited in the queue, nearby where the tree spreads its shade! Those times have gone. No more shall you travel that steep grade by tram to the Point, no more shall the roar of the motor engine cease as your eye carelessly roams over the broad road to the left. The tramlines have been torn up and a great barricade the street wide, bids with stern notice all and sundry to keep without. And the old-time scene, partly rural, partly seaside, has been cut off from the public gaze for ever.

The new commuter hot spot was shifted around to Lavender Bay. Here the ferries dropped passengers onto a temporary wharf where they could connect with the train that snaked around the bay. Commuters could also step from the ferry onto one of three escalators which carried 10,000 passengers an hour — it was an oft-quoted figure — up the steep cliff face to the new tram and bus stops at the top of the cliff in Glen Street. For some the creaking wooden escalators became as much an attraction during their years of operation as Luna Park would later. As Florence Innes recalls:

... the ferry service was the most wonderful because it ran every five minutes. Those ferries were much larger than the previous ones. One ferry was waiting to come into the wharf when the other one was already there. Every five minutes you could get to the Quay ... over a weekend the wharf was built around into Lavender Bay by the railway site ... then they built the first escalators. They were the longest and the biggest we had here ...

Here Comes the Train: A view looking north of the railway line and Milsons Point station. The first approach span is in the right corner.

The fit or fearful climbed the two steep, narrow (210 cm) stairways while the infirm and elderly used an electric lift.

The tram had been diverted along Dind Street to Glen Street to facilitate the exchange of passengers, but this had meant Glen Street also needed to be widened and houses demolished to provide for a bus and cab stand.

Bradfield timed the transport changes so well that there was hardly a disruption. At 11.30 pm on Sunday 27 July 1924 the trains and trams that travelled to the Milsons Point Arcade were stopped and by 4.30 am on Monday 28 July 1924 the new, functional, convenient — albeit temporary — system was up and operating ready for the first morning commuter.

In March 1925 the railway tunnel between Miller and Bank streets was complete and the first train passed through to the temporary goods yards at North Sydney. The excavated stone enabled the park at Lavender Bay to reclaim another half-acre from the harbour.

The shoreline from Milsons Point to Lavender Bay was rocky and steep, but the contract for the Sydney Harbour Bridge called for a series of massive workshops which Bradfield decided would be built to the west of Milsons Point on the place where Luna Park now stands.

The bottom of the cliffs was perfect for building the workshops as the site would give easy access to freighters carrying building materials from overseas foundries, at the same time allowing the finished sections to be loaded onto punts within a short distance of where they were needed. The major problem was that there was barely room for a railway line on the narrow strip of land available, let alone a trio of massive sheds.

Like the houses above them, the cliffs were a minor impediment to the march of the bridge. A series of explosions pared back 26,000 cubic metres of rock from the cliff face. Landfill was spilled into the sea, the shoreline was straightened and a flotilla of dredges got to work to clear beneath the water so ocean liners could pull right up to the factory doors.

For the next nine years the noise from the workshops echoed across the harbour and north shore. Machinery powerful enough to cut through 5 cm-thick steel plates shook the earth, diamond-tipped drills screamed and the combined racket from air compressors, steam cranes, rivet guns and ships' horns created a cacophony of sound that made the noise levels from Luna Park — so irritating to wealthy residents seven decades later — seem almost ambient.

Back up the hill, the new railway line and bridge approaches gouged a terrible path, eating into the sandstone, knocking down some houses, leaving others balancing on the precipice. Whole neighbourhoods became dusty wastelands. Railway lines burrowed into the stone under homes and residents cowered inside as explosions tore up their roads and shifted the earth around them. The chaos was unimaginable.

One side of Alfred Street was razed. Whole blocks of Fitzroy, Broughton and Willoughby disappeared as the approach swept down the hill toward the harbour.

Below Euroka Street, where Henry Lawson had lived in a two-storey stone mansion, neighbours disappeared and a tunnel emerged. The noise of demolition and construction was so loud that any dissenting voices from the small cottages, the boarding house rooms and the small businesses were hard to hear and the government was conscious that the expense of resumptions would blow out spectacularly if they did listen. Most disappeared with barely a whimper and rarely a trace. Victor Wills was watching:

'There was certainly no uprisings and there were certainly no demonstrations that I recall — it was something that happened … people might not have had much say in matters those days. It was a question of "do as you are told" or else … (businesses) moved further north and would have amalgamated or got involved with people in Mount Street and those places …'

Demolitions began in July 1923. Two months later the *Sydney Morning Herald* reported that 'great progress had been made … the last of the houses on the Blue-street frontage has been demolished, as also have two residences on Walker street'.

One by one the houses were taken down, loaded onto trucks and drays and carried away.

George Aiken worked for his father, G. E. Aiken, 'The Stone King', in these years. He drove his horse and dray from Camperdown, caught the punt across to Jeffrey Street, loaded it with materials and then carted it away to other building sites.

The men developed a special method of felling walls. Aiken

remembers that the workers would chip out the corner bricks, undermining the foundations, then knock out two bricks halfway up the wall. Using a piece of wood as a lever, they would pull down and then 'run like hell'. Cash one day photographed the moment when a wall fell on a worker before he could escape. The man had the foresight to dive into a fireplace hollow and saved his life.

THE NORTH SIDE

In early 1925 shopkeepers asked for money for the disruptions to their business but were rejected by a government who asked if it should perhaps collect money from those businesses which would prosper from the redevelopment.

At a licence hearing in February 1925 to transfer a pub from Alfred Street to Walker and Blue streets, evidence was given about the loss of trade and the number of people displaced. The *Sun* reported on proceedings.

> DOOMED HOUSES
> North Sydney's 438
> HOTEL LICENCE QUESTION
> 'At present 118 houses have been resumed,' Mr Perry, North Sydney Town Clerk said. 'There will be 37 more houses resumed by March 13, 74 by June 30, and 209 by December 31, making a total of 438.'
>
> Witness said the average population of each house in question was 4.638, the total number or residents to the houses was about 2032.
>
> Mr Holman KC (for the applicant): 'Has the North Sydney Council considered the problem of people displaced by the resumptions scheme?
>
> Witness: The matter has been considered, but no decision has been arrived at.'

The debate about compensation continued in government circles and newspapers for years and became a source of particular angst to the governing Labor party.

The loss of homes and businesses caused terrible stresses and acute financial loss for many. Some had only taken up properties in recent years and unscrupulous owners had demanded goodwill payments, but not offered a lease as they knew the bridge was coming.

Mrs G. Taylor had recently moved to North Sydney from Tasmania and took out a loan to furnish a boarding house at 17 Fitzroy Street, the real estate agent assuring her she would have a two-year lease, which he could not put in writing. Less than a year later the boarding house was resumed; hearing this, the tenants left owing her rent. Her husband was out of work and they had no means of meeting the loan repayments.

Local councillors and parliamentary members took up the battle on behalf of businesses that had lost their premises or found themselves on a dead-end street made almost inaccessible to passing

The Iron Giant: The view looking south from the end of the first approach span. All properties in the bridge's path were demolished, 1927.

trade. Tenants had no such voice. The ferry company was compensated for the demolition of the Milsons Point arcade and the Presbyterian Church was given a new site for the Presbyterian Scots' Church. Ordinary tenants and most businesses did not have a prayer.

By now the desks of aldermen, local members, the Premier and even Dr Bradfield were piled high with pleading, often heartbreaking, letters.

The government insisted there would be no compensation and over the years stuck to this line until in 1926 a deputation of waterside workers from Milsons Point approached the Labor government and asked that 'provision be made for the housing of some two hundred and forty workers mostly on the water side, who sooner or later, will lose their homes at Milsons Point, owing to bridge resumptions'. Premier Lang announced he would set up a board to examine the issue. A cabinet paper from 12 October 1926 records the Premier's response.

> It is true that previous Cabinets have decided against you and that the present Cabinet has decided against you also, but I will bring the matter up, and if it is possible to get you a Board I will consult with the five members of the district. If a Board is appointed, it may be able to do something to meet your demands. If it is proved that compensation should be given to tenants at will or weekly tenants in North Sydney, then the principle must apply to the whole State. I will endeavour to try and satisfy you that this Government wants to be just to all.

James McDunna of Arthur Street was part of the waterside workers' deputation and flexed his labour muscles in a follow-up letter to the Premier.

> A large number of the tenants are; like myself; strong union members and staunch labour supporters, and look to and expect our government to stand by us. We only ask fair jus-

tice, and unless you redeem your promise made to that deputation, and by doing so come to our rescue, we will be turned adrift penniless. After your faithful promise that we should be protected, I cannot imagine that you will allow such hardship to be imported on us.

I admit that our matters are small compared with the issue now before you, but to us they are of very great importance, for it means that our living is being taken from us, and the money that we had invested in these premises; residentials and boarding houses and other small businesses, is to be lost, we are to be impoverished to make way for a bridge that is to benefit the property owner.

McDunna was a wily constituent and became a thorn in the side of the bridge developers. Many, including the unionist, believed the bridge would be a massive boon to the property market in the north and indeed Bradfield had made many references to these benefits in preceding years. The Premier eventually appointed W. J. Kessell under-secretary in the Department of Justice to consider the question of compensation, and the piles of anguished correspondence were then routed to his desk. Within months Kessell took ill and the process stalled, causing another wave of frustrated letters that were to continue for the next two years as the government awaited his report — long enough for most of the displaced to have moved on.

However, some of the business people and the odd tenant continued to lobby. Most were seeking help for financial reasons; others were more emotionally compelling.

Mrs Kate Lockart was 75 and her husband 82 when their furniture business on Fitzroy Street was resumed. With no storage available they sold £400 worth of stock for £73 and found themselves without an income and in debt. For two years they wrote to anybody they thought could help. Mr Kessell acknowledged in his deliberations that the Lockarts were a 'hard case' but insisted they be rejected from compensation, scrawling on the bottom of letters 'if we pay anything I will form a precedent that will become very expensive'.

The last the government heard from the Lockarts came in the form of a letter from Mr Lockart. It is written in a painful, old hand from an address in Campbell Street, Milsons Point and addressed to the 'Honorable Minister for Public Works'.

> My wife wrote some weeks ago re compensation for loss of home and means of living — through resumption. In reply, you stated, that all the Dept. could grant would be the cost of cartage.
>
> The amount is small, but would be very acceptable as we have no means and are both too old to go out to work.
>
> We would be grateful if you would order the sum be sent to us, as we have a further account to settle for storage of a few remnants of furniture.
>
> I am, Sir
> Yrs faithfully
> J. H. Lockart.

Mrs Pitcairn lived at 141 Alfred Street, North Sydney. Her daughter took in music students and they sublet part of the house to a tenant, which earned the couple £3 a week profit. Concerned about resumptions, Mrs Pitcairn twice wrote to Dr Bradfield and was reassured in two letters by the chief engineer that they could stay there until December 1926, but were then thrown out in December 1925. Records show that many people were moved out up to a year earlier than the council and government had indicated. In February 1927 Mrs Pitcairn wrote a letter to Kessell from their new address at Elizabeth Street in the city. It is a remarkable document.

> Sir, I enclose 'Statement' re my one desire is sufficient to get a home again — there is too much competition in the city. My daughter cannot make what she did in North Sydney — indeed since we lost our home we have had to sell many things for the necessities to keep out of debt. Fate seems to have singled me out for disaster. My husband was killed in a

mining accident — trying to save the entombed man — then the war came and ruined us financially, the £250 left from the wreck, we put into '141 Alfred St Milsons Point' — my daughter had her pupils, the house was partly let — we were very happy and comfortable, all our own efforts. Again tragedy, through the 'Bridge', everything is taken from us — and once more we are stranded — At this time I had only one wish, 'to take my own life' — and only my religion held me back. There are only two of us, we have no man to help — 'Woe to the women who have to fight the battle of life alone — the world was made for men — I am glad I have only one life —'

    Yours faithfully

    M. H. Pitcairn.

Those who could not resort to emotional leverage, like the real estate agent J. W. Paddison, wrote letter after letter and finally took to sitting in Kessell's waiting room for a week on end in August 1927 awaiting some satisfaction. The under-secretary avoided him and Paddison went back to letter-writing.

Mr Jackson had a greengrocery business at premises in Alfred Street, for which he paid £35 a week rent. When the building was resumed he had no means of support for his wife and two children as no other suitable shops could be found. His life, like Mrs Pitcairn's, descended into an almost Dickensian tragedy. Kessell made this note:

'He [Jackson] is at present hawking vegetables from house to house and has absolutely nothing. His wife has been admitted to Waterfall Sanatorium with both lungs affected and he has been forced to put both children in the Burnside Homes. He has received no compensation. He was previously clearing about £4 or £5 weekly.'

In March 1928 the Premier was finally in receipt of Kessell's proposals regarding the various requests for compensation. The under-secretary noted that businesses and tenants who had no lease had no rights to compensation beyond cartage expenses as it would set an expensive precedent.

By this time the last properties had been resumed, but a few squatters caused work to be held up as they refused to budge. In early 1927 Bradfield wrote to Kessell stating that these properties 'should be obtained at once'.

The last two to go included the home of the belligerent McDunna who had written to Lang earlier. The chief engineer noted: 'Mr McDunna the occupant of No. 54 Arthur Street, was served on 30 August, 1926, with a notice to quit by the 30th of September, 1926. His rent is paid to the date of expiration of the notice to quit, but he owes from that date to the 17th January, 1927, the sum of £38.11.5.'

By 1926 Rev. Frank Cash had embarked on a photographic documentation of the destruction of his community. The locals supported the cause by letting him know when a demolition was in progress; the eccentric priest would then grab his camera and run to the street in question. In December that year the front page of the *Christ Church Parish Paper* featured a series of photographs of buildings being demolished. He wrote about it under the title 'The Parish Falling'.

> As the crow flies the Falling Walls on the frontispiece were in Arthur Street, about 100 yards from the Memorial Gates of Christ Church. But in a little while I hope to reproduce pictures of very big walls falling 50 yards from the Church, on the other side of Walker Street, nearly opposite the church.
>
> In these homes lived some of our most regular worshippers in Church, people who were always present at the early hour on Sundays. I have no doubt they sat around a fire on winter evenings, and watched the smoke going upward; now you see the chimney in the picture coming downward, very fast, and smashed into two pieces …

The old Brisbane House, former Christ Church rectory and Milson residence, amongst the finest homes ever built on 'Shore' was barred and vacant, like many others. Landlord Mary Malone and her seventeen tenants had disappeared. Its dressed stone, cedar fittings and iron gates were sold at auction to demolishers for £80.

The old Water Police Court at Dawes Point was also demolished. The court was built from materials recycled from the old observatory and fort at Dawes Point. Bradfield uncovered an old sandstone block in the rubble inscribed 'RR 1789'. This probably stood for Major Robert Roberts, the first Lieutenant Governor and was possibly the first sandstone block quarried in Sydney. The stone was donated to the Royal Historical Society.

In December Cash published photographs of a large home being demolished to make room for the new railway station on Blue Street. The home had been sold for £3 to timber merchants.

> Adjoining this house were four three storey houses. They were all very fine properties. I was present at the sale of them. You would scarcely believe a crowd of buyers could be so quiet.
>
> 'What am I bid, what am I bid,' cries the auctioneer. The men folk stood, as though they never heard the auctioneer's voice.
>
> At last a voice called out, £8 for the lot.
>
> An advance on £8 could not be secured.

One home reportedly sold for £2.

In August 1927, under the heading 'Falling Streets', Cash gave an update on the situation around the shrinking neighbourhood and the cost to his flock.

> The Parish is still falling down; demolition work is still going on within one hundred yards of the Church. On the East, the Parish boundary is 150 yards away, and on the North 200. How far the preparation for the Harbour Bridge has affected the neighbourhood, can be seen by any passer-by. Shops and

premises that were newly renovated two years ago or more, and were 'To Let' are as silent and uninhabited as they were, when the notice was first displayed.

One shop, about one minute's walk away, put up a fresh notice last week, *To let at greatly reduced rental.* Of course, our Church life is deeply touched. On a pleasant Sunday evening we get some 250 people, nearly 200 less than two or three years ago. The number of communicants at 8 o'clock on Sunday mornings averages little over 30 people.

Cash had lost another parishioner in the preceding month and noted it in the next item.

Reggie Clements
He was a little fellow of seven years, a bright-eyed boy in the State School near by; and happy in his Sunday School on Sunday. His life was not for long — seven years only, for a motor car knocked him down, and killed him on the afternoon of Saturday, 2nd July.

On the Tuesday following, his poor widowed mother and lonely little sister went with him to Northern Suburbs, where in the midst of a few friends, and an abundance of flowers, the little chap was laid to rest.

The mother could only go to work as usual the next day, very sad at heart, for she now has no husband and no son.

The south side
The advancing bridge made its presence known on the southern shore too. In 1926 resumed properties auctioneer, Cal C. Woodberry, stood on a box in the heart of the Rocks district, slammed down his gavel and cleared his throat. The sound silenced the whispering of neighbourhood women who stood a hesitant distance back, tribes of small children gathered at the hems of their fading skirts. A crowd of around 50 second-hand building supply merchants, who had been previously under the suspicious gaze of

the local women, turned their attention toward the auctioneer and his gavel.

Above the street others leant on balcony rails, peering down from their doomed homes toward the group of intruders as Woodberry raised his needling voice.

'Don't worry, they'll be gone by the end of the month,' he reassured the crowd of businessmen. 'If the tenants are not out by that date, buyers are free to commence demolition immediately after that date.'

'You have the authority from the Resumed Properties Branch,' Woodberry assured those hesitant to risk a couple of quid.

Potential new owners were reminded that they, too, had to have the affected properties demolished and land cleared. There was a bridge to build and everybody had to pull their weight.

The message was clear and as Woodberry announced a lot number and asked what he was offered, the women in the street and on the balconies must have turned their minds toward packing and loading their goods, farewelling neighbours, finding somewhere else.

The auctioneer occasionally had trouble raising the bids; sometimes homes went for as little as £2. Two pounds for the bricks, timber and fittings, with the guarantee of vacant possession. Eventually he sold off 84 homes — some of them as job lots — and when the numbers were added up the government had reaped a grand total of £429 and 10 shillings.

While two little cottages in Trinity Avenue, behind Trinity Church, fetched just £2 each, the big money, £33, went for 37 Princes Street, a 60-year-old two-storey house that had earlier been the home of Mr Alfred Byrnes, an officer of the Supreme Court. Some of the residents still remembered the time 10,000 people gathered below its balcony to hear an address by attorney-general, former Balmain umbrella repairer and future prime minister, Mr W. M. Hughes. Billy had been locked out of the city halls by his opponent Harry Holland, who went on to become New Zealand's prime minister.

However, few of the remaining Rocks residents had the political connections to make much noise about the resumptions and disruptions the approaching bridge caused. The tenants on the north side of the harbour lobbied hard and at least gained some recognition of their rights and their discomfort, but it says a lot about the sort of people who were displaced in the Rocks area that barely a whisper was heard. Only a few of the letters received by government officers came from this group.

The Rocks and Millers Point communities were more down-at-heel and transient, often by choice although not always. Just 25 years before Woodberry auctioned off the homes, some of the same residents had stood behind barriers and watched as their belongings were tossed onto large bonfires. Some returned to find the shells of their homes and the few remaining sticks of furniture scoured with carbolic water and indiscriminately whitewashed. One tearful lady discovered her piano had been given the once over by the municipal paintbrush. They were the lucky ones; others had their sordid dwellings summarily demolished and incinerated. These poorest of poor returned to a pile of ashes where their shanty had been. The evacuations and demolitions were forced on the city when the area was host to an outbreak of bubonic plague in 1900, which led to the compulsory acquisitions of many properties.

Sydney's first inner suburb, the Rocks began as a tattered assortment of hovels on the western slopes above Sydney Cove. Residents clung to the edge of the steep hill, drainage was terrible, disease common and poverty even more so.

Close to the port and far enough from the respectable people, the Rocks became a hive of tiny bars, brothels and criminality on such a scale that many an international visitor was given to comment on the unique depravity of the area. At a time when almost everything in Australia was believed to be inferior to the civilised parts of the world, it rivalled anything the Northern Hemisphere could offer.

Journalist Frank Fowler explored the area in his account of Sydney in the 1850s, *Southern Lights and Shadows*. He was not impressed.

The greater portion of the district called the 'Rocks', in Sydney, are in roguery and raffery, as vile as Whitechapel. Scenes of riot and debauchery … alleys, one running into another, and most of the houses in which are single rooms with earthen floorings, and utterly destitute of windows, chimneys and doors. Serpent-like gutters choked with filth …

He wasn't alone in his assessment of the area, which was generally avoided by the respectable members of society or anybody who cared for their own safety and health.

William Jevons, a journalist, assayer and economist, wrote an account of the area in 1858.

The houses … are small and comparatively ancient stone cottages, so unevenly and irregularly built that the doorstep of one residence sometimes approximates to the eaves of another. Where the erections are of wood their dilapidated, filthy appearance is all the more striking. The interior of these abodes usually consists of two dirty bare rusting-coloured chambers, of small size, and yet too large for the scanty articles which constitute their furniture. Of the inhabitants I will not say much; in some cases misfortune may have led and may keep them there; but in others the unhappy, debauched, wicked face, the slovenly dirtily clothed person, tell too plain a tale.

He continued in much the same vein for page after page, describing open gutters, dirt floors covered in excrement and even a portrait of an old and young woman 'striking pictures of the first and last ages of vice'. Jevons concluded: 'I am acquainted with some of the worse parts of London … and some unhealthy parts of Liverpool, Paris and other towns but nowhere have I seen such a retreat of filth and vice as The Rocks.'

Half a century later it was still so dirty the plague had found itself a fertile breeding ground. The clean-up that followed scraped some of the grime from the surface, but even in the 1920s the area was overcrowded with the underprivileged. A report in the *Sydney Morning Herald* shed no tears for those who lost their homes the day Woodberry came to the district: 'The reconstruction of the Rocks area was commenced 25 years ago during the prevalence of Bubonic plague, and the bridge work will complete the reconstruction by effacing the remains of the area, which was once one of Sydney's most fashionable residential quarters.'

The bridge itself aimed to land on the southern shore at the site of the old Dawes Point Battery before careering through the Rocks. Dawes Point took its name from Lieutenant William Dawes, who set up the observatory on the hill above the harbour.

On 17 March 1932, *The Times* in London issued a special supplement to celebrate 'An All British Engineering Triumph'. Sketching the history of the bridge it noted, 'The first task of those who were working on the spot was the demolition of property on the north and south shores, where a few houses, shops, and places of business stood on ground that was required by the builders. The population had to be moved, but not a great number of people was affected ...'

TENDERS

Bradfield is a fussy man and he wants his bridge to
be just so, but when his chosen tender company
pulls out at the last moment the entire project seems
doomed. Still, a young man who learned his tricks
during the Boer War is keen to try them out in
Sydney Harbour and good old English derring-do
wins the day.

The building of the Sydney Harbour Bridge had begun in July 1923 with the turning of the first sod and similar ceremonies. Or had it? The cynical at the time might have pointed out that Bradfield and his celebrating horde of ministers, councillors and flag-raisers were a cargo cult preparing for the arrival of manna from an aeroplane that had not yet been chartered.

Homes were demolished, tunnels dug, railway stations relocated, speeches and grand gestures made, but in reality the bridge was still little more than a rough sketch.

It might be a cantilever, it might be an arch; some even thought — despite explicit instructions to the contrary — that it could still be a suspension bridge. It might be built by locals, but it was more likely it would be an American or English company, although the Canadians had admitted expertise in the area and the Germans were eventually allowed to tender despite a widespread belief they might be the first to blow it up.

Everything was up in the air, except the bridge.

Tenders, if there were any, were not due to be opened until January 1924. They had to be examined and analysed, and even then there could be no guarantee one would be suitable or an agreement could be reached with the tenderer if it was. Still, nobody could deny

Bradfield and his project. They had become an unstoppable force, fuelled by ceremonies and commemorative acts. Questions about by whom and how it would be built were waved aside in the rush to move families on and prepare the ground on either side of the harbour for the coming of the great bridge builders.

All the speeches, toasts and photographs had brought matters to a head. Bradfield was smart enough to know it would be a brave politician to deny him and the people now — as they had done repeatedly in the past — especially as the government had already begun collecting the bridge tax. All he needed was a suitable tender and they were away.

However, all was not well with the tenders.

At the same time as the chief engineer, his secretary, Miss Butler, and dignitaries met to detonate the first charge in September 1923, an untimely death in England threatened to derail the great project.

As the Australians went about preparing the ground, Ralph Freeman, a brilliant young engineer for the Cleveland Bridge and Engineering Company, who was — after Bradfield — the single most important character in the construction of the Sydney Harbour Bridge, was back in London dealing with the biggest crisis of his professional life.

Born in 1880, the 42-year-old Englishman had twenty years' experience constructing and designing bridges and was marked early as the man for the job in Australia. He and Bradfield were two of the great engineering minds of the Northern and Southern hemispheres. This was their time and like the Australian, the Englishman was not going to let anything, including untimely deaths, stand in his way.

Freeman had cut his teeth working with consulting engineers Sir Douglas Fox and Partners on a number of landmark bridges. In 1901, when he was just twenty years old and fresh from college, the firm was called on to build a bridge in the heart of Southern Africa. Although few realise it, this structure played a significant role in the construction of the Sydney Harbour Bridge. That year the Cape to

Cairo railway had reached the Zambezi River at Victoria Falls. The transport link was the pet project of controversial Rhodesian leader Cecil Rhodes, who had pushed for its construction despite the disruptions of the Boer War. There were two possibilities for a crossing, one across the broad expanse of river above the falls, or a shorter route just below them across a white-knuckle drop of 130 metres. Rhodes decided train travellers should enjoy the beauty of the spectacular waterfalls and directed the railway to cross so close that it would travel through their mist.

Designer G. A. Hobson of Sir Douglas Fox and Partners was confronted with the relatively simple task of spanning 156 metres and decided to build an arch bridge below the cliff's edge with the railway running across the top of it. However, the enormous distance to the ground below and the fact that the cliffs on either side were almost sheer created a construction nightmare. Arches were traditionally propped up by temporary stays until they met in the middle, but this was impossible with the riverbed so far below. It was construction engineer G. C. Imbault who came up with an ingenious method of tunnelling into the earth back from the cliff edge and running cables through the tunnels to support the half arches during construction. Freeman was an assistant engineer on his first job and watched with interest.

Twenty years later Freeman and Imbault combined to tender for a bridge across the more sedate waters of Sydney Harbour and although it would be on a much larger scale, the pair believed they could hold up its enormous weight the same way as they had in Africa. Imbault had flown from Paris to London to meet with Bradfield the year before in London with Mr C. F. Dixon from the Cleveland Bridge Company and had spoken of the arch design.

Bradfield favoured a British company over American or other European bidders and was impressed by his meeting with Dixon and Imbault. They looked to be early favourites to get the job if their tender was as good as their initial pitch.

Imbault and Freeman were almost finished the initial tender of the Cleveland Bridge Company when disaster struck. Dixon died

FACING PAGE:
Big Plans: The chief engineer detailed his plans for a cantilever then arch bridge, along with a suburban railway system in the early 1920s.

THE BRIDGE

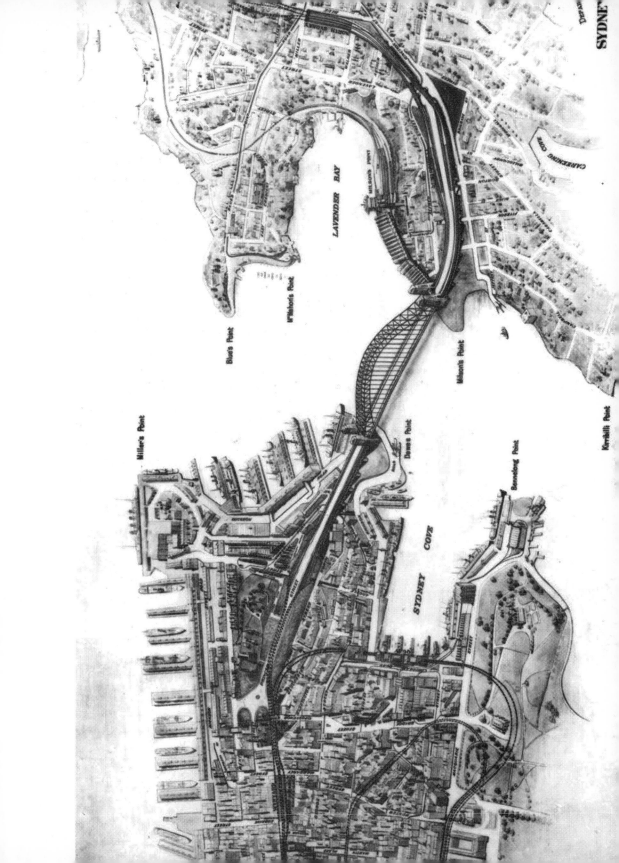

SYDNEY

LAVENDER BAY

Blue's Point

M'Mahon's Point

Milson's Point

Kirribilli Point

Miller's Point

Dawes Point

Bennelong Point

SYDNEY COVE

suddenly and the company's directors made a decision to withdraw from the project, cabling the news to Bradfield who replied feebly that he hoped they would reconsider for he had included an arch in the design specifications at the company's request. It was September, 1923, the same month the first charges were being exploded for the bridge approaches and two months before the closing date for tenders. The news was as much a setback for Bradfield as it was for the two Englishmen.

For Freeman, who had been working on a number of impressive designs for arch bridges, it looked as if a year's work had been for nothing. However, the Cleveland Bridge Company decided that the effort should not be wasted and granted permission for the engineer to take his plans across to steel construction company Dorman, Long & Co. to see if they would consider putting in a tender.

Freeman travelled to the country home of Arthur Dorman and met with the company's founder and chairman; its vice-chairman, Hugh Bell; and the general manager, Lawrence Ennis. He made his pitch and within an hour Dorman, Long decided it would broaden its steel manufacturing business to include bridge building and would submit a tender using Freeman's plans. It was an extraordinary decision to make in such a hurry and was later painted as an example of British derring-do. The cost of fitting out the company's factories alone would be in excess of £1 million, but Freeman was confident of his chances and Dorman, Long apparently wanted to prove to the world that the British, who had not built a major bridge in over a generation, were up to the job. Anyway, the design engineer told Australians in 1932 that the thought of a foreign firm — read American, Canadian or, God forbid, the Germans — constructing a bridge in the 'British Dominion' was unthinkable.

Dorman, Long despatched Lawrence Ennis to Australia with Freeman's seven designs under his arm. The company decided that the Scottish-born but American-trained engineer would move to Sydney to oversee construction if the tender was accepted. The English company had been given some much-needed breathing space when the Canadian Bridge Company and Goninan & Co.,

Newcastle, asked for more time. Eager to have as many tenders as possible, Bradfield moved the closing date for tenders back to January 1924.

By January parts of the north shore and city had worked themselves to fever pitch. The Rev. Frank Cash could hardly contain his excitement and that month's Lavender Bay *Christ Church Parish Paper* (price 3/- per annum) contained a more secular message than usual. The eccentric priest, his appetite whetted by the destruction of his parish and the construction about to take place at the bottom of his garden, had become more interested in the works of man than the works of God. This was the sort of creation that got the former metallurgist and gold fossicker reaching deep.

> The government publicly announced that at noon this day, 16th Jan, 1924, tenders passed, and the tenders have closed; but who can measure the tense eagerness of the parties chiefly interested? The best brains in the civilised world have been strung at high tension for this hour.
>
> The tender box which has been placed outside the room of the Under-Secretary for Public Works must bear an atmosphere of importance. The daily papers say, that it was to be fitted with double locks, and the Minister for Works would hold one key, and the Under-Secretary the other.
>
> Into this box were to be dropped the tenders for the North Shore Bridge, a structure, so experts declare, to be the most massive of its kind in the whole world.
>
> Picture this tense hour, the beginning of a decision in which millions of pounds are involved, the burden of which we are to share, the utility of which, when completed, we are to enjoy and admire.

WHICH BRIDGE?

Bradfield did not really need to wait for the under-secretary or the minister to put the key in the lock of the tender box. He had spoken with the tenderers and with the help of Kathleen Butler had been in constant correspondence with them. The chief engineer was familiar with the bridges they wanted to build and the bridge he wanted built. He had shifted from the cantilever design and was now sure in his mind that an arch was the way to go. He also had a fair idea that one company in particular was best suited to build it.

The box was duly opened on 16 January.

Bradfield and his staff went into overdrive.

The bridge boss, his young design engineer Gordon Stuckey and the ubiquitous Miss Butler examined each of twenty proposals from six companies and delivered a thorough, detailed, 63-page Report on Tenders back to the government four weeks later.

Bradfield had been waiting for this moment for 23 years and was moving with almost indecent haste. Miss Butler had her leave cancelled at the last moment. So much time had been wasted he was not prepared to squander another moment. He worked Stuckey and Miss Butler seven days a week and well into the night and noted their efforts in the final report, which landed on the government's desk on 16 February — exactly a month after the tenders had been opened. The speed of his deliberations was fuelled by all the knowledge and lessons he had learned in the past two decades. Bradfield and Stuckey had already done countless calculations on stresses for various bridges made of various steels. He had met the tenderers previously and discussed various structures, costs, stresses and other variables with them.

The Sydney Harbour Bridge Report on Tenders is an interesting window into Bradfield's rationale for choosing the final design for the Sydney Harbour Bridge

Although the final tender document called for an arch or cantilever bridge, the chief engineer had certainly come to favour the former. Still a couple of brave but foolhardy companies ignored instructions and included suspension bridges. 'Tenderers were not invited to submit independent designs, as has been frequently stated in the press,' the chief engineer noted in his tender report.

Wanting to appear fair, he claimed he had given the suspension bridges the 'same careful consideration' as the others, but Bradfield

was never going to allow a suspension bridge — which he believed to be too prone to movement — across the harbour.

At least six of the designs were for variations on the suspension bridges, including all three tenders of the English Electric Company of Australia Ltd.

The EEC had a hydraulic, electric and refrigerating manufacturing plant at Clyde in Sydney's west and had marketed itself in the local press as the only 'local tender', but Bradfield in the opening remarks of his tender report argued that it did not have 'the experience in the fabrication of the class of bridgework required for the Sydney Harbour Bridge'.

The other five tenderers — Goninan & Co., McClintic Marshall Products Company, Sir William Arrol & Co., the Canadian Bridge Company and Dorman, Long & Co. — were noted by Bradfield as 'among the foremost bridge fabricating establishments and contracting firms in the world'.

When it came to the details of proposed bridges, Bradfield's fancy and determinations were obvious. Goninan & Co.'s £10 million suspension bridge was first to be examined and first to be rejected. It was too expensive and experimental; not only that,

Variations on a Theme: Dorman, Long prepared paintings of the proposed arch across the harbour with and without the granite pylons, which were largely cosmetic. 1924.

'the bridge has nothing to commend it as regards design, appearance or fabrication in Australia'.

Thanks, but no thanks.

The English Electric Company of Australia's plans for three suspension bridges were designed by noted New York engineers Robinson and Steinman. Bradfield noted that the latter was probably the world's leading authority on such bridges, but in all reality the EEC never stood a chance. Despite making it clear early that he did not believe a local company was up to the job and that the tender document had specifically called for a cantilever or an arch, Bradfield went through the motions of examining the bridges and conceded they were indeed sturdy but concluded:

> It must be borne in mind, however, that there is a tendency for the cables and suspenders of a suspension bridge to vanish from view on account of their slimness, when seen from a moderately distant point. With the main cables barely visible and the wire rope suspenders invisible, the bridge would not have a pleasing outline and the angularity due to the increase in depth of the stiffening truss at the quarter points and over the towers would detract from its appearance.

At times Bradfield sounded like an interior decorator with an engineering degree, but taste is a relative thing. Twenty years earlier he had believed an arch bridge would be an 'eyesore'. His ability to be influenced by a good argument or better idea is a tribute to his wisdom; however, at times his aesthetic stances appeared pedantic and one in particular proved to be extraordinarily expensive for the people of New South Wales.

The chief engineer not only demanded a sturdy bridge, he wanted it to look sturdy, which is why he insisted on granite pillars for the successful tender even when they added a significant premium to the price. It was a grand gesture. He believed strength, like justice, must be seen to be believed and Bradfield's Harbour Bridge rejected notions of subtlety or discretion. It would be a monument proud of its own form and function.

The McClintic Marshall Products Company offered five bridges, including three cantilevers, an inverted arch — which Bradfield noted was, in reality, a suspension bridge — and a three-hinged arch (two hinges at the base of the arch and one in the centre). One by one the McClintic Marshall bridges were dismissed by the engineer. The first cantilever design allowed too much deflection or flexibility. The second cantilever met the design demands and 'though a sound engineering proposition, is unhandsome' — which it most definitely was. It also cost too much. The third cantilever was a noted 'improvement' on the second; however, Bradfield believed 'it cannot be said to altogether harmonise with its surroundings'.

The notion of 50,000 tonnes of steel reaching 150-odd metres into the sky and somehow harmonising with the beauty of Sydney Harbour is a difficult one to grasp, but there is no doubt that the cantilever structures were boxy and lacking in any grace.

The fourth McClintic tender was a three-hinged cable suspension bridge designed by the famous New York commissioner of bridges, Gustav Lindenthal, and looked like a smaller version of the Golden Gate Bridge, which would open fourteen years later. Bradfield did not want to dismiss the respected bridge expert, but noted that a similar design by Lindenthal had been 'discarded' for the Quebec bridge — the one Bradfield had famously climbed in a storm to feel its vibration — in favour of a cantilever model. He also wrote that the three-hinged cable suspension structure had been under consideration for the Hell Gate Bridge but was rejected in favour of a two-hinged arch structure.

The fifth McClintic proposal for a three-hinged braced arch was almost there, but not quite. Bradfield wanted a two-hinged arch and argued that this design, prepared by American engineer C. A. P. Turner, did not produce 'a satisfactory optical explanation of the transference of the enormous stress from the crown of the arch to the abutments'. Again, it might be strong but it didn't look it. And anyway, it cost too much.

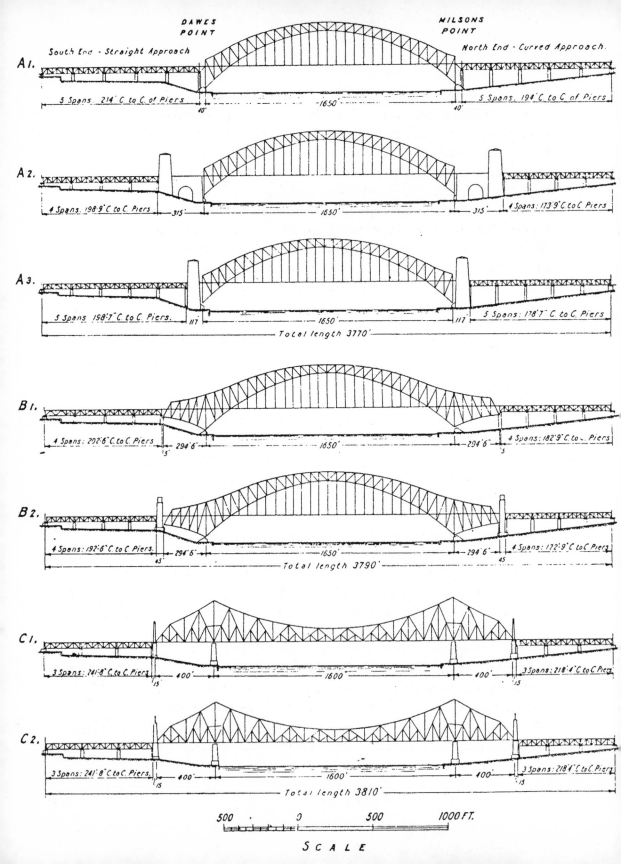

DAWES POINT   MILSONS POINT

A1.
South End - Straight Approach   North End - Curved Approach.
5 Spans, 214' C. to C. of Piers   40'   1650'   40'   5 Spans, 194' C. to C. of Piers

A2.
4 Spans, 198'9" C. to C. Piers   315'   1650'   315'   4 Spans, 173'9" C. to C. Piers

A3.
5 Spans, 198'7" C. to C. Piers   117'   1650'   117'   5 Spans, 178'7" C. to C. Piers
Total length 3770'

B1.
4 Spans, 202'6" C. to C. Piers   294'6"   1650'   294'6"   4 Spans, 182'9" C. to C. Piers
15'   15'

B2.
4 Spans, 192'6" C. to C. Piers   294'6"   1650'   294'6"   4 Spans, 172'9" C. to C. Piers
15'   15'
Total length 3790'

C1.
3 Spans, 241'8" C. to C. Piers   400'   1600'   400'   3 Spans, 218'4" C. to C. Piers
15'   15'

C2.
3 Spans, 241'8" C. to C. Piers.   400'   1600'   400'   3 Spans, 218'4" C. to C. Piers
15'   15'
Total length 3810'

500   0   500   1000 FT.
SCALE

The Canadian Bridge Company offered a cantilever and an inverted arch or suspension, but they weren't quite right to Bradfield's eye. The designers made a bad error in adopting the 'K' bracing for their bridges. They were not to know, but three years earlier the chief engineer had decided that an 'M' bracing was aesthetically better. An entry into his work diary on Wednesday 2 March 1921 stated: 'Decided to adopt a M braced truss for the Sydney Harbour Bridge in preference to a K braced truss although the latter will be somewhat cheaper and easier to erect. The appearance of the M truss is much better; the K brace has too much sameness whilst a combination of K for cantilever and M for suspended span is not satisfactory especially when the change in systems occur.' Two days later he had run his thoughts past Miss Butler, and the head of Railways, Mr Fraser. He noted in his diary that all three 'selected same design as myself as having best appearance and showing the motive of design throughout'.

It was only a minor detail, but Bradfield had waited a long time to get his bridge and he wanted one which was just so, so out went the Canadian bridge with its K trusses.

For their part, Sir William Arrol & Co. said all the right things, noting in their tender document 'we can suggest nothing better than Mr Bradfield has put before us'. Flattery appeared to work as the chief engineer quoted the line in the first sentence of his review of their tenders. The company produced a cantilever and an arch as required, the latter of which was almost identical to the current bridge, but it was rejected on controversial grounds. The tenderer wanted to use a new steel developed by the British Admiralty during the war, but Bradfield and his design engineer Gordon Stuckey argued that the working stresses given were too great and the tender was flawed.

On reading this, Sir John Hunter of Sir William Arrol & Co. famously stormed into Bradfield's office to confront him but a showdown was avoided as the chief engineer was not in. He later attempted to sue Bradfield and may have had a legal argument as other experts argued that the stresses were not too great. However, the libel action was eventually dropped. Arrols had tendered for a

FACING PAGE:
Love Me Tender: Dorman, Long prepared seven proposals for the bridge and it was drawing A3 that was chosen by Dr J. J. C. Bradfield. 1924.

bridge twenty years earlier and now felt they had twice been badly treated by the colonials of New South Wales.

And so to Ralph Freeman's work.

Dorman, Long & Co. submitted seven designs including five arches and two cantilevers, although most of the five arches were simple variations of the one design. The first arch had no abutment pylons and was judged 'aesthetically too severe for its settings'. Bradfield wanted towers.

The second had pylons but set them back from the arch as part of a larger abutment structure. The chief engineer deemed them 'too massive'.

Bradfield then came to Dorman, Long's Tender A3 and gave it a four-paragraph assessment. Like Goldilocks he had found the bed that suited him best; not too large or severe or unhandsome. It was not only strong, it looked strong. It had pylons and it had them in the right place. It also helped that A3 was 'in accordance with the specifications and the official design'. The chief engineer noted simply: 'This is the tender recommended for acceptance.'

A variation on the A3, which offered concrete pylons instead of granite facing, was rejected even though it would save £240,000 as Bradfield argued 'the difference in appearance between the two bridges, one with granite facing and the other with white artificial stone facing, more than offsets the difference in price'.

Not having pylons at all would have saved over £700,000, but the engineer wanted his pylons no matter what the cost and argued they gave a monumental tone to the great utilitarian structure. Anyway, he had already driven down to Moruya on the south coast of New South Wales and chosen the stone two years earlier.

Bridge A3 was by no means the cheapest bridge, at £4,217,721.11s.10d, but it was a bargain compared with Goninan's cantilever-suspension priced at £10,712,015.19s.8d.

The bill for the bridge did not include approaches, which were estimated to add another £1,275,721 to the bottom line.

New South Wales taxpayers were about to fork out about £5.5 million for a harbour crossing.

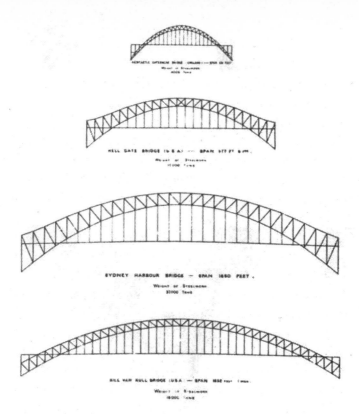

Bradfield went to the trouble of having his own picture of the Harbour Bridge painted by his draughtsman and published the first picture of the new bridge in the report, with his signature in the corner. He finished his report with a flourish:

> In making my recommendation I have kept in view the past and future as well as the present. One characteristic of modern thought is the increasing tendency to study the past, and in looking backward we find a nation's manner of life and civilisation written in those works of its rulers, which have survived the time …
>
> Future generations will judge our generation by our works. For that reason and from considerations of the past, I have recommended granite, strong, imperishable … for the facing of the piers … humanising our landscape in simplicity, strength and sincerity.

Arch Rivals: Scale drawings of the Gateshead (Newcastle-on-Tyne), Hell Gate (New York), Sydney Harbour and Kill Van Kull or Bayonne (New Jersey) bridges.

Of no moment whatever in considering the acceptance of a tender, but which still is, perhaps, worth recording, at times of national rejoicing ... [the bridge will be] a fitting tribute to our soldiers unparalleled in the annals of any nation.

Bradfield attached a second picture of the bridge with the military forces badge illuminated on its side so that everybody could see his patriotic vision.

The chief engineer finished his Report on Tenders by denouncing those who called for an Australian tender, explaining that they should be happy to have the cheapest tender in combination with all-Australian manufacture — although the majority of the steel would be produced in Britain — and anyway it was the people of the city and northern suburbs who paid the bridge tax, he argued, not the people of New South Wales or Australia.

Bradfield signed off with thanks to Gordon Stuckey for helping him check the designs, and to Miss K. M. Butler. 'Since 16th January, these two officers have cheerfully worked incessantly, Saturdays and Sundays, assisting me to present my report to the Minister at the earliest possible moment.'

So, Sydney was to get Dorman, Long's Bridge A3, which Bradfield claimed 'is my design as sanctioned by Parliament and as submitted for tenders'.

The issue of who designed the bridge would rear its ugly head further down the track, but A3 hadn't just fallen from the sky. Engineering is an empirical science and elements of the bridge and its proposed construction methods could be traced through history.

Gustav Lindenthal felt miffed when he saw that the winning design Plan A3 was remarkably similar to his Hell Gate Bridge, New York. While only a fraction of the size of the Sydney Harbour Bridge, on a quick glance the Hell Gate is almost extraordinarily similar, right down to its decorative stone pylons. Because of strong currents in the East River and the need to keep the area free for ships to pass, Hell Gate was even constructed using the cable method devised by Imbault.

Lindenthal was informed by many of the same ideas as Bradfield when building the New York bridge; he wanted a structure that gave high clearance for shipping but was also an elegant landmark. He also realised that sometimes strength or weakness can be an illusion. The original plans did not call for the arch to be connected to the towers above the deck, but the designer believed that the public would be reassured if it did, even if the additional chords were entirely cosmetic and served no engineering purpose.

The American said later he thought the Sydney Harbour Bridge was inspired by his arch and that he had no idea the tender specifications were rewritten to include an arch when he prepared his work for McClintic Marshall.

Today in Sydney one company uses a harbour bridge image which on closer examination reveals itself to be the New York bridge. Perhaps the company was working off the tender document, because the English engineer Freeman would argue later that the outline of a bridge Bradfield provided was just a tracing of the American bridge.

In April 1924 Bradfield's secretary, Miss Butler, was seconded to Bradfield's assistants Gordon Stuckey, James Holt and Owen Powys and the quartet left for London to check the plans and calculations at Dorman, Long & Co. headquarters. As she had been in 1922 when he was overseas, Miss Butler was again Bradfield's eyes and ears and given control over the trio to the point that she could send any of them home should they step out of line. Two days after the trains and ferries started unloading their passengers onto the new dock at Lavender Bay, the chief engineer himself got on a boat and followed the others to London, taking with him his oldest daughter, Mary, who became seasick and disembarked at Perth to catch a train back to Sydney.

In London the group discussed the design and fabrications, inspected plans and plants and oversaw the testing of the rivets for the bridge (the whole of the Sydney Harbour Bridge is constructed using rivets and not welding). They watched as exacting specifications were worked out for the tapering and widths of the rivets and as the first cast of silicon steel of the bridge was rolled out into plates and 'billets' or long sticks. The latter were drawn into wire and spun into cables for use in construction. Everything was tested, as Bradfield noted:

> When in England a visit to Dorman, Long & Co.'s Steelmaking plant, rolling mills and constructional works at Middlesbrough and at Redcar, near Whitby. The Sydney Harbour Bridge is unprecedented in size, and the rivetting will be the heaviest yet undertaken. Many of the rivets will be 11/4 inches in diameter, and over 9 inches long between the head and snap. At Middlesbrough many experiments were undertaken to ensure that the rivetting will be as perfect as possible. The best results were obtained with rivets having 1/32 inch taper in their length, the rivet holes being drilled 1/32 inch larger than the diameter of the rivet. Special pneumatic tools for closing the rivets were designed and experimented with to ensure perfect workmanship, and many experiments were also made in heating the rivets in electric furnaces, also in coke and oil furnaces …

Dorman, Long, their consultants Sir Douglas Fox, Sir Ralph Freeman and Sir John Burnet and their key employees were involved in a series of meetings with the visiting Australians before Bradfield signed off on the plans and left London in November 1924, reaching Sydney, after stops in Canada and the USA, in January 1925.

BUILDING THE BRIDGE

A granite quarry in Moruya, a series of worksheds where Luna Park now stands and a job so tricky that sometimes the men found themselves hanging on by their eyelashes. Building the bridge meant tunnelling into the earth, disturbing a convict holding cell in the process, and climbing into the sky. It was not for the faint-hearted.

Dorman, Long & Co. was officially granted the tender in March 1924 but details of construction and design were not finalised until later that year.

While the company prepared to build the arch and approach spans it was left to Bradfield, as head of the relevant railways and public works areas of the project, to connect the rail, tram and road arteries to the bridge. While most people concentrated on the space above the harbour and its immediate vicinity an enormous amount of construction was done 'off Broadway'.

To get the roads and railways up to the bridge the local engineers and workmen had to construct a complicated series of bridges, tunnels and bypasses in the city and on the northern side.

Even in the 1920s, when green bans and development applications were unheard of, this meant negotiating with a number of special interest groups. Again the chief engineer's political skills were invaluable.

To mark the hundredth anniversary of the opening of Scots Church in 1926 Bradfield stood before the solemn-faced gentlemen of the general assembly and humbly suggested he be allowed to demolish the place of worship so he could widen York Street.

His speech was the chief engineer at his best. He praised the

men and their institution then beat them senseless with the size of his Harbour Bridge project and the impact it would have on Sydney, before giving a little tweak to one of his favourite catchcries:

> Consider no mean plans, for such plans have no magic to stir any man's blood, but in your plans aim high in hope and work and dream of Presbyterianism in Australia in terms of the future when Australia will have its 60 million inhabitants or more, when Sydney will be the Queen City of the British Empire.

Bradfield then stirred their blood with talk of a new church.

Posing for Posterity: Management from Dorman, Long and the Sydney Public Works Department come together for a photograph on the northern pylon, looking south. 1928.

... the inanimate materials of which would be constructed, could be contrived by the skill of the architect and engineer into a fane of beauty expressive of the divinity and spirit of God, of the 'I AM' who spake to Moses from the burning bush, which bush with the legend 'Nec tamen consumebatur', your Church Arms, expresses to you the Presence and Eternity of God.

He got his way, as he usually did. Sometimes Premier Jack Lang, himself no slouch when it came to the powers of persuasion, found himself swayed by the power of the chief engineer's oratory and passion.

He would come down to the Premier's office with his plans under his arms, and was prepared to expound them by the hour if given the opportunity. I gave him every encouragement, as he was so different to the average public official. I realised that he was a dreamer. But behind it was his conviction that he was planning the greatest city in the southern hemisphere ... As he talked you could almost see a new city emerging.

Lang remembered that Bradfield's plans provided for two main arteries from the bridge through the city.

They were up to 100 feet [30 metres] wide. One was to sweep from York Street through Martin Place to the Eastern Suburbs. The other was to carry down York Street to the Western Suburbs. Everything in the way had to go. Sydney was to have its own Fifth Avenue. He visualised it as being more beautiful than Paris. But behind all his dreams there was a sound common sense.

Bradfield had first unveiled his plans in 1917 at a town planning conference. Lang was prepared to let him have his way, but lost office in 1927 and much of the opportunity was also lost. The Commercial Bank and Bank of New South Wales began rebuilding their headquarters in Martin Place. When Lang was re-elected in 1930 he offered to resume the properties so the chief engineer could have his way, but this proposal was defeated by his government.

Bradfield did well with the Presbyterians and the Premier but could not sway the high priests of St Andrews Cathedral when he proposed removing a few metres of their frontage to construct the entrance to Town Hall station. He was involved in quite a public spat until the matter was resolved by the incoming Premier Bavin.

While these earthly negotiations were being conducted above ground, below it Bradfield's brilliant city rail loop was tunnelling away. By early 1923 Hyde and Belmore parks resembled open-cut mines as the link from Central station finally got under way — some five years after a previous attempt had been abandoned. Work was also recommenced on electrifying the western suburbs line, but the eastern suburbs link was again put on hold.

There was enough public angst about the loss of trees and destruction of the park during the construction of the underground

Tight Curve: A view of the bend in the railway line on the northern approaches leading to the bridge, which complicated the design. 1930.

Hang on: The six steel erectors lift a lower chord for the north-east half arch into place while painters, assemblers and inspectors watch. 1930.

railway that Bradfield again had to use his public relations skills; he and Miss Butler began flooding the *Sunday Mail* with articles about the grand plan for the bridge and city. Meanwhile the twin tunnels burrowed perilously close to the foundations of iconic retailers Mark Foys and Snows, increasing the general anxiety about the work.

During these years 360 km of electric railway, including 32 km of new track for the city and Harbour Bridge, was laid following plans Bradfield had set out years earlier. North Sydney and Milsons Point stations were built at the time, the latter moved up the hill from its original location. Later Bradfield reported the cost of completing the railways alone was £25 million and as the economy began to wither in the late 1920s the cost of the scheme became a political controversy that threatened the completion of the project.

THE BRIDGE

The Fuller government lost office after the laying of the foundation stone and it had been left to Lang, the incoming Labor Premier, to raise the finances to pay for the bridge through loans from London.

In 1929 a new chief commissioner removed Bradfield from his role as chief engineer in the Railways Department, but Cabinet stepped in to make up the £1000 a year he lost by raising his salary and moved the Sydney Harbour Bridge Branch under the umbrella of the Public Works Department. Unfortunately a lot of Bradfield's railway works were abandoned at the same time. Circular Quay station was not completed for another 30 years.

In the meantime the enormous retaining walls along Elizabeth Street on the south side and a series of approach bridges on the north side were built to lift the rail and roadways over Euroka and Bank streets while the tunnels between Miller and Bank were completed. Over the next years more retaining walls, tunnels and bridges were built to reroute traffic to the bridge approaches and arch bridges were built over Burton and Fitzroy streets in Milsons Point, but work slowed down in 1930 because of the same belt-tightening that saw Bradfield dumped from the Railways.

Bradfield was delivering on his side of the bargain, despite some concerted political campaigns and crippling economic problems.

It was now up to Dorman, Long & Co. to deliver the bridge.

DORMAN, LONG & CO. START WORK

In March 1924 Lawrence Ennis, who had sailed to Australia with Ralph Freeman's plans for a bridge under his arm, signed the contract on behalf of Dorman, Long. Ennis then returned immediately to London to begin the strategic planning and preparations. Bradfield had nursed the project up to this point but it was the English director of construction who would take ultimate responsibility for ensuring the job was completed.

Ennis was a larger than life figure who strode through life and the job with confidence and good cheer. A project of this size was not for the faint-hearted. His maternal family had been engineers

Getting There: The creeper cranes were assembled on top of the pylons and advanced out as they built the bridge. The pylons were completed later. 1931.

but while he was still young his father took them from Scotland to a farm in America. The call of steel was stronger than the call of the field and all six sons eventually left the land to pursue careers as engineers.

Ennis was employed as a messenger boy during the Niagara Falls bridge construction and was bitten by the bridge bug. Over the next 42 years he built structures around the world, including the bridge which carries the Bombay Pipe Line across the Ganges at Allahabad. He joined Dorman, Long in 1903 as superintendent of the construction shops at Middlesbrough and later became general manager of the steel plant.

He sailed back to Australia in 1925 to oversee construction and remained until the bridge was finished.

Ennis called the Sydney Harbour Bridge 'the most difficult bridge construction I have encountered in my 40 years in bridge work'. Still, he enjoyed the thrill of construction and said that working on a bridge 'invigorates the poorest intelligence and captivates the imagination of everyone concerned'.

The early days in London were spent in 'long conferences' between himself, Ralph Freeman and George Imbault as they worked out every detail of the manufacture of the steel, its transportation and erection, before setting out final plans for the bridge.

Having worked in the field and in the mills, Ennis understood steel manufacturing and bridge building, so he was able to bring his expertise to both ends of the project. Imbault and Freeman worked with him to decide the best bridge they could build within the limits set by the size of steel members that could be produced and transported. Ennis later wrote:

> The fact that the bridge was to incorporate members greater both in size and weight than any hitherto fabricated and erected meant that much experimental work was necessary before the first details of the fabrication and the scheme of erection could be settled, and before the purchase of plant and

Rock the Cradle: The first deck-hanger is lifted to the arch in a special lifting cradle designed by Dorman, Long's construction engineer Lawrence Ennis. 1930.

machinery and design of the shops could be proceeded with. For example rivets of a size never before used had to be driven, and experiments were carried out in this connection, not only in regard to the actual driving, but in the heating of the rivets.

During this period Bradfield visited London with his engineers to sign off on the plans.

Dorman, Long began work in November 1924, but the arch did not begin to move out over the water for another five years. Everything associated with the bridge seemed to be without precedent. Plans needed to be discussed, machinery devised, methods tested and much of the early work was a process of slowly feeling the way. To rush could be fatal. Still, in the first six months after signing the contract, the firm spent £1 million on plant and equipment, including a special testing machine of 1250-tonne capacity — 'the largest in the world' according to Ennis — which would check the one-eighth scale models of the bridge.

The granite

One of the company's first acts was to place an order with the Government Dockyard at Walsh Island, Newcastle, for three ships, each of 400-tonne capacity, for transporting granite from the quarries at Moruya to Sydney Harbour. When Dorman, Long won the contract for the bridge, part of it stated 'that the State Government would provide, at Moruya, a quarry from which the granite for the bridge pylons could be taken, free of royalty'.

Even gathering stone, which was only for the facings of the pylons, necessitated the construction of a town and an international recruiting effort. Bradfield had chosen Moruya, 200 km south of Sydney, after a day trip through driving rain and floods in May 1921. Around 50,000 tonnes of numbered stones were dug and shaped in the quarry before being shipped to Sydney.

The fine-grained blue granite in the area had been famous for many years. A 15-tonne block was shipped to Hyde Park in 1878 to

form the base of the Captain Cook statue, an extraordinary feat which almost ended in disaster when the small schooner carrying the enormous load collided with a barque at sea. The stone was also used for the Bank of New South Wales head office and, under Bradfield's guidance, the Martin Place Cenotaph, whose 23 stones were cut from a single 2000-tonne block.

While Moruya had the stone, Australia did not have the expertise to mine it on any great scale. Dorman, Long claimed to have exhausted the supply of local stonemasons and 'found it necessary to bring a large number of men from Scotland'. In 1924 advertisements appeared in British newspapers for workers to come to Australia and work at a 'coastal quarry'.

Work began clearing the scrub from the rock face of the quarry in November 1924, a wharf was built in early 1925, a standard gauge

A Road in the Sky: Cross girders were fitted to hangers in preparation for the construction of the road later named the Bradfield Highway. 1930.

railway system was laid to the wharf and a tramway for the aggregate. A steam jib crane ran on the rails. A power house, dressing shed, crushing and screening plant were all built and seven different cranes transported to the site along with the rolling stock, and pneumatic tools for dressing the stone.

By 1926 the quarry had 240 men of thirteen different nationalities on the payroll.

Bob Colefax was born in Moruya and was a pay clerk in the quarry. His father was the timekeeper.

Spit and Polish: With the bridge complete, workers scrub the granite pylons in preparation for the opening. One man was killed during the task. 1932.

… when I was there the maximum number was 240 … The men were paid weekly and the total money for the pay roll was approximately fifteen hundred pounds a week.

… there were ninety stonemasons, who of course were the principal members of the work force. Then there were quarrymen to get the rude stone out. The first part of the quarry workings they had a huge crushing plant where they broke up the granite spalls and converted it into aggregate for making the concrete for the building of the piers and the pylons.

I would say just at a quick guess there would be up to twelve quarrymen. Then of course there were the auxiliary men such as quite a few labourers, powder monkey … we had a huge power house and there were the engineers. We had to construct a water supply for the quarry and also for the village that was subsequently built there for the workmen. We had carpenters and so forth. We had a plumber. Practically every classification of tradesman that you could nominate.

Dorman, Long constructed temporary timber accommodation for the workers and by 1926 around 70 cottages were ready and Granitetown was born. The 300-strong community lived without power and for some time had to exist on water pumped from a near-by swamp. Soon, however, they had proper town water, their own post office, a cooperative store and a good road connecting the village to Moruya.

Harry Rootsey was a local stonemason, born in Bega and raised in the Sydney suburb of Botany before getting a job in the stone dressing shed.

The work was very heavy because they were big blocks we had to get. Anyhow it came all right and we got used to it.

They [the blocks] were quarried first and they were sent to us rough … Each block was made out of the rough.

We had pneumatic tools, chisels. You would get a rough block and you would have to square it up with four pegs.

You would get the three lowest points of the stone and put a peg in the lowest part, the next one and the highest point you would take the pegs across and sight them. That is how you get a square when you sight it up with a straight edge across each end.

You would get a plan. You would get a sketch of the job and the size of it. Then you were on bevels, different bevels, fourteen-one, fourteen-two. Each one has got a bevel that goes up the side and that is how you go from big at the bottom to small at the top.

It all had to be accurate … they had to fit in. They had to be right because you couldn't mess one up and shoot it away when you got on the job. Not like shooting a bit of brick or timber away.

All by hand … when we took them out of square with the pegs we would put a servicing machine on, it was what we call a four-point. That was worked by compressed air and that jumped up and down and knocked the stone down to level. Then it would all be done by pneumatic hammers, smaller chisels and tools of the trade that we used to have.

Granitetown boasted an Italian quarter where a dedicated cook prepared home-styled Italian food for the stonemasons who could not stomach bland Australian fare. The locals even built a recreation hall and according to author Christine Greig, the Moruya Centennial Hall became a popular place for Highland dances and other cultural pursuits over weekends.

A school was built in Sydney and shipped to the site, opening in September 1926 under an arrangement between the Education Department and Dorman, Long. In 1927, 66 students were enrolled.

Back in Sydney work began in earnest on 26 March 1925 when the Premier, Sir George Fuller, and all his department heads, ministers and Dorman, Long bigwigs Sir Arthur Dorman and Sir Hugh Bell turned out for the laying of the foundation stone at the base of the southern abutment tower, which was, coincidentally, the same day Bradfield cut the ribbon to let the first goods train through to the temporary yards at North Sydney.

Ennis personally mixed the first batch of concrete in June 1925.

THE WORKSHOPS

The state government had granted the builders land on the northern side of the harbour for the Bridge Fabrication Shops, which consisted of three sections or sheds: the light shop which measured 180 by 40 metres and held four cranes, each of 25-tonne capacity;

the heavy shop, which was 150 by 46 metres and had two cranes, each of 120-tonne capacity; and the template shed, which was 60 by 40 metres wide.

Ennis wrote about the shops in a bridge souvenir booklet:

Material was unloaded from steamers by our wharf cranes and transferred to the stockyard, there to be sorted and stacked by two semi-goliath travelling cranes. The steel was then dealt with by two straightening machines, the one with a capacity for straightening plates up to 57 mm thick and the other capable of straightening angles 305 mm x 305 mm x 32 mm. After being handled by heavy shearing machines and cold saws for cutting to length, and planing machines for planing to width, the larger of which had a travel of 20 m, the material was marked for drilling from the templates, which had already

A Big Job: This army of painters used 272,000 litres of paint to give the bridge its initial three coats of dangerous lead-based paint. 1932.

been prepared. This process required a high degree of skill and accuracy, for upon it depended the ultimate correctness of the fabrication.

On completion of the drilling, riveting and assembling, the ends of all members were carefully machined before 'butting' together for the reamering of the field joints. To ensure a perfect fit, all members connecting together at the main truss joints were assembled in their respective positions on the floor of the shops, prior to their despatch for erection and lifts of upwards of 200 tonnes were handled by the two shop-cranes operating in unison. At all stages of the fabrication and erection checks were carefully made by instruments, particularly of the relative positions of the members during the process of 'butting together' …

The slight angles were extraordinarily important as the 'arch' bridge does not, in fact, contain any curved pieces of steel and is the result of the careful bevelling of joints.

Ennis said later that fabrication of the bridge members was as complicated a job as their construction.

It would have amazed, aye stunned, the people of Sydney had it been possible for them to have seen at times what was going on and being done, behind the galvanised walls of what ferry travellers were pleased to call 'Dorman's tin sheds' and in which my staff and I have spent many long, weary, and anxious hours, night and day, guiding and teaching the men to attain the knowledge and experience necessary, in order that when members were sent out to the erectors they would have no difficulty in fitting together hundreds of feet up in the air.

Even though the first shipments of steel arrived from England in March 1925, the workshops at Milsons Point weren't completed until the next year.

In the meantime the English firm built a narrow-gauge railway on timber trestles over George Street and up a 150-metre incline from the harbour to haul materials back to the start of the approach spans.

There are five approach spans either side of the harbour weighing an average of 1200 tonnes. Five-tonne steam trains were used to construct falseworks or frames of American Oregon timber, and once these were in place 25-tonne cranes were brought in to lift the steel members and construct the approaches. Ennis noted that:

> often it is necessary to build a succession of cranes, each one of a heavier lifting capacity than its predecessor, to accomplish the final purpose.
>
> These cranes, after having first been erected on timber towers, travelled forward upon the steelwork, which they had placed in position, thus building their own track as they went along.

While the approach spans were under construction the company dug four enormous holes in preparation for the bridge's four foundation bearings or skewbacks.

THE SKEWBACKS

The bridge starts and finishes, rises and falls, on four cyndrical pins or hinges, each 36 cm in diameter and over 4 metres long. It cannot be locked into concrete as the steel expands and contracts in the sun. The arch can lift 18 cm on a very hot day.

The hinges rest on saddles or skewbacks that have to take the extraordinary weight of the steel structure and transfer it through the earth. Without these foundations the bridge would spring out.

The four bearings, manufactured in England, weighed over 300 tonnes each and were so large they had to be transported by special train using two lines of track from the Darlington mills to the Middlesbrough docks. The Dawes Point bearings were shipped out a few months before those for the Milsons Point side in 1927.

Bradfield had tested the rock around Sydney Harbour, sinking

FACING PAGE:
*Looking Down:
Ferries blow
smoke over the
harbour and
city as they wait
for passengers at
Circular Quay.
Business was
soon to drop off.
1929.*

bores 25 metres either side of the harbour, and had found a deep, solid bed of sandstone. Keen to protect the future foundations of the bridge the engineer had two 4-hectare reserves created in which no coal mining could take place, but he assured people at the time there was plenty of opportunity for coal mining further along the harbour.

In 1926 workers began to dig the four large holes which would anchor the skewbacks. Each hole was 27 metres by 12 metres, and 9 metres deep. Three of the holes were dug into sheer rock, but the discovery of shale on the city side meant they had to be a little deeper than usual, while on the northern side they were stepped.

Once the cavernous holes were complete the concreting engineer, Dr Oscar Faber, designed a system of pouring concrete in hexagonal slabs 12 metres by 2.4 metres by 1.4 metres, which was calculated to reduce shrinkage and best suit the primitive concrete mixing facilities on site.

The most delicate part of the operation involved placing the skewbacks or bearings. The erection of the south-east bearing began on 27 March 1927 and was not finished until a month later on 23 April 1927.

The engineers and builders were dealing with enormous weights, unprecedented concrete pours and minute angles. The slightest error here and the half arches would not meet. Using theodolites mounted on a tower at the centre line of the bridge, the skewbacks were lined up toward that centre point in space.

The 130 cubic metres of concrete used to fix the foundations of the skewbacks was made of a special mix designed to bear the load of the bridge without cracking. It had to be laid in one continuous pour.

The first pour began at 6 am and involved 14 hours of backbreaking work, using only shovels and special wheelbarrows.

The process was repeated four times.

TUNNELS, CABLES AND CRANES

Once the skewbacks were in position the north and south pylons were built up to road level to meet the approach spans which were

A Maze of Steel: The arch consists of 39,000 tonnes of steel, but the entire structure used 52,800 tonnes of the material, most of which was shipped from England.

under construction. By June 1928 Dorman, Long were ready to start building the arch but some in Sydney were losing patience and the critics suggested that if it had taken this long to dig a few holes in the ground then the project would never be completed. Ennis recalled the distractions when the bridge was finished and wrote in the paper on the day of the opening ceremony:

> I can remember that during the construction of this not very spectacular work we were subjected to much 'armchair' criticism as to our slowness in getting on with the job. Indeed, so despondent were the critics, that many discussions arose from their comfortable surroundings, as to whether the bridge would ever be built. In addition, many pessimistically inclined engineers in Australia and overseas expressed the opinion that the erection of the arch of such magnitude was a foolhardy

THE BRIDGE

attempt to do the impossible and these criticisms became so definite that some members of the New South Wales Cabinet at the time expressed alarm, and I was called upon more than once to reassure them.

To erect the bridge the builders needed special cranes which could not only lift the heavy weights, but actually be in position to lift them for the first panels near the shore and the later panels in the middle of the harbour. They devised two cranes which would climb out on the structure as it was erected, in the process overcoming access problems.

Messrs Wellman, Smith and Owen of London manufactured two creeper cranes that Ennis described as the 'most important erection units'. The idea was that these cranes would construct their own path. As they put a new panel in place they crept onto it to put the next section in place, creeping their way into the centre of the harbour. Each weighed 575 tonnes (which alone would place enormous weight on the unsupported arch) and had a lifting capacity of 122 tonnes on its main hoist but carried a number of other smaller cranes for different jobs. Just placing the creeper cranes on the pylons so they could begin the journey cost an estimated £30,000 and involved the construction of smaller cranes.

'We now felt that the real undertaking was upon us,' Ennis wrote.

The bridge was about to step out into the void of the harbour. It was impossible to build support piers so the half arches were held back during construction by 128 steel cables which wound across the top of the half-completed pylons and into deep horseshoe holes in the sandstone.

Again it was not a novel construction method but the scale of it was daunting. Freeman and Imbault had used the method on the anchorages of the Victoria Falls Bridge a quarter of a century before but this time the bridge that the cables would hold was 50 times heavier. Ennis noted:

Consisting of 217 wires, the cables were of a diameter of $2\frac{3}{4}$ inches, a length of some 1,200 feet, and an average weight of $8\frac{1}{2}$ tons. When tested they revealed a breaking strain of 460 tons per cable, but in practice were called upon to sustain a strain of only 115 tons.

Dorman, Long manufactured 25,700 km or 2200 tonnes of wire for the bridge.

Workers armed with hydraulic jackhammers were sent tunnelling under the foreshores' stone. Just as the skewbacks are critical to the bridge as it stands, these tunnels were critical to the bridge during construction. The cables were fed from the east side to the west through the sandstone bedrock and took the weight of the bridge until the arch could be completed. The U-shaped tunnels were 36 metres long and dug at a 45-degree angle. A man could stand easily inside and the walls were lined concrete.

Clarrie Erdman, an orphan son of an American teamster, got work on the bridge and found himself tunnelling under Sydney.

One day I saw an ad in the paper wanting men for sewerage work, putting in a new sewerage line, I can't remember whether it was at Bondi or Bronte. Any how I went out there and I was ten minutes too late. I decided to go back to the city but on the way back I thought I would have a look at the Harbour Bridge … I was standing at the gate having a look around to see the progress and a chap passed me and he said, 'Are you looking for work, son?' I said, 'Oh yes I am.' He said, 'Hang on a minute, I might be able to get you on.' He went away for about a quarter of an hour and he came back and he said, 'I want you to go up there and see a man called Mr Foley.' Mr Foley was like a riding ganger, we'll say. I went up and saw Mr Foley and I only had on an overcoat, singlet and trousers, I was pretty poor in those days. Mr Foley said, 'Take off your overcoat, son,' so I took off my overcoat. By the way I was only about twenty-three years of age then … he said, 'Righto, put

THE BRIDGE

it down there and go and get a tin and pick up some rivets.' I was doing that for quite a while and then Mr Foley came to me and said, 'I want you to go up there to Mr Barr.' Mr Barr was the foreman carpenter on the gantries. So I worked on the gantries for quite a while. Then Mr Muir, he was the superintendent on the Dawes Point side, put me in what they called the tunnels, the support shafts where the cables were that supported the span. I worked on that for quite a while.

I was on what they called an Ingasaw Rand rock drilling machine. There were about four or five of us down there in the tunnels … they were down about fifteen to twenty feet, I suppose about five or six metres [when I started].

Erdman stayed with the job until they were down to the bottom of the tunnel:

… I think was about two hundred and forty feet.

When I got down to the bottom that is when I left.

They were square tunnels. I had nothing to do with the concreting, only the drilling of the rock. There were others shovelling out the rock and we were drilling. There were four or five of us on the drills, two men to a drill.

You had to hold the drill up in your hands. There was no stand …

When they got to the bottom … they cut out a hole in the bottom because the water started to seep in. They had pumps on it … After we got down a certain depth we came to concrete and they were cells where they used to tie the prisoners up … Where they put the convicts … Tied them up to flog them I suppose it would be. There were rings in the wall. They called it Battery Park, or Battery Hill, or something like that.

The cables were threaded through the completed tunnels and gave the builders great flexibility in dealing with the shifting weights and tensions during the construction. Everything was watched, measured and monitored. The strain of the creeper cranes deflected the arch, but so too did the weights they lifted.

THE ARCH TAKES SHAPE

Sighting targets were marked on the bridge members and these were monitored by surveying equipment while the cranes lifted the loads into position. Ennis recalled that the bridge moved most markedly as the half arches neared their meeting place.

Pretty as a Picture: The bridge has no curved pieces and is formed by straight iron chords fitted at precise angles to create the arch shape. 1932.

As the weight of the lift was being taken by the crane on the end of the half arch the deflection of the half arch could clearly be observed before the lift started to go up. We thus ensured that no undue deflection was caused over and above that allowed for in the calculations. Several times we had anxious moments when undue deflection took place, and a halt was made while the cable anchorage system and structure generally were carefully inspected.

THE BRIDGE

… On the completion of the eighth panel of the arch on the south side we were within an inch of correct alignment, both vertically and horizontally. At practically the same stage of erection on the northern half arch it was found that the truss had tended to slew-westwards. To correct this, the cables were slackened half an inch at the north-west point of attachment. This figure of half an inch was of course only determined after careful investigations had been made, and this sufficed to bring the two half arches practically dead into correct alignment. There was 8000 tons erected on the northern arch at the time, and this was suspended on the cables when the adjustment was made.

Erection of the first half arch began on 26 October 1928 and involved lifting the first lengths of steel and attaching them to the skewbacks on the Dawes Point side. The first panel was the strongest and heaviest of all fourteen. The lower chord alone

Low Level: This view north from St Philips church tower after the opening ceremony shows how even the approach spans dominated the low city. 1932.

weighed over 1000 tonnes and was beyond the capacity and reach of the creeper crane so it was built up in sections; the first piece of steel to be attached to the foundations only measured 6 metres long but weighed 85 tonnes. The support cables were not put in place until the end posts were constructed, so temporary arrangements had to be made to hold the initial members in place using a crane on a barge. The end posts weighed 200 tonnes each and the entire panel 3050 tonnes. According to Ennis:

> The nose of the arch now projected over the water. And, from this stage, members had to be lifted direct from a barge in midstream, an operation needing great care in view of the continual passing of ferry-boats and deep-sea liners, for which the fairway was available during the whole period of erection.

Work picked up speed as the builders became more comfortable with the construction process and the creeper crane began its first tentative steps out onto the top of the arch. 'On 26th November, 1929, we had the satisfaction of erecting a record tonnage of 598 tons in one day,' Ennis recalled.

RIGGERS AND RIVETERS

Assembling the bridge was a huge task undertaken by a handful of men. These were riveters, boilermakers, steel constructors and riggers. Each had a dangerous and often uncomfortable but always crucial job.

Harry Tom Tomrop was born in Russia in 1891 on a sailing ship captained by his father, his American mother died at birth and Tom was raised at sea. He worked as a rigger in New York on the city's first skyscrapers before moving to Australia. He was one of the twelve 'tin hares' of the bridge, the men who assembled and guided the steel into place. Tomrop had worked all over the world but said that assembling the creeper crane on the pylons rated as one of the most difficult and dangerous jobs he had ever attempted.

We had to erect the creeper crane ... that was the most awkward job of the lot ... one of the biggest jobs I have ever been on in my life. You had to hang on by your eyelashes you know. It was tricky and you couldn't just stand there you had to hang on. [I told a] mate of mine ... that I was working on the creeper crane. I had only been there for about a week. He said, 'I wonder if I could get a job there?' He was right down and out. I said, 'Well you will have to see the boss. You see Len Tucker.' ... Anyway he got a job and he only stuck it about two hours and he left himself. He really didn't know what it was like.

Tomrop says the danger didn't stop there.

Manual Labour: The ironbark track timbers for the electronic railway lines on the steel structure were prepared by carpenters in the age old manner. 1931.

When it was too windy and so on a couple would go up on the arch and then say to the foreman that it was too windy. We had to make the staging more safe. If you saw any loose ropes you fixed them up then we would go down to the hanger. We would do all sorts, hauling blocks, or do a bit of splicing. We had to splice wire and ropes. That was all part of the job.

Tomrop and the other tin hares used podgers, which were pointed spanners, to hang on to the members and would climb the structure by sticking the end in the rivet holes like a mountaineer. He often rode the steel up from the harbour.

Len Tucker … was the man on the telephone and he could talk to the crane driver to tell him what to do, to higher it up or stop. That was his job. At the same time he was in charge of us. There were about six of us …

When we got on the arch itself, like on the top chord, there were a lot of us. We used to line it up, maybe only one man, sometimes two … My mates would stand with the guys keeping it [the steel members] steady to stop it from blowing about. Of course the fellows were riding it up. Sometimes it wasn't just them riding it up, on calm days they used to let anybody ride up … As soon as the job was in position they would get down to it and put a podger in and would bolt it down and so on. They would go down in the cage to the punt again and as soon as another job came out of the workshop he would sling that and the same processes goes through.

Stan London was a boilermaker, one of the men who fitted and bolted the panels into place after Tomrop had ridden the steel into position.

Well naturally the job was assembled in the shop first. The first span was made fully in the shop and before that came out the next span was made and fitted to the first span to make sure there would be no difficulty when it went aloft. It was inspected in the shop, all the holes were reamed out to make sure everything was perfect so we would have no troubles when it was up aloft. Naturally they had pins turned up that were a driving fit into the holes. These pins made sure it was a free go for the bolts to be put in without any effort whatever … The rigger would tap them in as the creeper crane held them in position.

There would be so much weight of the section that the pins would get locked in the holes too at times and they had to be drilled out …

The boilermaker's job was to put the bolts in. Then the inspector would come along and sometimes say the plates were not close enough. He had a feeler gauge he could insert in the holes and it had a little foot. If he could insert this little foot which possibly would measure a thousandth of an inch, I can't say for sure on that one, then they weren't tight enough. It had to be that he couldn't get it in at all. In other words the plates had to be … dead tight before they were allowed to rivet the job … it was definitely a job whereby every joint had to be so tight that no corrosion could take place later on, being sea air and that sort of thing. They were very particular about it, most particular about those plates being tight.

In many cases, if there was a slight distortion in the plates you would put a bolt in every hole and you couldn't even get the plates together. Sometimes there would be maybe a sixty-fourth [of an inch], even a sixteen [of an inch] I have seen them, difference. So the riveter would have to come along, put a rivet in. As you know when you get up beyond a critical point the rivet grows in length, well in reverse when you put it in and the riveter knocks that rivet down it contracts. Well the contraction, naturally, would pull the plates together. Often I have seen possibly dozen of rivets put in so that the plates would pull up together and then we had to cut them out. Then the riveter would go through and the inspectors would come along and test each rivet individually. Possibly there were hundreds in at one joint alone. So there was a lot of work done, that had to be really done, that was wasted in a way because they were that particular about making these joints extra tight.

The boilermaker is responsible for the joint. When he finished bolting up the section the inspector would come along and okay it. You would have your spanner with a six foot length of pipe on it and your labourer would stand on the end of that and hang on if it was outside. A lot of work went on inside the chords, the bulk of the work really. The labourer would stand on it and weigh it down and you would get up on it and weight it down too. There was terrific pressure in the steel.

Bob Ross was a Scot from Glasgow who started cooking rivets at the age of thirteen. The rivets were cooked on the arch in portable coke ovens. Sometimes they were thrown to the riveter and caught in a sand-filled bucket, but at other times the hot slugs were fired along a pneumatic tube.

Of course … as you are going up the bottom of the arch, or the top of the arch, we had to have automatic pass boys to pass our rivets up. Well they were in the shape of a milk cart standing about 3 foot or 3.5 foot high and it was connected to the air. You dropped your rivet in the top of it, the flap would close and you would slap your foot on the pedal and she would go up like a rocket. If he left his end open, the holder-up, he was likely to get a smack with it. George [Scott], a couple of times, forgot to close it and I could hear someone swearing so I knew he had missed something.

You put your rivets in a fire, in the coke … you turn your rivet over until you get the head hot, just white but not runny. Then you turn it back until you get the end of the rivet as hot

3.
8·1·31·

as you can, because by the time it gets down to the riveter it gets cool a bit, he likes it nice and hot so he can knock it down.

If there was a heavy wind you had to be very careful because you were walking on the heads of rivets. You had to make sure of your feet because once you slipped there was nothing to hang on to. They only put a line up and you know what a rope line is, sagging all the time, and it is not much help to you. It is not like they have now, a safety line. Who I used to feel sorry for was new chaps coming to work on the arch that had never worked on a bridge before. Quite a few of them had to turn it up before they got half way up to their job and you couldn't blame them.

George Evernden, an English-born ironworker, was part of the riveting crew.

Well my job was in a riveting squad and a riveting squad consisted of three men, sometimes four. There was the man who cooked the rivets. My position was holder-up for the boilermaker, I used to accept the rivets when they were ready for me and I used to put them in and the riveter round the other side rounded them off. The fourth man, whom we occasionally needed, was a man to pass the rivets ... Other times we used to put them down a sort of a chute and they would come into a kerosene tin at the end of the chute and I would take them from there, with a pair of tongs of course, and put them into the hole. I would hold my rattler dolly [a tool that holds one end of the rivet while the other is being shaped] on them while the riveter the other side used to round them over and complete the job. If those rivets weren't completely heated, they would have to be taken out because they would sweat a bit. Once they have sweated they become loose in the hole. The inspectors used to come round and inspect the job after they had cooled off a bit and if they were loose at all they had

PLATE 6.
SYDNEY HARBOUR BRIDGE, MANUFACTURE AND ERECTION.

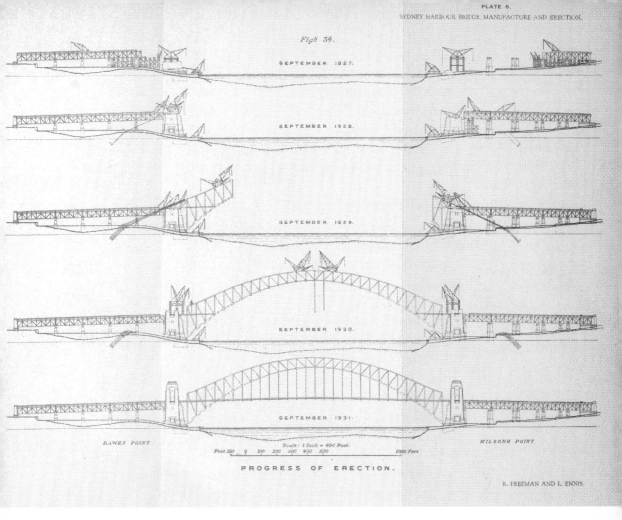

Fig. 34.

SEPTEMBER 1927.

SEPTEMBER 1928.

SEPTEMBER 1929.

SEPTEMBER 1930.

SEPTEMBER 1931.

DAWES POINT

Scale : 1 Inch = 400 Feet.
Feet 100   0   100   200   300   400   500   1000 Feet

MILSONS POINT

PROGRESS OF ERECTION.

R. FREEMAN AND L. ENNIS.

to be taken out straight away … It was a very deafening job, we worked inside the chords. We used to straddle the chords to do the rivet heads and used to try hold ourselves in position to complete the job, to hold the rivet firmly while the boiler-maker knocked them down the other side. On one occasion when the first tower went up for the road way the squad that I was working with was put on to that job and there were a few rivets I couldn't reach off the staging myself and I had to sit on a box to reach them. When I put the machine on overhead and turned the air on it threw me back over the staging and I fell. As I fell I grabbed the staging and I held on for grim death and my two mates … the man who cooked the rivets,

By Inches: Draughtsmen's drawings sketched the bridge's progress as it rose from the north and south shores and stretched across the waters of the harbour.

BUILDING THE BRIDGE

and the boilermaker grabbed me. I think they got more of a shock than I did. It happened on the Friday afternoon which gave me the weekend to get over it. Naturally we knocked off straightaway, the boilermaker, myself and the cooker, we were all upset and we went home.

In 1929 the arbitration commission heard an application for a wage claim for the workers on the arch. Harry Tomrop gave evidence and Bradfield backed them in their claim.

Judge Beeby granted the workers on the arch a pay rise, concluding:

> The work is unusually laborious and hazardous and of a nature imposing nervous strain which, fortunately, men are not often asked to endure. Some of them work in confined spaces and in strained positions, whilst the work of riggers is unusually difficult and dangerous. The men are necessarily picked workmen of peculiar temperament. For the next 18 months from 100 to 150 workmen will be engaged from day to day on a venture which is exciting the interest of the engineering world. A community which asks such an unusual service must be prepared to offer unusual wages.

CHARACTERS AND CALAMITIES

Vince Kelly is falling from the arch, Karl Zarenzoff, the Russian strongman, is trying to find a colleague he can hang from the arch and all the time the workers are hanging on for grim life. Sixteen men die during construction; Kelly manages to hit the water feet first and is back at work soon after.

Practically every workman on the Harbour Bridge knew Jacko. He was the Bridge watch dog, and a proud one at that, because he is the first dog to cross the structure. Up on the arch he looked down on all other dogs. For years he did the rounds of the Bridge at night and day with the watchmen. He knew all of the workmen, and when a stranger appeared he would bark long and loudly. One night a watchman found the dog barking up at one of the lower chords of the Bridge on the Dawes Point side. On investigation a man was found asleep inside the chord, where it was warm and sheltered from the rain and biting westerly wind. On dark and wet nights when the watchman's lamp was not very effective, Jacko would run backwards and forwards along the tracks to guide his master. When feeling lonely some days, Jacko would make his way up the arch to the creeper-crane driver's cabin or would lie down beside one of the painters for company. Jacko is equally as sorry as the workmen that the job is finished. Now the leading question so far as the workmen are concerned, is not who designed the Bridge, but who is going to have Jacko.

Daily Telegraph Sunday 19 March 1932

October 1930

Vincent 'Ned' Kelly is hurtling toward the afterlife. Tumbling toward a certain death. Wind screaming in his ears, tearing at his clothes, G-forces pulling at his arms and legs, the grey harbour water, tense and cold, steeled for impact. In one sickening moment he has overbalanced and then there is nothing other than an almost certain death 50-odd metres below. He had been fixing rivets, lugging a massive pneumatic gun connected to a cumbersome air hose when his rubber-soled shoes slipped and the flimsy platform disappeared from under his groping feet.

Kelly barely has time to let out a grunt of surprise. By the time he has dropped the rivet gun, the last fixed object has flown past. His hands clutch at nothing but the whistling air; there is no time to scream, only a second left now to decide if he will die. He is out of control. Turns a somersault that rolls the clouds and the water and the bridge. There is only one slight chance he can defy the odds. He knows he has to control the fall, straighten his body, point his toes down and raise his arms. Become a sort of human spear. It is critical that he meet the water with as little of his body as possible. Point the toes. Raise the arms above the head. He has to get straight and he has only seconds to do it. In a breath he is travelling at more than 30 metres a second.

Twenty-five years later, R. G. Snyder will publish a paper in *Aerospace Med* which finds one thing that Kelly knows instinctively: body position is crucial; and one he doesn't: the human body cannot withstand impact with water when travelling faster than 35.3 metres a second. Kelly is almost at terminal velocity and even if he stays below it he has considerably less than a 10 per cent chance of surviving. Suicides have more chance of living than a falling worker whose every atom is fighting to survive. Suicides jump, usually feet first; working men, like Kelly, enter the void out of control.

He … has … to … get … straight and he has less time to do it than it took you to read these few words. And now he is frightened. If Kelly hits the water in a lateral position the injuries to his chest will be similar to being hit by the shock wave of a bomb blast, lacerating the lungs, rupturing the heart and spleen, causing brain haemorrhage and massive internal bleeding. If he doesn't drown in the water he will drown in his own blood.

But Kelly is tipping sideways and there is no time to correct. He waves his arms desperately. Forces his body upright. Or almost. He places his hand over his face and the next thing he knows he is exploding into the water.

A BREED APART

Men rose to the occasion. In the wake of a war and in the mire of a depression there was no room for fear or frailty. The light was fast dimming on the Australian economy and a job was a job. A man was a man. Still, the sheer enormity and audacity of building something so big and daring was too much for some. Just erecting the approaches that lift the road to the start of the arch took men to fatal

High Diver: Boilermaker Vince 'Ned' Kelly is congratulated by Mr Davidson MLA. Kelly fell from the deck into the water and survived to return to work. 1930.

THE BRIDGE

heights. Seven men lost their lives before the arch had left the ground. Many lost their hearing, their lives, and one lost a testicle.

The scale of the bridge project was bigger than anything Australians had undertaken. There was no vertigo in the workshops, but the deafening noise and earth-shaking scale of the steel cutting machinery tested a worker's nerves to the limits and were a constant threat to his mortality. Explosions rocked the quarries in Moruya where the stone was cleft from the ground in enormous blocks. Above the harbour things could shift in a minute; gentle zephyrs became gales, great steel beams swung about in the sky, guided only by the strong arm of a tin hare. Crane drivers worked blind, guided by phone and whistle. Shoes slipped and slid on the steep, slick back of the metal arch. There were no steps or handrails as there are today. Men skipped from rivet head to rivet head, twisting their feet like ballet dancers to grip, hand in pocket and cigarette on lip. Before the roadway was hung the workers were taken 141 metres and higher, reaching out into the void to guide the next enormous girder. Even the roadway was 59 metres above sea level — that's 5 metres higher than Niagara Falls.

Vera Holliday worked in the Dorman, Long pay office at Dawes Point. She filled in the compensation forms when workers were injured and she recalled the rivet boys occasionally getting a hot foot when one of the super-heated metal slugs shed its scales into an open boot. Buckets of water stood by for such occasions and were never close enough for the hopping man who would have pulled his boot off with his teeth if he could.

In 1930, when the arch had been joined, Vera was offered the chance to inspect the men's work and view the harbour from this magnificent vantage point.

> The big moment really came and he said to me, 'Come on Vera, come over the top of the arch.' I just couldn't … but I would have loved to have gone but I just couldn't. I had seen too many men come down from there white-faced when a sudden gust of wind had come and they had had to hang on

for dear life. I thought that could happen to me and I would rather be down here.

Vera had done the paperwork for the men who died or were hurt on the site, remembering one who 'fell face down and that was not at all nice to think about. I put those well in the back of my memory, the actual facts.'

The men knew, too.

Some swallowed their fear, fixed their eyes straight ahead and got on with the job. Riggers, tin hares and dogmen were used to heights but in a city where the buildings had yet to pass 50 metres, working the arch took the men where few had been. Some revelled in the adrenaline rush of riding the hook of a crane 140 metres above the harbour. Forced to ride the cradle — a small fenced platform — up and down to start and finish work, the daredevils sat up on its railings, hands free to roll a cigarette, while the others piled inside like sheep. In a pen. What a way to come to work, dangling in a cage on the end of a crane, bashing against the iron girders, swaying out on a spectacular ride long before Luna Park rose from the dirt floors of the workshops.

When the photographers lugged their heavy gear onto the arch, men would pose, hanging on by one casual hand as they did this or that 141 metres up. They were supermen, elevated above the sea-level humans.

You can or you can't work at heights. Because it was the Depression, some who couldn't did their best, but no amount of money could quell the fear. Pat Crawley came to the job late, hired to clean the decorative granite pylons on the ends of the arch. He could handle the heights, but remembers one who was not so fortunate.

It was a bit frightening at first, the height worried you. You had to be down on your haunches and you had to wash all the top. I remember distinctly one day, the first day we went up, there was a chap there, I can't think of his name but he had seven in his family, and he said, 'Look Pat I don't think I can stand this height. If I stop up here I will fall over.' I said to him, 'Well the height is not worrying me so much, I will do round the edges and you do the inside.' He did that all day but he didn't turn up the next morning. He had to turn it in, he couldn't stand the heights.

It must have been a terrible night for that frightened man, thinking about the needs of the seven mouths he had to feed and the stomach-clenching fear he felt every time his mind returned to the job. Fear drove him back into a world of soup kitchens and food coupons and onto a dispiriting unemployment line when up to four in ten men were without work. Walter Ellis was one of the really brave men, the ones who were scared and overcame their fear.

The first week that I was employed there I was running down bolts and nuts and greasing them for the upper structure. In that week I was told one morning by Mr Sam Harris that I would be going up in the cage to the top. He gave me my mate, who was a riveter, a Mr George Stobbart. As we went up halfway the crane driver in his joking way deliberately let the brake off and it used to make us bounce. Of course I became terrified because previously I had never climbed any higher than say a peach tree or a locust tree. When I got to the top the swivel of the hook was spinning around and I was that terrified I did not know how I would get off. Eventually somebody helped me out and through, I suppose, bravado, I overcame the situation. But my first job was more terrifying that the travel up in the cage. I was given a twenty-eight pound hammer to knock a drift through the side plate of the bridge of the first chord, which I did do and I did it magnificently. From then on of course I grew up at the bridge and it had no fears for me. I was a holder-upper for the full term from the first section to the fourteenth section, with my mate George Stobbart.

The crane driver's black humour was not the only time Ellis found himself hanging on and terrified.

> I had a very near escape … half way over on the middle section we were working on the laterals, which are in the middle of the bridge on the bottom section of the top chord. Now me being a holder-upper, I caught the rivet this particular morning to place in the hole for my mate to rivet down. But unfortunately I did not change my spike piece, which is the bottom of a piece of two inch water pipe and it must be sharp to dig into the steel where the top section, which is the plunger, holds the rivet up. Now this point being blunt, when I turned the trigger on for the air to go through for the plunger it skated and it took me with it. I went down from the scaffolding roughly about six foot. I hung on like grim death, being so young and vigorous. There were two … riggers in the vicinity and they came racing over and they pulled me up by the rubber hose and I regained my footing on the scaffolding. Then, of course, I naturally went home for the day. The following morning I backed up again. Of course youth and being young and vigorous, good reflexes I was able to shape up the next day without worrying about the day before.

Stan London also remembers some hairy rides in the cage. London was one of the youngest workers on the arch. One year out of his apprenticeship, the young man made the trip into town from Parramatta three times before finally getting a start.

> I made several visits down to the bridge to get a job, but Mr Hipwell, he was the outside manager for Dorman and Long, refused me on two occasions. Eventually he said, 'Well, you are rather persistent so I will give you a start. There is a certain element of risk and you are a young man with a life ahead of you.'

A Sorry Affair: Almost 200,000 crossed the bridge to demand the Howard government apologise to Aboriginals for past wrongs. They were ignored. May 2000.

Party Time: The bridge is a focal point for Sydney's celebrations and on New Year's Eve 2000, the Olympic year, it was a big show.

Bridge Climb: For decades youths climbed the bridge under the cover of dark.
Despite increased security, Frenchman Alain Robert did it in broad daylight. 2003.

Fast Track: Dr J. J. C. Bradfield's Model A Ford was the first car to cross the bridge. Mark Weber's Williams F1 machine was the fastest. November 2003.

London was 22 when he started and was given the job of bolting the new members into place before they were riveted.

I had the fright of my life, one winter's night. You know they used to take us up in an open cage about three feet high. It was a rectangular base with a vertical post either side and angles all round it and we used to sit on that and hang on to something. There were four steel ropes that came over the top ... It was dark, a winter's night, and cold as charity. I was sitting on the rail. We used to pack twenty of us in, like sardines, and I used to sit on the rail and wrap my insteps around the middle one and hang on to a bloke if I couldn't grab one of the ropes ... This night we were chatting and all off a sudden the rope

Caged in: Construction workers had the choice of walking up the steep, slippery arch or getting a lift in the cage, which jolted and swung about wildly.

must have jumped off the coil on top. Well it might have only gone twelve inches, but the jib seat went too … Lou Moore, he was … a rough diamond, he said, 'Well if anyone says they didn't shit themselves he is a bloody liar.' It just dropped and everybody wanted to grab for the hook because we thought the bottom was going. If you grab the hook you are safer, but no one could get it because there was that many in this contraption they had for taking us up and down. That was the biggest scare I ever had, I reckon, it put the wind up me.

To cope with such work men became larger than life, if they weren't already. Most of the people whistling high above the harbour were shipbuilders and waterfront workers, they came from as close as Balmain and as far as Belfast, migrating from the shipyards when the work dried up in the early 1920s. Nuggety barrel-chested blokes, larrikin lords of the sky. Men whose whole lives had been spent around iron and salt water.

Men were hired from all over. Returned servicemen were favoured by government policy and many of the men who had spent their youth fighting signed up for the project; some of their sons did too. Unionists were favoured and, as the Depression bit, so too were family men. It was a colourful world populated by men from around the globe. The American who breathed fire, the Frenchman who ran the betting school at lunch and strange men whose hand-made lives grew fantastic detail among the steel and steam, cranes and craters.

Bluey Whitehead was one such bloke. He fancied himself as a sideshow strongman and introduced himself as Karl Zarenzoff, the Russian muscleman. He was an ironworker in the big sheds down where Luna Park is now. Charles Brown remembered him:

Bluey proclaimed himself to be a very tough guy and a very strong man. He used to get bags of rivets and lift them from the floor in his teeth. We used to make beds of nails for him to lie on and we used to get a board with the nails in and he would brace his shoulders and his arms and he would say, 'Hit me on the back.' So we would give him a whack with them. He would say, 'That's the stuff'.

Ian Ferrier also remembered Zarenzoff, or Bluey:

> He would lay down on a board with all nails protruding through, take his shirt off and lay on that. They would put a rock on his chest and one of the chaps would hit it with a sledge hammer and break this rock. The rock wouldn't break as easily as we thought. The idea of these rocks and nails was you would take the weight off with your elbows on the ground. This one hit too hard and Bluey came up with this board sticking to his back and blood coming out.

At lunchtime Bluey would get a group of the ironworkers and apprentices together and they would ride the steep escalator up the cliff above the workshops to the tram terminal. With his boilersuit unbuttoned to reveal a rippling chest, the strongman would convince a citizen to let him tie a rope and shackle to the bumper bar of his car and taking the rope in his teeth would drag it along the street. They loved that. But Bluey had grander visions, as fellow worker Charles Brown recounted:

> Well all of these successful exploits seemed to encourage him and he wanted to go to greater heights. He thought it would be a marvellous thing if he and I were to join together in another exploit. What he proposed to do was to go to the top of the arch, that is on the top chord, and he was going to hang by his legs from the top chord holding me in his teeth. Now whilst he thought that was a hell of a good idea, I wasn't too keen on it myself. I think that is where about we fell out and the end of his exploits with me.

It might have been a joke, but Brown didn't think so. Ferrier said that Zarenzoff had a dry sense of humour.

Dangerous Tasks: Tin hares climbed up on steel members and clambered into impossible positions using a sharpened tool that fitted in the rivet holes. 1931.

Another thing I remember about him. It was the day they closed the arch of the bridge. Well day-by-day there was a report on it in the papers, 'The bridge is getting closer, the arch is getting closer.' It was supposed to be closed when the temperature was right. This day, about mid-day, or eleven o'clock in the morning, or whatever, the arch became closed. When the signal was given the siren in the workshop went 'Cock-a-doodle-doo' ... There was a rush from the workshop outside, out on the wharf, the harbour front, to see. Everybody was looking up but of course they couldn't see that much different. I went back and there was Bluey Whitehead standing with his arms folded, just leaning back. I said, 'Didn't you go outside and see, Bluey?' He said, 'Oh, haven't you seen an arch close before?'

Ferrier himself went up onto the arch one day and then climbed the jib of the creeper crane. His mates took a photograph of him hanging by his hands way out over the harbour and it was passed around the workshops.

The daily grind

It wasn't all fun and the machinery in the shop could claim a life or a limb in an instant. One young married man was wearing sandshoes and slipped while operating the massive drill used to put rivet holes in the thick steel plates. The machinery caught his trousers, caught him by the crutch and crushed one testicle. The white-faced workers saw him taken away by ambulance but heard later that the man had recovered and successfully fathered a child.

While you were supposed to be 21 to work on the arch, many of the people in the workshops were young men, keen for a bit of fun even in the brief moments they got to escape the noise and strain of the work, as Charles Brown recalled:

> We only had a half an hour [for lunch], but it is amazing how much you could fit into half an hour. At times some of the boys, myself, Charlie Nunn, Jack Rue and a couple of the others, would get out onto the wharf in the very hot weather and we would dive off the wharf into the harbour. They used to warn us that there were a few sharks around, but being so young and a bit more daring than we are now it didn't seem to worry us all that much. Again there was a couple of Crown and Anchor boards always going there. You would always have your pennies, or if you had more money, three pence on the board. They filled in the lunch hours.

When the winds came up they blew through the workshop and chased the men from the arch. Men would keep an eye on the observatory tower at Millers Point where a black ball was raised and dropped every day to tell ships' navigators and the Town Hall clock that it was 1 pm. If it was raised again that meant a storm was coming and the arches would be cleared. If there was rain and it was too heavy the men stood by for two hours, one on company time, the other on their own, to see if work could continue. If it couldn't they were sent home without pay. The sleek arch of the bridge did not have the steps you see on it today and became impossibly slippery.

As a holder-upper, Cliff Anning spent most of his time in the noisy, swaying darkness, inside the chords of the arches, feet splayed and braced against the heads of rivets already placed while he held up the rivets for the riveter working outside. Inside stunk from the lead paint used to mark off the rivets. Anning would be burnt by hot scalings that fell from the slugs, cook during summer and shiver during winter, but even this seemed to be something of a comfort zone compared to some of the jobs the men were asked to do, like climbing the jib arms of the creeper cranes — a place higher and considerably more precarious than the arches themselves.

> Well I did have a thrill once, you can call it scared. I had to go up and we were working on some little job on the jib, I just can't remember what. I know I had to get about three-quarter way up to the top, I think it was to check on a couple of bolts. When I got up there I just noticed up the harbour big clouds coming down. I thought to myself this was going to be good and all of a sudden it hit us, a westerly gale. Well I just had to hang on for a quarter-of-an-hour, twenty minutes. It didn't subside much but I worked my way down and was glad to get down.

George Evernden worked in the steel chords too. In 1982 interviewer Richard Raxworthy, who recorded the reminiscences of most of the bridge workers quoted here, asked Evernden if he remembered the conditions.

Oh my word I do, they were very deafening. There was practically no light at all … I used to stand at the head of the rivets to try and get balance to hold the rivets in firm position. Sometimes there was a bit of staging, but mostly we had to find our own footing …

We had to wear leather gloves to stop the sparks flying off the rivets and the scale. After you put the rivets in when you turned the pneumatic riveter on, the machine on, the sparks used to fly and I would often have burns on my neck and arms …

Inside the chords it got very hot. On windy days of course we couldn't stay up there. We used to have to hang on like grim death. It could get very windy up there, which is only natural. It was very hot inside.

The wind might not have threatened your life in the workshops, but it added another degree of discomfort, as Ian Ferrier recalled.

The floor was a dirt and ash cinder floor and would get very dusty at times. They would have to water it down, bed it down a bit at various times, especially if they got a wind off the harbour. The wind would whistle through those workshops and it was bitterly cold. This dust would fly everywhere. It was dreadful at times but, however, they were the conditions you worked under, had nothing else to do.

Today's employers provide all manner of comforts but the bridge workers were given a job and not much more. There were no change rooms, no showers and only the most rudimentary protective gear. Men might boil a billy to make tea, but would kick it over if a supervisor approached as it was against the rules. Cigarettes were rolled in your own time. The start of lunch breaks were a sight to behold. The men in the sheds had time for swimming and hijinks, the men on the arch barely had time to make it to the ground. Pat Crawley recalls the scene:

THE BRIDGE

… the whistle would go to blow for lunch, dinner or knock-off and you wouldn't hardly see a man, then all of a sudden you would see heads coming from everywhere. Every little hole there would be a man in there, a boiler maker, painter, or something like that … they would come out like rabbits, everywhere. I have never forgotten it … I can see it now, the whistle going and the heads coming out … They would be inside the steel work and wherever there was a hole you would see a head pop out, it was amazing.

Not everybody bothered to go down for their toilet and lunch breaks. Jack McCrae remembers a man who found a variety of uses for his tools.

Joe Wheeler was the crane driver on the Wilson runabout crane on the Dawes Point side. This crane lifted the granite blocks out of the three small ships that used to come up and down from Moruya and his job, along with the dogmen, was to place all these pieces of granite in their order and in their correct courses. However, Joe was a bit of a conservative man and when he took his place on the crane, say early in the morning commencing time, he didn't leave it until five o'clock. He did all his own firing of course, throwing the coal into the furnace, as this was a steam crane, this involved using a square mouthed shovel … Along with the shovelling of the coal into the furnace Joe also used to use this shovel as a means of easing himself, because the lavatory was some considerable distance away. This was a very handy tool this square mouthed shovel because as well as using for the firing of the crane and Joe's movements he also used to use it for frying sausages, after it was sterilised of course.

There were no portable toilets on the arch. As Hugh Dunn says:

… It's a long way up … and if you wanted to go to the toilet they shut their eyes to the fact that you got a bag and you did it in a bag. Anyhow, this holder-up of mine he did it in the bag and he folded it up and threw it over. As soon as he threw it over it opened up and went round and round and round and straight on the top deck of a ferry. I often wonder what happened about that.

Others told the same story but maintained the bag landed at the feet of the English foreman. Despite the hard times, or perhaps because of it, some of the men found time to have a punt, as Ian Ferrier recalled.

There was an ironworker there, a dogman on the crane, a Frenchman, known as 'Frenchie' or 'Froggie' as they called him. He used to run this Crown and Anchor game every lunch time. He would go around there yelling out, 'Hoy there, hoy there, hoy there.' Then over to the Crown and Anchor. You would bet from a penny up, three pence, shilling, whatever … He was a very excitable chap, Frenchie, and as I say he was a dogman on the crane, and there was some mishap and somebody got injured. He was very upset. He was that upset he couldn't run his Crown and Anchor game at lunch time that day …

Of course there was another chap there who was an SP bookmaker, used to take bets on the side. You would walk by with a bit of paper and just leave it where he worked. He would look up to see if the foreman was around and go and get the paper. Bentley his name was. He was an off-sider for a boilermaker there and he used to take the bets. In those days, as you know, there were no transistor radios to get the race results. It was in the only pony days and sometimes the races would start at eleven o'clock in the morning. People were putting their bets on, a shilling each way or six pence each way, whatever, I think two shillings would have been a big bet. There was a barber's shop out on the wharf at Milsons Point and generally barber's shops and hotels are the main source of getting information from races. This barber's shop would get the results somehow and they would get the message through a little window, through a little hole. Beside the workshops was a shunting line for the trains and there was a hole cut in there and the message would come through there what the result of the race was. Another time I remember when the trains would come into Milsons Point and they used to come up the line to shunt, the train driver would give the message over as to what won the race. That was another source of information.

THE HUMAN TOLL

The scale of work was inhumane. Immortal tasks always are. To achieve such magnitude and height, lives were risked. It's like climbing the 8000-metre peaks; death is always a possibility. You did not need oxygen to paint or rivet the arch, but a mistake up there would prove every bit as fatal as an error on a mountain.

Sixteen men died building the bridge. Almost all were dead before the arch joined, in fact only two died on the arch. Five lost their lives building the approaches, two working on the pylons, two in the workshops and two a day's journey from the harbour, in Moruya.

Henry Waters, a dogman on the cranes at the Moruya quarry, died while riding on the back of a loco crane in April 1926. In March the next year Percy Poole, a 30-year-old quarryman from Young, New South Wales, was crushed while working on the granite face.

Reg Saunders worked at the quarry when the two men were killed.

It seems that the powder monkeys had blasted a very large mass of granite and it was balancing on the quarry ledge. The quarrymen were working down below and all of a sudden that mass of granite became unbalanced and the shout went round, 'Look out!' They all sprang away from the face except one man who sprang back against the face. When the stone fell it crushed him against the face of the quarry. His name was Percy Poole, I knew him personally. My brother-in-law George Leslie Watt, now deceased, was a big strong young man of about twenty-six. Fifteen or sixteen stone built like the Greek god Apollo. He picked Percy Poole up like he was a ten year old boy and carried him down to the dressing station, but the man was dead. Another incident was when Henry Waters, who was a contemporary of my father, had the job of being a dogman for a crane. A dogman is a man who fastens the hooks onto crane loads. Harry Walters used to form the habit of riding on the carriage of the crane rather than run along after it. On this particular day Mr Joe Sevright, a crane driver, didn't see Harry sitting on the body of the crane and he swung this mobile steam crane around and it crushed Henry Water's thigh. He died very soon after that.

Rough Work: The first deck hanger was nearly capsized in a storm on the harbour but was successfully erected onto the arch the following day. 1930.

Scot Robert Craig had the unwelcome honour of being the first man killed in Sydney, dying in 1926 during the construction of the approach spans. Craig was in his early to mid-sixties when, on 14 September, a ballast hopper he was emptying at Milsons Point tipped over and crushed him.

The Milsons Point workshops claimed their first victim in 1927. Swedish-born Angel Petersen, 23, fractured his spine when a stack of steel fell on him. He lingered in the Prince Henry Hospital for six months before dying in July.

By 1927 the bridge approaches had not reached the shore but still involved working at potentially fatal heights. In December 1927 a Glaswegian worker who used two names, Edward McNeill and Nathaniel Swandells, was riveting from a temporary staging at the north-east pier when he fell 18 metres. He was only 22 and was taken to the Mater Hospital but never regained consciousness. Another Glaswegian, William Woods, fell two months later from the same side.

In August 1928, Edward Esmond Shirley, a 27-year-old Tasmanian carpenter, died in Royal North Shore Hospital, after the scaffolding collapsed at the Fitzroy Street arch.

Seven men were dead while the great steel arch was still only a work on paper. It wasn't until 1929 that it began to grow from the page. Irishman and returned serviceman Thomas McKeown died in March that year as the first arch members were put in place, but he too was working on the approach span. McKeown was a rigger and lived at Phillip Street, Enmore. He was working on the city side with Edward Lund, Thomas Doody and Holdger Noysen on a painter's staging, but somebody had apparently forgotten to fix the gantry and the platform tilted under the workmen. The other three clung to a girder, but McKeown grabbed a chain to stop himself from falling to a certain death.

His awful predicament was recorded by the newspapers in chilling detail.

The chain was running downward, and McKeown commenced a desperate battle for his life. He climbed hand over hand but the chain was running out too fast for him to make any progress. As he was carried down his left hand and left leg became entangled in the chain. It drew taut, severed both limbs and he hurtled 100ft downward. Then the whole staging, weighing about 3 tons collapsed and fell also. Those who witnessed the accident were horrified. The other men hung momentarily to the girder and then drew themselves upward to safety. McKeown's body, after a formal pronouncement of death at Sydney Hospital was taken to the City Morgue by the Central District Ambulance. The deceased was one of the most popular members of the Iron Workers Assistants Union and had served in the Great War and the South African war.

Sydney Nipper Addison was 25 when he worked his last day. A boilermaker's assistant, he was married and his brother was the ambulance officer on the bridge. The baby-faced Englishman worked with Stan London. 'He had been at sea this young bloke and when he was sent to work with me I said, 'Gee, I am young, but you are younger still,' London recalled 50 years later.

The pair worked right on the ends of the arch. After the new members were slotted into place by the tin hares, London and Addison would bolt the plates together, using a spanner with six-foot pipe attached to give extra leverage. The workmen were precariously positioned and London hated the way the unformed arch vibrated as the heavy creeper crane moved forward on the apparently unsupported arch.

I had a feeling of claustrophobia really, feeling this movement, I knew the crane was going up and I knew the further it went out the greater risk of those ropes pulling out of the rocks. That was always paramount in my mind. I thought if that ever gave away there would be a hell of a mess. In fact, just getting on and off the job was dangerous.

The pair became mates and London went to Nipper's wedding; having come from England to work on the bridge he didn't have a lot of friends in Australia. When the new Mrs Addison took her vows she knew her husband had a dangerous job, but she could never have imagined that three weeks later she would be a widow.

Cliff Anning remembers that the Englishman had a close call before his death.

Well I remember him a week or two before that. He slipped this other time. Probably he was screwing up and he tumbled down but he didn't go over the chord this day, he fell against the post. I thought he was very lucky that day. Whether the man was careless or didn't keep his mind on the job I wouldn't like to say.

Even half a century after he lost his mate, London was moved to tears as he recalled grappling desperately to save him. It was raining on 6 March 1930 and the two half arches were separated by 250 metres.

You always had rubber-soled boots. Crepe was just about coming in at that time too. There were some leather boots with crepe soles. By the way the firm never ever found any gear like that for you, only gloves. You had to find all your own gear. My mate, Nipper, he used mostly sandshoes. The day he fell off I grabbed him by his sandshoes. There was the chord coming up there … it came up in two sections with a spliced plate up the centre of it. This picture shows me leaning over and he is inside and sticking the bolts in and I am just fitting the washer and the nut on. He would then come out and put the pipe on the spanner. He would be down the bottom and I would be up the top where the nut was. After we had pulled it right round he would pull to the edge of the chord, about eight or ten feet, I forget, ten feet say on the bottom chord. This is where he fell off, the bottom chord, just where the roadway comes out from the arch, that joint just below. I said, 'Righto Nip we'll take another purchase.' Cook, the inspector, was coming the other side from the scaffold thing he was on and he let a yell out. The spanner hit me in the chest and I rolled and I grabbed at Nipper. Well you can imagine a man's weight, I couldn't hold him.

Silly to get so upset isn't it.

I should have held him. Nipper turned on the way down. He was a terrific diver, he could dive off the tower a beauty. I was leaning over watching him and he straightened and he couldn't hold it and he started to turn. He hit the water straight on his back and it must have cracked his neck. His neck was broken when they brought him up. The diver was in a helmet and a suit.

We all went home that afternoon, we didn't go back up. It was the next day the diver said he was leaning over, he would have floated eventually I suppose, in a crouched position with his arms just moving but his neck was broken.

Cliff Anning also saw Nipper fall.

… it was out on the fourth or fifth panel and we were working on the stitching plate underneath the chord. They were working up above screwing the job up. All of a sudden something caught my eye and I thought it was a bag of bolts going by. Then I heard a commotion and I realised something was wrong. I looked over and I saw a fellow just hit the water. He disappeared for about one or two minutes and then floated to the top with his head and hands outstretched looking down into the water. I suppose for a minute or two he was like that and then he disappeared.

It was a heartbreaking day for everybody, particularly London who was forever haunted by the fact that his friend had slipped through his hands. Clarence Hipwell, Dorman, Long's superintendent of

steel works, sat London down after the accident and poured him a medicinal brandy. A nip of booze passed for counselling in those days.

Addison's English wife was hospitalised after her husband's death. 'She went a little mental and was put in a mental home,' according to London.

Despite the death, work was not stopped for the day but the men all chipped in half a day's pay to cover Nipper Addison's funeral expenses.

Frederick Gillon died in July 1930, when scaffolding above Junction Street, North Sydney, collapsed. The Bathurst-born worker was 25.

The high divers

In October that year, Vincent 'Ned' Kelly, who was working on the southern side below the roadway, had his famous fall. Thomas 'Mo' Moore was also working on the deck. He didn't see his fellow worker go but heard the commotion.

Later in life Moore and Kelly were best of mates who shared many interests, but as young men this manifested itself in fierce competition. Hard men, Balmain wharfies, they knew all about heights and water, having made a name for themselves as divers and swimmers. They combined work and fun, pulling jobs around the docks at the harbour and Botany Bay, each pushing the other to greater feats of daring in their spare moments.

Mo Moore was born 1883; his first son was born the day work finished on the bridge in 1931 and the boy would work up there too, maintaining the structure his dad had built. Mo was only 5 foot 9 inches but had the presence of a bigger man. A boilermakers' union delegate on the north side of the bridge and a first-grade union player with Balmain, he was a renowned diver with the Australian Troupe of High Divers and famed for his triple somersault corkscrew. He went on to train some of Australia's Olympic diving team. All the men on the waterfront remember the day he jumped from the Titan steam crane jib at the wharves. A loudmouth bet him five, maybe ten bob — the details have faded — that he wouldn't do it. He underestimated the union man. Mo not only dived the 33 metres; when he saw that the wagerer was leaving without paying, he swam ashore, chased the bloke to Birchgrove Park and demanded his money with his fists.

Mo was as hard as the times, a man of solid muscle and little sentiment.

Being a diver often came in handy. There was the time one of the men fell off the ferry travelling from the north side to Circular Quay in the middle of winter. The worker was weighed down by his overcoat and began to drown, but Mo jumped in and saved him. He got the Royal Humane and Shipwreck Society Certificate for that at the Town Hall, but according to family legend found the ceremony a bit stifling, so an impatient Mo walked from one side of the stage to the other and out the door without picking up the medal. His wife had a job cleaning at a pub on the Quay and told the kids that some days as she crossed on the ferry after work Mo would slide down a rope from the roadway of the bridge and onto the deck of the ferry. It's probably apocryphal but nobody who knew Mo would doubt that he had such daring in him. When Nipper Addison fell from the bridge and they couldn't find the body Mo tried diving for him but found he couldn't get deep enough, so he tied a bag of rivets to a rope and pulled himself down. His son was told his dad found the body before the water police arrived, but it seems this may not be true as others remember the police finding it.

Ned and Mo always said if they fell from the arch they'd go in feet first. Might even throw in a somersault or two if they had a chance.

On 23 October 1930, Ned got his chance to find out what happens when you take the big dive and Mo strained to see how he would go. When Kelly hit the water Mo had to be restrained by the other workers as he wanted to dive from the roadway to save his mate.

The story of Kelly's fall has grown wings and a few feathers over the years, but these appear to be the facts.

Kelly was using a heavy riveting gun that was connected to an unwieldy hose and kicked back with some force when the pneumatic pressure was applied to the head of the rivet. He was working under the roadway on a floating scaffold when he went over the edge. Perhaps it was the kickback from the gun. Some suggest he was dragging the gun and stepped backwards over the edge, although in the dockyards in later years the story went that he had climbed onto the rope rail of the scaffold to reach for a rivet above his head when the kickback pushed the platform away.

Either way, Kelly's fall and survival was one of the most celebrated events among workers on the bridge and took on a folklore all of its own. Some say the force of the water split his boots and pushed them up his legs to his thighs. Some say the shock gave him a stutter, although others said he had always stuttered and they wondered why the shock did not cure him. The story lived in the dock-

Niche Work: Construction worker Tom Evans surveys the bridge as a ship passes below. He witnessed a number of terrible accidents at work. 1932.

THE BRIDGE

yards of the harbour and echoed in the metal hollows until much of it was unbelievable. Fifty years later the men who were there had varying recollections.

Tom Evans was a rigger, responsible for getting the painters into position on the bridge so they could apply the 'red lead' paint that protected the steel.

> I remember Kelly ... Kelly one day dropped a spanner in the harbour and he turned around and said to me, 'I suppose a man will be going over there one of these days, like the spanner.' I said, 'Oh don't be damned silly.' Well it wasn't long after I heard that Kelly fell off the pedestrians' walk. What can I say any more than that he hit the water with a splash and he sent the spray up about ninety feet.

The spanner in the harbour echoes an element of the Kelly story that is often told. Many say the boilermaker survived because the surface tension of the water was broken by something he dropped; tourists on the bridge are told that he took a tool out during the fall, but none of his contemporaries or the man himself mentioned this at the time or after.

Dave Irvine, an Irishman, got his training at Workman and Clerks in Belfast, the small shipyard, known as the 'wee yard', which was next to Harland and Wolff's where the *Titanic* was built. When things got quiet there he wrote to Dorman, Long in London who told him there was work in Australia if he was prepared to travel there and apply. He was hired as a foreman riveter in 1926 and while he did not work on the arch, he knew the boilermakers who did.

> I knew Kelly well, we called him Ned for short ... I had spoken to Kelly previously on several occasions and he told me that he anticipated what he would do in the event of falling off. That was exactly what happened, he fell in feet first. They reckoned his boots were all so and so and so and so, which they were, I saw them on the front. Mo was on the top and it

took six men to hold him back because he wanted to jump in after him to save his life … Kelly of course was back within two weeks, back to work.

Harry Tomrop saw the accident.

His foot slipped and he went over the rails of the staging he was working on … he fell backwards and he hit the water. Before you could say Jack Robinson he was up again and swimming. George Kidder, one of the 'tin hares', my mate, who was on a punt, he dove in the harbour trying to save him. Then he did go to hospital, he kept saying he was all right. Falling that distance you knew damn well he couldn't be too right.

Stan London, the youngest man on the arch, was on the deck when Kelly fell.

He stepped off. He was on the scaffolding, he had three planks ten inches wide and about two foot nine inches, three feet up. There was a rope went round. He put his rattler [rivet gun] on and was going to walk along to get set in the position to knock these rivets down. Kelly wasn't a big man at all, he was a little fellow and he stuttered. They say if you have a shock it cures your stuttering, but it never cured him, he still stuttered afterwards. He was backing along shifting his gear and when he bent over his back missed the rope and he stepped clean off it. Luckily he broke the water with his feet, or a bit side on. He broke three ribs, if I remember correctly, and was off for a hell of a while after but eventually he was back on the job. He was one of the guys, with Moore and myself, who dived for my mate [Nipper Anderson].

Returned soldier Frank Villagrand worked with the concreting teams on the massive arches which support the approach spans. Hired in 1930, his work was rationed to four days a week, but the £4 he earned was enough to support his and his brother's families. He saw Kelly being pulled from the water and placed in an ambulance.

> ... he fell off the deck which is maybe one hundred feet or more above sea-level. I would say the top is about one hundred and two or four feet above sea-level ... being an experienced swimmer and diver he knew how to fall in the water and threw himself around to go in feet first. Held his hands over his head, which I used to do as a diver myself. He entered the water and went down and came up and swam to a boat that was nearby. He wanted to go back to work, but they wouldn't let him they made him go home, they thought the aftershock might upset him. However he was one of the very few that recovered from that accident.

Tom Evans also witnessed the rescue.

> He swam from where he fell in to the punt. Faulkner [who was killed in an accident five months later] and others who were dogmen down there were going to dive in and pull Kelly out, but he swam that way to the barge and they managed to pull him onto the barge.

The papers reported that Mo Moore, 'a man who once dived 100 feet for a bet of 10/- was about to dive to Kelly's assistance, but was restrained by other workers' and that a man called Reginald Coomber tried to save him but 'in his anxiety to effect a rescue he pushed Kelly under the water, adding to his difficulties'.

Maybe the last word should be Kelly's. That night he was in the Mater Hospital when a reporter for the *Sydney Morning Herald* found him in apparent good cheer and recorded his story.

> I am often working near the edge of the bridge, and on many occasions I have thought to myself, 'Now if you ever fall ... you had better make sure that you hit the water feet first or

head first.' So, when I slipped and fell today, I concentrated upon saving my life. That is all that I thought about. It was the only thing in my mind; the desire to live. I knew that I was very near death. I hit the water. I went under. There was a roar of water in my ears. My lungs felt as though they would burst. Then I came to the surface. I was alive, marvellously alive.

I tried to clutch something, but there was nothing there to clutch and down I went. I turned a somersault and then I remembered that I must concentrate upon entering the water either head first or feet first. I waved my arms and screwed up my body in an effort to do this. I began to fall down feet first and I almost felt satisfied. I clasped my right hand over my nose and mouth. And then I hit the water. Unfortunately I was not quite upright, otherwise I don't think that I would have been hurt at all. I did not go under very far, and it seemed only an instant from the moment I fell from the bridge to the time that I was struggling on the surface. Struggling and alive.

When I hit the water and went under I felt afraid for the first time. During the fall I had kept saying to myself that I must fight for my life, but when I was submerged I almost felt that all was lost. I could hear nothing, see nothing and feel nothing except the terrific pain in my side from my broken ribs. My brain was not functioning. And then I was on the surface again, striking out for the buoy. With almost a shock I realised that I was alive. I could have shouted for the sheer joy.

His mate Mo Moore used to have a line he used when asked about Kelly's accident. 'He was fine, it was pay day and the miserable bugger still had his hand on his wallet.'

Kelly was back at work after seventeen days off and was presented with a watch by Lawrence Ennis on behalf of Dorman, Long & Co.

Kelly continued to work around the harbour where he was famous as the man who fell from the bridge. A workmate from later years, Con Johnson, remembers him telling stories.

> He could not pronounce F's and some other letters. Ned told the story of when his wife came to see him in hospital, I think he added a bit of colour to the story, he reckoned his wife said 'that was a silly ducking think to do, Ned'. Ned did come closer to drowning on dry land than he did in the Harbour. After the bridge Ned was working at S. G. Whites, which was known as the bullring, and was on the toilet reading a paper one morning when a large tank with 18,000 gallons of sea water tipped over. The water rushed down the passage and Ned was flushed out of the toilet like a drowned rat. He said he thought it was a 'ducking tidal wave'.

Vince Kelly died in 1982 but every day his name is spoken from the girders on the arch by guides telling the story of his great fall.

THE FICKLE HAND OF FATE

You didn't have to be working at great heights to be in danger. Workers on the ground or water had always been in danger of things falling from above. The punt that used to transfer workers lowered from the cage when the arch was progressing had a small reinforced ceiling above the steering house, but despite many close calls and a number of rivets smashing through the decks of ferries, it was considered a little effete for the workmen to take cover under the steering house roof.

George Scott, a holder-upper, had a near escape once.

> I was working down on the approach down on the bottom chord and a rivet fell from another on top and ricocheted on to my face and broke my two sets of false teeth and gave me a black eye and you can see the mark there. Incidentally no compensation for broken teeth or anything in those days. No.

Only just compo for being off, but not for my teeth and they were broken beyond repair.

John 'Felix' Faulkner, a 40-year-old Canadian rigger, was working on the roadway in March 1931 when he was hit by a half-tonne plate which fell from the top chord and crushed his right leg. Harry Tomrop witnessed the accident.

Oh that was a shame. Bad luck I suppose, this plate slipping down and happening to hit him. I was only a few yards away. He was laughing, putting the plates down on the roadway and he just gave a signal to the crane driver with his hand. He was laughing and doing a good job. It was bad luck, you know.

He was bleeding all over the place. There was an iron worker and he happened to be near the top and he came down and tried to stop the blood. By the time they got him down and got him to hospital he had lost a lot of blood. The wife and I were going to the hospital to give him some blood. I had some experience once before giving blood to a mate of mine who had had some accident, in New York it was, and done him the world of good. After I had given my pint I felt a 100 per cent, so I thought it would be all right you see, I wasn't afraid of using a bit of blood. Anyway I went down there and Faulkner was still on a stretcher and the sister said it was too late, I was too late.

Tom Evans, a rigger, also witnessed the accident and might have been the ironworker Tomrop spoke of.

As the chords went out they had strengthening plates on both sides. The plates were bolted on to each section to strength-en the bridge as it went out. It had to have all that support otherwise it would have collapsed because it was only held up by nuts and bolts and rivets. What was happening up on the top of that chord I can't say, but I have some anticipation that

they were trying to put a shackle in that plate and lower it down with the crane. Down below Faulkner was sitting on a girder, straddle legged over this girder. As the plates came down so he was dogging it in between girders down to the punt that was collecting them in the harbour. Somehow or another this plate got out of control and it came down wriggling like a snake and hit all the bridge, that is the hangers, on the way down. It came down and struck across Faulkner's femoral artery and his leg was hanging loose. I was the first one to get over the rail and lift his leg up and steady him and he was quite conscious the whole time. The first thing I did, because we couldn't get a tourniquet on his leg, was ask for a stretcher. We got him on the stretcher, with the assistance of others … to lift him over the rail onto the roadway and we

Rope Trick: Henri Mallard was one of very few photographers allowed access to the bridge during construction. His still images are among the best taken.

took him to the lift. We had a lift at the back of Dawes Point end, but we found when we got into the lift we couldn't get the stretcher in, it was too long. So then we took him up on the big crane, with the small crane in front of it, we took him up with the small crane, and then we backed the whole lot down to the Dawes Point end. We lowered Falconer down with the crane and then transhipped from that crane to a working steam crane that was on the Dawes Point end. From then all I remember was one of his mates ran to him and that was that. They took him to Sydney Hospital but I think he died afterwards, about three o'clock in the afternoon. That is all I know in regards to poor old Faulkner.

It is a funny thing about Mrs Faulkner. I remember her coming down, whether it was that day or days afterwards, with a baby in her arms … I never had a chance to speak to her, but I know she spoke to several other workers. It is a peculiar thing, I got a rigging job with CSR at Rhodes … A young fellow came along with a pot of paint and a brush in his hand. This is twenty years or more afterwards. I was the charge hand at CSR at that particular time and as he came up and approached us and got near us I said to him, 'What's your name?' He said, 'My name is Faulkner.' I said, 'Faulkner?' He said, 'Yes.' I said, 'Did you father get killed on the Harbour Bridge?' He said, 'Yes.' I said, 'Well I am one of the men that went to your father's assistance.'

Two weeks after that accident, James Chilvers, 54, from Stockton, was killed unloading steel angles from a punt at the Milsons Point workshops. One angle fell, hitting a piece of wood which knocked him on the head. He fell into the water and drowned.

Before the month was out John Webb was dead, too. The Englishman was painting on the cross girders inside the south pylon when he fell.

In October 1931 the bridge was basically complete, but the deaths continued. Robert Graham, a 41-year-old labourer from

Robertson, did not fall and was not crushed by anything from above, but died when he was hit by a tram in Alfred Street, North Sydney.

In February 1932 the *Daily Telegraph* ran an article about preparing the bridge for the opening ceremony.

> So far, the Bridge has withstood all tests. Next week the engines will be shunted off, and brooms and hoses will be used to make the deck clean for the official opening.
>
> It is estimated that the cost of cleaning the pylons is £7,500. A big gang of men, using steel brushes, is working overtime on the job.

The clean-up was, perhaps, the last job before the bridge's opening and unfortunately it claimed one last life, that of Jim Campbell, a colourful foreman rigger who had shown John Andrews the ropes when he started.

> He was a Liverpool-Irishman, a Liverpudlian I think they call them. He was a great rigger, well respected. A real tough, good old bloke, he was a marvel. Well he went down to do a special job, lift down some temporary girders, and this little tripod that was helping to lift down the block and tackle sort of stuff. Somehow or other he straddled it and it kicked up and he went right from the top down, hit a big light stanchion, through the sleepers of the railway lines and finished up in the middle of the pylon. I will tell you some stories about his funeral …
>
> We went to the church first. Fred, my next door neighbour who had got me the job on the bridge, got my driver to drive a car to the service down at Milsons Point, down at Lavender Bay. Of course all the boys were real good-hearted blokes but rough and ready, they went to the service but by the time they got to the service they were all drunk. They piled into the church and while the sermon was going on I hear someone at the back say, 'Christ I am not going to

bloody well listen to this all bloody day.' There was shushing all round the church and they walked out. After the service was over they marched up to Crows Nest. We went up in the car of course and joined the cortege. We saw the riggers walking up and some cars stopped to offer them a lift. These riggers all piled in and they had plenty of grog in them by the time they got up to the cemetery. When we got to the cemetery, this was before the crematorium was built, they all jumped out of the cars and ran like mad. We wondered what was going on but when we got there we saw there was a little toilet block. I suppose by the time the riggers got there, there wasn't enough room for all of them and so they encircled the outside of that little toilet block to urinate, they had to. Everybody was shocked, but of course this was those days. Well the sermon started at the grave and these fellows were still drunk, some of them, and one fellow, as the sermon went on, went to light a cigarette. This is true what I am telling you and if only I could have recorded it on camera. He went to light his cigarette and the other fellow on the other side shook his head, put his hand up to his mouth telling him not to smoke. It was definitely out of order at that stage. The first fellow thought he was asking for a cigarette so he takes out his packet of cigarettes, chucks them over the grave, over Jim, to the other fellow who caught them. The mourners nearly collapsed, they couldn't believe what was happening. Anyway all the bosses were there, the big shots, Muir and Bradfield. It was terrible. As they put Jim down the parson, Reverend Frank Cash, picks up a little bit of clay soil. It wasn't dust to dust, it was clay soil there. The reverend picks up a … bit of clay and puts it on the coffin as it is being lowered. Jim's nearest friend, I think his name was Cole, was in tears because they were inseparable mates and he picks up a bit of clay too, in respect. As it hit the coffin it went boom, boom. Well all these rough and ready, good-hearted blokes, all sincere, thought this was part and parcel of what they had to do. Well they all picked up a bit of clay and as the coffin was being lowered it was boom, boom, bang, bang. Clods of earth and clay were coming from everywhere and it sounded like a drum tattoo. I am not telling you a lie, I saw it and if I had only photographed it. That was Jim's funeral and he would have loved to have seen it because that was the type of fellow he was. He would have had a laugh. As he was being lowered down if they had a glass top to that coffin he would have laughed and said, 'That is just what I wanted.'

I understand [that] later on the pipes played on the way up to Crows Nest. I just can't recall the pipes being played, but I understand they were.

The piper was Jock McKay, the stonemason on the pylons.

In a paper by Freeman and Ennis given to the Institute of Civil Engineers, the English bridge builders reported:

In the course of the whole contract nine lives were lost, in every case the consequence of some misjudgment on the part of the man. No loss of life or personal injury occurred as the result of any failure of plant or tackle. Two fatal accidents occurred in the quarry; one in the foundations; one in the workshops; three on the approach span section; and two on the arch erection.

Only two of the men who died working on the bridge were married. Workers compensation for a dead worker paid the dependants between $800 and $1600 plus $50 for each dependent child. Workers without dependants, which was the majority of the men, were awarded $40 burial expenses only.

A proposal to allow the next of kin of those who died during the construction of the bridge to march during the opening ceremony was rejected by the committee in charge of the celebrations as it would introduce 'an altogether inharmonious note into an official ceremony'.

10

DESIGN CONTROVERSY

Bradfield is the hero of his hometown but over
in London the man who learned his tricks in the
Boer War, Freeman, is feeling a little neglected.
A spat develops which pits the Australians against
the English in a battle so bitter it draws in
governments and drags on for another 70 years.
Who suggested an arch and who did design the
bridge?

In 2004, 72 years after the completion of the Sydney Harbour Bridge, a television commercial dramatised the moment J. J. C. Bradfield received the inspiration to design an arch — when a lemon slice rises in his drink.

It's a light-hearted fiction which bears more relation to Joern Utzon's inspiration for the design of the nearby Opera House, which came from contemplating the segments of an orange. However, the question of Bradfield's inspiration — in fact his entire role — in designing an arch bridge has never been satisfactorily settled and in the early 1930s was an international scandal that was engineering's equivalent of the bodyline controversy in cricket. Some maintain to this day that the design of the bridge is not Bradfield's at all, but is the work of the Englishman Ralph, later Sir Ralph, Freeman.

The bitter wrangle became the subject of a government inquiry, cast doubt on the PhD in Engineering granted to the Australian engineer and saw Dorman, Long threaten legal action against the state government.

To most Australians at the time it was a shocking turn of events. Until that time few had even heard of the interloper claiming to have designed Dr Bradfield's bridge. Who was the man and how could he claim to have designed a bridge which the great Australian engineer had been involved with for decades?

Consider, however, the Englishman Ralph Freeman, sitting in his London office, drawing plans for the Sydney Harbour Bridge arch, which he claimed he conceived at least two years before the tenders closed. The consulting engineer had suggested the arch to the Cleveland Bridge Company when the specifications called for a cantilever, and he took those plans to Dorman, Long & Co. in late 1922 to enable them to make the successful tender.

His office generated all the original diagrams and calculations which were sent to the Australian harbour bridge engineers for checking. Freeman first met with Bradfield and his men in 1924 to discuss the specific designs and suggested the bridge change from 33 to 28 panels, which profoundly altered the structure. He also changed the designs of the approach spans.

In 1926 he travelled to Australia to view the project and apparently enjoyed the company of Dr Bradfield, writing him a note from the SS *Orama* while it was docked at Fremantle.

Dear Dr Bradfield
I was just about to write you a farewell letter when I received your cable this morning.

Many thanks indeed from Mr Pain and myself for the kind thought which prompted your good wishes and more for the many kindnesses to us during our stay in Sydney …

Will you allow me to take this opportunity of congratulating you on the splendid work you showed us on the interurban railway system and more particularly on the inception and development of the bridge project itself. Only a visit to Sydney can make one grasp the immense importance and value of the work you have done.

I hope that the work Dorman, Long & Co. are doing and have to do in the future will accord with the greatness of the undertaking and the confidence you have reposed in us.

With kindest regards to Miss Butler and yourself,
Ralph Freeman

*By Design:
Dr J. J. C.
Bradfield and
Ralph Freeman
look uncomfort-
able as they pose
with Lawrence
Ennis and
Alfred Martin
when the arch
closed. 1930.*

The handwritten note was warm in tone and gave no hint of Freeman's apparent concerns. Still, it had annoyed the Englishman that everywhere he went in Australia people referred to Bradfield as the designer of the bridge and barely knew his name.

Dr J. J. C. Bradfield's cult had grown stronger as the bridge took shape. He strode Sydney with a confidence and celebrity that remained unchallenged. He was the bridge builder, the poet's patriot, the Premier's Napoleon and the people's hero.

A consultant to the contractor expects little glory, but for Freeman there was so little it really started to irk.

Freeman was distant from the physical project, but felt as much ownership of the bridge as Bradfield. He said that when first

THE BRIDGE

approached about tendering in 1922, when he was working for the Cleveland Bridge and Engineering Company, he replied that he would be interested if he could prepare an arch design. 'I was convinced that an arch was the right bridge for the site. From that time it took two years to develop the design and sufficiently accurate estimates of the weight of steel necessary for a tender to be submitted.'

It is history now that the tender process was changed to include an arch bridge and that it was Freeman's arch which was chosen. He and construction engineer G. C. Imbault had worked closely together as the process of erecting such a large bridge impacted on the design. It was a process they had begun twenty years earlier with the Zambezi bridge.

Freeman had an army of engineers, draughtsmen and support staff working under him in London; they produced plans and drawings and these were all sent to Australia for checking.

However, whenever anything appeared in the Australian media it had been redrawn and had the signature of Dr J. J. C. Bradfield in the bottom right-hand corner. This had been happening since the Report on Tenders was released in February 1924, in which the beautiful bridge he'd designed had been painted and photographed and credited to Bradfield.

It was the way things were done in those days. Half a century later, Gordon Stuckey, Bradfield's design engineer, described the chief engineer as:

> A complex character, a man of very great vision as you can see, but he insisted that he alone had all the credit. He didn't bother himself much about detail or calculations and that, he was in bigger things than that, but I give him all the credit for getting the job going. He wouldn't have anybody else, no committees, he was responsible to the minister alone, that's the only way. No committee or anything could have done it, he was chief engineer and he was the sole one responsible and he only went to the minister that's all and I only went to him through nobody and that way it worked.

Stuckey chuckled as he recalled 'the old fellows liked to sign everything'.

Bradfield certainly didn't like anybody getting in the way of his limelight. He appeared in almost all of the official photographs of dignitaries associated with the structure and wrote all the articles — apart from some written by Miss Butler — about the bridge for the public and the engineering community.

Then, in 1928, the English *Engineering* magazine published an article written by Bradfield which gave no credit at all to the Englishman. Freeman now found himself ignored in his own back-yard and was humiliated. He reacted quickly, writing to the editor and asking him to suspend publication of the second instalment of the article while he spoke to his Australian counterpart about a few matters. He duly wrote a 'Private & Confidential' letter to Bradfield in Sydney from the Broadway Buildings offices of Douglas Fox & Partners, Westminster.

Dear Dr Bradfield,

Since the contract for the Sydney Harbour Bridge was let to Dorman, Long & Co., there have appeared, especially in the Australian Press, numerous articles describing the Bridge and referring to the Engineers connected with it.

I feel sure that you do not realize that any reference to my connection with the Bridge in these publications is so rare or in such indefinite terms that few people appreciate from reading them that I have any association of importance with the bridge.

My attention has been called repeatedly to this and I have mentioned it to Mr. Ennis and other officials of Dorman, Long & Co., but I have hesitated to write to you as I assumed the difficulty would be able to be righted without my intervention, and there is the risk that correspondence on a matter of this sort may lead to possibly misapprehension, which I am specially anxious to avoid.

Though it seems scarcely necessary to do so, may I assure you that there is probably no one who appreciates better than I the greatness of the work you have done in connection with Sydney Bridge and who is more willing at all times to give this work the most generous recognition in his power.

I believe, therefore, that it is only necessary to mention to you the matter to which I have referred for you to take such action as is appropriate in order to put it in its correct aspect, and may I add that recognition coming from you of my part in connection with the bridge would be esteemed more than any other notice of my work.

Freeman went on to point out that he had worked on the designs of the bridge for six years now, dating back to 1921 and made the following request:

For the future as far as Australian periodicals are concerned, may I ask you to use your influence as far as you can to prevent publication of the statement that the 'design' of the bridge is yours, unless it is made clear that thereby is meant the inception of the bridge and the direction of its execution. I recognize with the greatest satisfaction that a fellow engineer to whom I am proud to be known has such great achievement to his credit, but in the understanding of engineers I feel sure you will agree that the statement that the 'design' of the bridge is yours would mislead.

In the English or American Technical Press may I ask you to do more than this. It is not altogether easy for me to suggest the appropriate step, but I should appreciate it very much if you would refer to the inadequate recognition that earlier publications have accorded to my share in the work, and that you would personally like it to be known that the designs of the bridge submitted with Dorman, Long's tender were prepared under my direction.

Freeman went on to suggest that if any more articles did appear in the *Engineering* magazine that 'I hope that in these you will not allow publication of the technical details of the design to an extent which would cause such information to lose its value or novelty if later on it is desired to submit it as a paper before one of the professional engineering societies. If this occurred the Society concerned might refuse to accept the paper.'

Freeman believed he should have the right to publish technical details of his bridge.

The letter left London in May and arrived in New South Wales in mid-June. Bradfield was not tardy in his reply.

> Dear Mr. Freeman,
> Your letter of 2nd May reached me some days ago simultaneously with a letter from the Editor of 'Engineering' with reference to yours to him of even date … The Editor states that he is at a loss to understand your request for him to suspend publication of following articles, but that it is now too late to stop the second article, which has been set up. I have to confess that I also cannot understand your attitude in writing to him, nor what warrant you had in asking him to suspend publication of articles written by me. I alone have the information, and subject to the Minister's approval, the right to write such articles.

Freeman must have had a sinking feeling as he read the opening remarks, but it was to get worse. Bradfield continued, 'while I am specially anxious that in the execution of the great work of the Sydney Harbour Bridge all honour shall be paid where it is due, at the same time I feel that, as the one who has been the most intimately associated with the Bridge project for many years the requests you make cannot justly be entertained'.

Bradfield went on to say his association was bigger than Freeman's and dated back to 1900.

He wrote that in 1913:

I made a detailed study of the types of bridges suitable for the location, cantilever, suspension and arch, and published designs for same, but believing that the world's engineering firms would not tender for an Arch Bridge of such magnitude, I had written the Specification for a Cantilever Bridge only, as the suspension type was not in my opinion quite suitable from technical consideration for the traffic to be carried.

Bradfield did not seriously entertain the idea of an arch bridge until 1922; indeed, up until his visit to the Northern Hemisphere he would not even consider one and made this note in his diary on 25 April 1922 while in Chicago.

> Mr G. Lewis Taylor, Chief Engineer. McClintic Marshal Co. Pittsburgh called at 9.15am and discussed the Bridge with him. Said he never saw such complete detail in a specification before and was very much impressed with the Plans which were good from every point of view. He agrees that the M braced truss is more pleasing than a K braced truss. Asked if would consider a steel arch of 1600 [foot] span to save weight of shore span; after discussion agreed it was not practicable. Discussed suspension versus cantilever bridges and other style matters.

Bradfield went on to tell Freeman some six years later:

> In America in 1922, when giving information to prospective Tenderers, as required, I asked several firms if they would be prepared to tender for an arch bridge of 1650 feet span. I also asked English firms, among whom was the Cleveland Bridge Company (Mr Dixon interviewing me in London), whose tender was successfully taken over by Messrs Dorman, Long & Co., Ltd. Two American and three English firms stated they would tender for such an Arch Bridge, the Cleveland Bridge Company among the rest, acting, I understand on

your advice as Consulting Engineer. In the end only three firms tendered for the Arch Bridge.

Arch Enemies: George Finey's cartoons mocked Dr Bradfield's and Freeman's claims to be the sole designer of the bridge. The issue was engineering's equivalent of Bodyline. 1929.

Bradfield admitted he did the figures and rewrote the specifications for an arch after the meetings abroad:

> There was in no sense a competition. Tenderers were not asked to submit any other types of bridges. The salient features of the two bridges were all set out exactly in the Specification, but Tenderers were allowed to exercise a certain latitude in details.

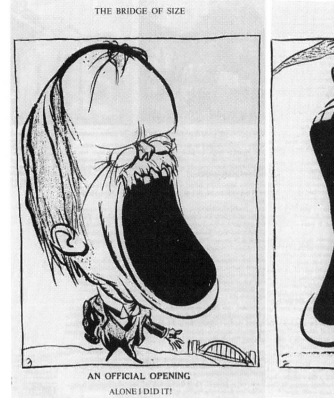

THE BRIDGE OF SIZE

AN OFFICIAL OPENING
ALONE I DID IT!

THE BRIDGE OF SIZE

AN OFFICIAL OPENING
ALONE I DID IT!

Bradfield either could not or would not understand Freeman's complaint that he was not receiving credit for his work, indeed, that Bradfield was receiving all the credit, but then the Englishman's request that he be known as the bridge's designer was asking too much from the Australian who had overseen its development over 26 years. He believed that Freeman was getting his due recognition. 'It was recognised in my Report on Tenders that the Contractors' Consulting Engineers were Mr. Ralph Freeman, of Sir Douglas Fox and Partners, and Mr G. C. Imbault, and on every subsequent occasion this recognition has been made.'

Bradfield pointed out that he must approve every element of design and construction and his office independently check details of the bridge.

> … we are producing between us the steelwork of a structure of worldwide significance, the details of which are in the first instance prepared by you, but are subject to my revision before approval. You are the Consulting Engineer to Messrs. Dorman, Long & Co., but not to the New South Wales Government. The responsibility falls directly upon the Contractors and myself as Chief Engineer for the New South Wales Government.
>
> I have had to set out the position according to my point of view at some length in order that you may be fully apprised of matters of which you may have been unaware. In light of this information you will see that your request that I should proclaim in the Press of the world that the 'design' of the Bridge is yours would be incorrect if construed in any sense. Your advice to the Cleveland Bridge Company in 1921 was unknown to me, but before Tenders were received other Engineers were of course performing similar work on the specified lines for other Tenderers …
>
> I would be pleased to have your reply to this letter which please understand is written in the most friendly spirit of one desirous of giving you full credit for the work you are doing,

but I cannot do all you ask. I have not shown your letter to
Mr. Ennis nor will I until I receive your reply.

   With kind regards, Yours sincerely …

The letters may have had a superficial politeness but it was not to
last long. They continued to correspond and Freeman came to
Australia in March the following year where the pair had an icy
showdown. Neither would compromise. The Australian claimed
later that the Englishman demanded the entire credit for the design
and a note written the day after their meeting appears to confirm
this. Their relationship had deteriorated to the point that the pair, it
seems, could not even agree to disagree.

   Dear Dr. Bradfield,
   Referring to my letter to you of 13th September 1928, and
   our conversation yesterday, I have to thank you for accepting
   as correct the statements contained in that letter and suggest
   that you should write to me as follows:-

      I recognise that, subject to the official specification pre-
   pared by me, the design of the Sydney Harbour Bridge as now
   being erected by Dorman, Long & Co. Ltd., including the
   steel structure, piers and foundations, was made by you as
   Consulting Engineer to the Contractors.

      I authorise you to take a convenient opportunity to make
   this public on the understanding that due recognition is made
   of my position as Chief Engineer to the Public Works
   Department responsible for the specification and for the
   selection of the type of bridge to be employed.

      In any publication I may make or authorise I will record
   the fact that the design of the bridge was prepared by you.

Freeman had clearly reached breaking point. Bradfield's reply to the
note was brief. He refused to comply.

   The Englishman announced that he had had enough and this
would become a public duel: 'Dear Dr. Bradfield, I have your letter

of yesterday and regret that you cannot subscribe to the terms suggested in my letter of 5th March. There now appears to be no alternative to defending my claim in public.'

The private exchange became public with almost indecent haste.

The first the public knew about the spat, or any tension was in March 1929 when the *Sydney Morning Herald* rushed onto the streets with an article which claimed that Freeman not Bradfield was the designer of the bridge. This was an astonishing claim.

By 1929 it would have been hard to find an Australian who took even the most passing of interests in current affairs who had not heard of J. J. C. Bradfield. This was a matter of colonial pride. Wasn't Bradfield the man who was the equal of the world's greatest engineers? Wasn't he celebrated internationally? Certainly the public had been told so for years.

There was a certain amount of patriotic pride on the other side of the ledger too; Freeman often referred to the fact that the bridge was the first major engineering undertaking the British had embarked upon in a generation and that he was determined no foreign firm take on the contract in any part of the empire. Just as he was determined that the Australian engineer not take the credit.

The argument threatened to undermine the harmonious relationship between the English builders and the Australians and eventually did.

Bradfield pointed out in his defence that Dorman, Long & Co.'s director, Sir Hugh Bell, at the laying of the foundation stone, toasted the Australian: 'To Dr Bradfield, the designer of the bridge, I give every credit.' Seven years later the relationship between the English firm and the Australian government had become so strained the builders stonewalled inquiries from the Minister for Public Works and threatened legal action if Bradfield was described on a plaque as the designer of the bridge.

For his part, Freeman found an ally in the *Sydney Morning Herald*, which was not only happy to run his articles but also backed his claims in editorials.

The newspaper appeared, to Bradfield, at least, to have sided with the Englishman before the outbreak of public hostilities. In January it had written an article claiming that Freeman had designed the Newcastle on Tyne and Sydney Harbour Bridge. Now the publication knew it was onto a controversial topic and ran hard with it. This might have evolved out of jealousy; Bradfield was clearly closely linked to the *Sydney Mail*, the chief engineer and his private secretary, Miss Butler, having filled its pages for years with articles about the bridge.

Bradfield had felt during the delicate negotiations to get the enabling act passed that the *Herald* had acted as devil's advocate, often promoting schemes at odds with his, and even noted in his diary that he had met with the paper's editor in November 1922 're the attitude of that paper'.

Whatever the *Herald*'s motivation, it took a line and stuck to it.

If the contents of the first article, published on Monday 11 March 1929, were not incendiary enough, the headline made sure nobody was in doubt as to what was happening.

The paper offered its readers the 'Harbour Bridge Designer's Story' and 'Engineer's Romance'. Bradfield's name was not mentioned once in the story, which was written by Freeman and began: 'In order that any contribution of mine to the Sydney Press regarding the Harbour Bridge may be properly appreciated it is necessary to explain my connection with this undertaking.'

Freeman laid out his credentials, stating he worked with G. A. Hobson designing the Zambezi Victoria Falls bridge and had 25 years' experience. The English engineer said he first worked on plans for the Sydney Harbour Bridge when the Cleveland Bridge Company of Darlington approached him in 1922, not 1921 as he claimed to Bradfield in his first letter.

After study of the conditions I came to the conclusion that an arch bridge would be preferable, and proceeded to make designs. In the following year (1923) a new specification was issued asking for tenders for a cantilever bridge or an arch bridge.

Meanwhile my designs for an arch bridge had been proceeding and with the assistance of a large and competent staff, by the autumn of 1923 the work was well advanced.

Freeman noted the specifications showed only an 'outline' of an arch or cantilever bridge, leaving it to the contractor as to what type of bridge they wanted to build and that Clause 20 stated 'it is to be expressly understood that the contractor undertakes the entire responsibility not only for the material and construction of the bridge, but also for the design, calculations, specifications and plans furnished to or by him …'

Two further instalments appeared on the following days and it was only on publication of the third article that the Australian chief engineer was mentioned, when the Englishman added as a footnote:

> I cannot conclude these articles without paying a tribute to the great services Dr Bradfield has rendered as chief engineer for Sydney Harbour Bridge on behalf of the Government of New South Wales. To him also is due the credit for the conception of the bridge project and the decision as to the type of bridge to be built. These are achievements of the highest importance. I must add that the contractors and I, as their consulting engineer, are indebted to him for many valuable proposals arising from his independent inspection and verifications of all that has been done.

Freeman was openly baiting Bradfield, who was quietly enraged. On reading the first he fired off a letter to Dorman, Long & Co. via Ennis in Sydney asking if it had approved of the articles or agreed with their content. The English ducked and weaved on the issue.

Ennis wrote back on the same day:

> In reply to your letter of 11th March, I have to inform you as follows:—
>
> (1) The articles are not published with the approval or

endorsement of Messrs Dorman, Long & Co. Ltd., the Contractors for the Sydney Harbour Bridge.

(2) The articles are not published with my approval and endorsement as Director of Construction.

(3) Messrs Dorman, Long & Co. Ltd. as Contractors for the Sydney Harbour Bridge have not approved or endorsed the articles published.

(4) I may add that the articles have not been submitted for approval or endorsement of Dorman, Long & Co. Ltd. as Contractors for the Sydney Harbour Bridge or of myself as Director of Communication; but Dorman, Long & Company have publicly repeated the statement, which appears in the Memorandum accompanying their tender, that the designs of the bridge for which they tendered have been prepared under Mr. Ralph Freeman's personal directions.

By 14 March the New South Wales government had become involved. The Minister for Public Works and Railways, Mr Buttenshaw, restrained Bradfield from a public reply but called for a report from his chief engineer. The former minister, Ball, was not so reticent and said he believed that the whole controversy hinged on the definition of the word 'design' and that it was his opinion the bridge was 'a Bradfield–Dorman, Long design'.

Bradfield, meanwhile, steamed over his report for the minister and typed up eleven indignant pages which he presented the following Monday.

He again laid out his long association with the project and repeated that the arch bridge was first raised during meetings with prospective tenderers during 1922.

> ... several American and British firms stated they would be willing to tender for an arch bridge of similar span to the cantilever, influenced perhaps by the fact that the Hell Gate Arch of 1000 feet span had recently been successfully completed.

One of these firms was the Cleveland Bridge Company, but I did not receive any information relative to the arch bridge beyond the intimation that they were willing to tender therefore, from that or any other Company, nor did I have any correspondence or discussions with or meet Mr Freeman.

Bradfield pointed out that 'designs' of a cantilever or arch bridge 'Plans 1 and 2' were included in the specification and plans.

The make-up of the various members and the details of construction are left to the judgment of Tenderer, but these must conform in every respect with the requirements of this Specification. Mr Freeman in his first article quotes only the first part of this clause of the specification with the object apparently of showing that he is the designer of the bridge. It is obvious that the meaning of the clause is that the contractors must assume responsibility for the design, not as the designers, but the builders of the bridge.

The controversy was sparked in part by the fact that Bradfield had issued strict specifications for the bridge, but avoided detailed drawings of the design as a cost-saving method.

... it would be inadvisable for the department to make complete detail steelworks drawings, which might not suit both American and British practice, and which might have to be revised when a tender was accepted, on account of some variation in the steel adopted, or other reason proposed by the successful tenderer. In the case of the Quebec Bridge, Canada, upwards of £150,000 was uselessly spent in this way.

Bradfield pointed out that the specifications included '20 sheets of plans' and 'completely governed the calculations and details of the structure, design, workmanship, model tests, fabrication and erection, materials of construction, including even the composition of the paint, the second coat of which is now being made to my specification issued to tenderers on February 8, 1923 ...'

The minister, Buttenshaw, gave Bradfield approval to take the report to the press and the *Sydney Morning Herald* duly published extensive but edited extracts that Saturday under the heading 'Dr Bradfield's Reply. MR FREEMAN NOT THE DESIGNER. TENDERS CALLED ON MY DESIGN.'

Two days later Freeman came back counterpunching in the same newspaper under the headline 'Where is Dr Bradfield's Design'.

My claim to be regarded as the designer of the bridge is not in the least disturbed by the report you publish, and I intend to leave no stone unturned in order to substantiate that claim.

In justice to myself, my staff, and my profession I must do so.

Dr Bradfield in his report not only endeavours to deprive me of the credit to which I am entitled, but definitely asserts in the 'conclusions' of his report that the credit is due to him. This compels me not only to prove that I am right, but also that he is wrong.

There is nothing novel in an arch bridge as such. It is possibly the oldest type of bridge built by man, and as a metal structure was one of the first.

Any good text book on bridges contains numerous illustrations of steel arches. Records available to any engineer give full particulars of many arch bridges of moderate and large spans.

The largest arch bridge yet built is the Hell Gate Bridge in New York, the span being 977 ft 6 in, opened in 1917.

The outline elevation for Sydney arch given in the specification is plainly reproduced from the outline of the Hell Gate arch. It is exactly the same type of bridge, has the same proportionate rise of arch and reproduces a quite extraordinary feature of that bridge, viz, an odd number of panels.

THE BRIDGE

Freeman pounded the pulpit over Bradfield's claims to have 'originated' the design and sounded quite heated when he wrote 'Dr Bradfield states that the specification "would enable me to mould the details as I desired." He has no right whatever to "Mould" or otherwise alter any detail whatever.'

Freeman went on to claim that, 'Dr Bradfield did not inspire a single feature of the design' and was backed up by an editorial in the newspaper.

The pair were so intemperate by now that each was overstating his own case. Bradfield came out in the paper the following Thursday stating that he had made a drawing of an arch bridge in December 1922 before tenders were invited and this was included in the specifications. In fact his diary reveals that he had asked Bill Lush to complete an elevation of an arch bridge in early October.

> Mr Freeman's claim that he 'designed' the bridge is based on a definition of the word 'design' as meaning the selection of the quality of steel to be used and the preparation of the calculations and drawings required. These matters are not the 'design' of the structure … Long before Dorman, Long & Co., or Mr Freeman came into the matter the location of the bridge, the determination of the grades, the length of span, the trusses, bracings and other vital points previously mentioned in this report had to be determined by me and Dorman, Long & Co., Mr Freeman and everyone else were and are bound by these determinations.
>
> It is not my intention to engage in a contest with Mr Freeman as to whether, he or I is the 'designer' of the bridge. The statements made in my report are correct notwithstanding the views of Mr Freeman. I cannot admit that this great structure as it will exist when finished will, as Mr Freeman would apparently have us believe, be due to him as its 'designer'. No one man can take the whole and sole credit for either its design, fabrications, or erection. I certainly cannot be expected to admit that I and my staff have taken no part in the

design of the bridge now being erected by Dorman, Long & Co. even on the narrow aspect of design to which Mr Freeman wishes it be confined.

The debate settled down for some time after this, only because there was nothing left to say, but the wounds were still raw and the Australians left in no doubt about the English position on the controversy when another article setting out detailed plans and drawings of the Sydney Harbour Bridge and its method of construction appeared in the *Engineering* magazine in July 1930. Dorman, Long fired off a furious letter to the New South Wales government.

> This article and the plans and drawings mentioned were published without our knowledge or sanction and the confidential information on which much of the article is based must, we assume, have been given to the paper by the Chief Engineer of the Bridge, as the continuation of earlier publications under his name, and no one else has access to the information.

By this stage it seems the English company could not bring itself to mention Bradfield by name.

> We are naturally annoyed at the premature publicity given to information confidential to you and ourselves and at disclosure of plans and diagrams which are the copyright of this Company and of our Consulting Engineer, Mr. Ralph Freeman, the actual designer of the Bridge.
>
> The article in question was published without any application by the above newspaper for our consent, and does not give the customary acknowledgment to ourselves or to Mr. Freeman as the original sources of the drawings and the information.

Dorman, Long concluded that the firm was confident the government had not approved of the article, that is that Bradfield had acted alone, and asked that such articles be prohibited until the bridge was handed over by the English to the Australians.

Bradfield explained to the government that in fact the whole incident was a misunderstanding. He had provided information for a chapter in an English boys' book of engineering with approval from the minister with 'due and correct acknowledgement to the Contractors and their Consultants' and the editor of that book had handed it on to *Engineering* without his knowledge.

The chief engineer said it was regrettable there was 'no acknowledgement in these articles of the source of the information or of the Contractors' association with the work', but did not stay on the back foot for too long, pointing out that the drawings were prepared in his office, the photographs the property of the department and the scheme of erection the same as set out by him in the 1924 Report on Tenders. 'I cannot conceive of any foundation for the statement that the drawings and details are the copyright of the Contractors and their Consultants' he wrote, and went on to claim that he controlled all such material.

In the meantime, the Australians tried to get to the heart of the issue with the Director-General of Public Works, G. W. Mitchell, assigned to report on the incident to the Minister for Public Works. Mitchell's under-secretary was given access to the correspondence between Bradfield and Freeman, probably from the Australian engineer, and twice wrote asking Dorman, Long for a submission on its attitude to the design question.

In August 1930 the Sydney office of Dorman, Long passed on a curt cable from London.

> Replying to your question relative design contained in your letter 30th July to our Sydney office. We definitely state that for bridge being built, general and detailed design and calculations as stipulated by form of tender and contract were prepared for this company by or under the direction of Ralph

Freeman, as stated in our memorandum accompanying our tender, which is now contract document.

Mr Ennis wrote at the bottom of the message, 'we have nothing further to say', and signed his name.

Mitchell told the minister that he believed the English were being 'evasive', which was 'tantamount to an admission of the weakness of their case' and clearly came down on Bradfield's side.

At the same time the local branch of the Institution of Civil Engineers offered to arbitrate on the matter but terms of reference could not be agreed on.

Freeman was due back in Australia for the closing of the arch that year, but any further outbursts were headed off by the institution, which published a letter in the *Sun* when the Englishman arrived:

> It will be noted that Dr Bradfield has not calculated any portion of the actual bridge whose erection we have seen, but nevertheless every calculation, drawing and detail has been checked and approved by Dr Bradfield's engineering staff.
>
> Therefore it may be submitted that Dr Bradfield and his staff are the designers of the bridge scheme and that Dorman, Long & Co. Ltd, together with their consulting engineers, did calculate, detail, fabricate and erect under the supervision of Dr Bradfield the actual bridge, the arch of which we see about to be closed.

The warring engineers were told that the 'newspaper controversy' was against the institution's ethics and they would be expelled if it continued.

The papers prepared for the government inquiry were bound and presented to the Mitchell Library in Sydney and reveal that there had even been an investigation into the validity of Bradfield's thesis for his doctorate in engineering, which had been based on the bridge and suburban railways system plans. The chief engineer had submitted his work on 2 January 1924, two weeks before tenders closed on 16 January.

When it came to crediting the design of the bridge on a plaque, Dorman, Long threatened to sue if Freeman wasn't mentioned and the Minister for Public Works decided on this wording:

> The Bridge was constructed for and the approaches by the Public Works Department of New South Wales. The general design and specification were prepared and the whole supervised on behalf of the Government of N.S.W. by J.J.C. Bradfield, D. Sc. (Eng.), M.E., M. Inst. C.E., M.I.E., Aust., Chief Engineer. Contractors for the design and construction of the main structure Dorman, Long & Co. Limited, Middlesbrough, England. Lawrence Ennis, OBE, Director of Construction for the Contractors. Ralph Freeman, M. Inst. C. E., M. Am. Soc., C.E., Consulting and Designing Engineer for the Contractors. Sir John Burnet and Partners, Architects for the Contractors. The Honorable M. A. Davidson, M.L.A. Minister for Public Works. G. W. Mitchell, Director of Public Works.

Two days before the plaque was unveiled Bradfield found himself an unusual champion. Given the opportunity to write an article for *The Times* of London's Sydney Harbour Bridge Special Section, the Governor of New South Wales, Sir Philip Game, used the space on the front page to celebrate Bradfield's achievements. 'The noble single arch bridge spanning Sydney Harbour which is to be opened to the public on March 19 is truly Dr Bradfield's child. He has been in the very closest daily touch with its progress since the work began and if he is a proud man on March 19 he has every right to be.'

Mitchell's report to Buttenshaw was never made public, but when Bradfield retired from the public service in 1933 the acting Premier, Mr Bruxner, lauded him as the designer of the bridge and released extracts from the document which state: 'My definite opinion, based on documents, papers, interviews, and personal contact with various officers of the department is that Dr Bradfield was the designer of the Sydney Harbour Bridge, and no other person, by any stretch of imagination, can claim that distinction.'

Not everybody was so sure and the former Minister for Public Works, Mr Ball, who had guided the enabling act through parliament, released a statement the next day contradicting the Premier.

> I regret that this has again been raised. I thought the tablet placed on the bridge, which was agreed to by Dorman, Long, and Co., and Dr. Bradfield, put an end to this dispute. I have previously stated that I regard the design of the bridge as a joint work of Dr. Bradfield and approved by the Public Works Committee.

Ball noted that the original specifications for a cantilever bridge were not changed until after Bradfield's visit abroad and told this story:

> I well remember that Dr. Bradfield's view at the time was that the details of the design should be left with the bridge contractors in order to get the keenest competition and best results, the details to be approved of by Dr. Bradfield. This necessitated Dr. Bradfield and a staff being sent to England to check and approve of details supplied by Dorman, Long & Co. I also remember one very important detail which was altered after the tender had been let. I was taken by Dr. Bradfield and Mr Ennis to Dorman, Long's works at Mascot to view the full-size model of the hinge pin then designed to carry the full weight of the bridge and traffic. It was four feet in diameter. I know that Mr Ennis did not like the original design and requested that their own consulting engineer, Mr. Freeman, to review the matter. When Dr. Bradfield was in England this was gone into, and Dr. Bradfield approved of the present design and agreed to an extra allowance being made for the altered design, which I had to approve of. What is in

existence today is nothing like the original design, and it is undoubtedly a distinct improvement. Anyone with engineering knowledge knows that the design of the four hinge pins, which carry the whole weight of the bridge, is one of the most important factors in the design and construction of the bridge. This is one of the reasons why I say the design of the bridge is the joint result of Dr. Bradfield and Dorman, Long & Co.

Although the controversy over the design of the bridge arose because Bradfield wanted to avoid the expensive process of preparing full working drawings before a tender was accepted, the chief engineer had a tendency to overstate his role in moving from a cantilever design to an arch.

A study of his diary during the 1922 trip to England reveals that Bradfield was brought around to the idea of an arch bridge; it also shows that Freeman was only one engineer advocating the idea.

As noted earlier, the first mention of an arch was made in Chicago by the chief engineer at McClintic Marshall Company, Pittsburgh, and rejected as 'not practicable' but six months later Bradfield had changed his mind; indeed, in his report to the government about the trip he stated:

> In 1912 only cantilever and suspension bridges of the magnitude and capacity required for the Sydney Harbour Bridge had been constructed, arch bridges approaching such a magnitude had not been attempted owing probably to difficulties in erection supposed rather than real. Since that date the Hell Gate Arch Bridge of 1000 feet span has recently been completed across the East River, New York. This arch bridge is an handsome structure carrying the heaviest railway traffic and for which an arch bridge is eminently suitable.
>
> In response to my enquiries, several firms of repute are prepared to take the responsibility of erecting an arch span of 1600 feet across Sydney Harbour, and I have no hesitation in

saying that an arch bridge of this span can be successfully erected, whilst the problem of design and manufacture are not more difficult than for a cantilever bridge.

Bradfield's specifications included the outline of a 33-panel bridge identical to the American structure.

How did he get to this point?

A month after the meeting in Chicago he climbed the Quebec bridge and seems still to have his heart set on a similar cantilever design. In July he met with the chief engineer of Armstrong Whitworth & Co. 'He proposed an arch bridge — I pointed out headway was restricted at each side of the harbour and that the Public Works Committee had not approved of my similar design on account of this. An arch bridge would require less steel than the cantilever bridge.'

The following month he met with Mr Dixon from the Cleveland Bridge Company but said later he had no idea that Freeman was consulting them at this stage. His diary shows a shift in attitude to the style of the bridge: 'Discussed with them possibility of erecting an arch bridge across the harbour of 1600 feet span. They are prepared to submit for an arch of this span.'

Freeman said he sent Dixon to the meeting with the idea of an arch, armed with the knowledge of new steels and the erection method used in Africa twenty years earlier. Eight days after the meeting Bradfield noted that an issue of the *American Society Civil Engineer*, 1918, vol. 82, contained information about the Hell Gate Arch.

The following day he met with Dixon again who this time was with his construction engineer, Imbault.

Mr Imbault was brought from Paris for the interview. He is one of the members of the Committee preparing British Standard Specifications on Bridge Designs. Mr Imbault says the specifications as drafted is very satisfactory. When a tender is accepted the successful firm and myself would work out the design in detail. He prefers an arch design and has himself prepared a design for an arch span across the harbour.

Six days later Bradfield boarded the SS *Diogenes* as a born-again arch man and began work on cost estimates. Stuckey, his design engineer, remembered being instructed to prepare new design specifications.

Later that year when the Cleveland Bridge Company cabled Bradfield telling him it was withdrawing from the tender process because of the death of its chairman, Mr Dixon, he replied, 'Hope you will be able to reconsider your decision because arch bridge was specified at Dixon's special request'.

Gordon Stuckey said some years later:

> We completed two [designs] we completed a cantilever while Bradfield was away the first time, he only knew a cantilever, he'd seen the Quebec and so cantilever it was, but Cleveland Bridge talked him into the arch and he put it in the specifications as a sort of alternative, but I was always very keen on the arch on account of the wonderful abutments we've got there, the sandstone. I reckon it was made for it, so while he was away the second time the specifications had been amended to provide for the arch, while he was away we did the arch in nickel steel, we didn't know anything about silicone steel they brought that in later in the tender, we didn't have any silicone steel in the specifications.

In 1934 Freeman revealed to the Institution of Civil Engineers that the Hell Gate Bridge was 'undoubtedly the precedent for Sydney' and Lindenthal, the designer of the bridge, noted wryly in a letter to the Institution of Civil Engineers that the Sydney Harbour Bridge's 'resemblance to the Hell Gate bridge was striking', he added that its influence was given no credit. The American also said he remembered Dr Bradfield visiting in 1922 and that there had been little discussion of the Sydney project, but concluded with a compliment to Bradfield on choosing 'an arch bridge, like the Hell Gate bridge'.

To this day articles appear in the press citing either Bradfield or Freeman as the designer of the Sydney Harbour Bridge. In some respects it is a question of the order of chickens and eggs. Freeman certainly was responsible for the exact design of the Sydney Harbour Bridge we know today but that bridge would not be where it is, how it is or even in existence if it were not for Bradfield and his decades of work on the subject. The Englishman designed the bridge the Australian told him he could. With both men dead the feud should be buried with them and both roles recognised, for neither has sole claim to designing the bridge. Bradfield has more claim but Freeman's influential role cannot be ignored.

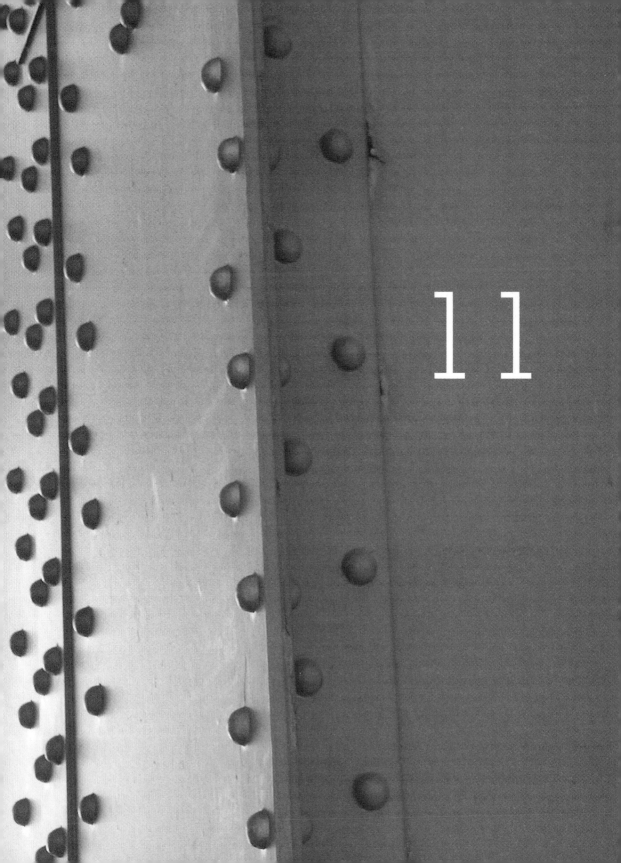

11

LENNIE GWYTHER'S GREAT ADVENTURE

Our narrative finds another hero in a nine-year-old Victorian boy who packs his swag and saddles up a horse called Ginger Mick for a solo journey to see the bridge opening.

Here's a plump little lad on a plump little pony — Leonard Gwyther, who rode all the way from Gippsland or Switzerland or somewhere to Be With Us on this Great Occasion. And here, striding along as if they didn't give a damn for anyone, are a hundred ordinary blokes. They are in this galley because they helped to build the Bridge, and that seems a pretty good reason why they should procesh [sic].

The Bulletin 23 March 1932

Lennie Gwyther is riding out into the Australian morning, a hero on a horse, a child of the nation as it imagines itself: young, strong, adventurous and carefree, confident but not cocky. In the months ahead he will be fêted and celebrated; invited into the halls of parliament and onto the elegant balconies of municipal town halls. The talkies, as they still call them, will set out to interview the monosyllabic nine-year-old and pressmen will record his feats in language reserved for explorers and conquerors. Lennie's quest will make the news in Melbourne, Sydney and London. Crowds will line the street as he enters towns, thousands of eyes will rest on his back as he pushes further along, carrying their excitement and focus, but today, in his home town of Leongatha, people barely have time for a curious glance as they pass. Everybody has something else on their minds.

Lennie sits and waits on his horse, Ginger Mick, near the showground, his short, skinny legs hanging, his thin lips quiet. He waves away a fly and whispers a few words to his anxious mother, who has the three little ones to control and is only too well aware of the fact that the son sitting above her on his pony will soon be out of her control and sight for too long.

Still, his father, known as 'the Captain', has said the boy can go and that is that, no matter what his mother or neighbours say or think.

Lennie has a distant stare. He has heard the bridge's call. His nine-year-old engineer's soul hears her straining against the bedrock of Sydney sandstone, hears the heavy metal cacophony of her labour and now he must go to pay homage to the idol.

Today, 3 February 1932, is Show Day for the small farming community nestled into the rolling hills of South Gippsland, almost 1000 km south of Sydney.

From the early hours they've been riding into town, down from the La Trobe Valley and up from the windswept Victorian coast. As the morning sun announces its harsh intent people swarm toward the recreation reserve, keen to find a place to tether the horses and a shaded picnic spot. Coming along the road the families are alarmed to see the whole area burned out by a grass fire.

It's been that sort of summer. Every time the wind comes up from the north there's the unnerving smell of smoke.

At least the fire will have driven the snakes from the grass.

Despite the drought and the Depression the show is almost as big as last year's, which was the best on record. Livestock entries are nearly as high as in 1931, in fact there's more poultry, fat cattle, swine and dairy produce than the year before. The ladies of the district have been working hard too, with 169 entries in the needlework display and a record fourteen entries in the art division. Stewards from the Agricultural and Pastoral Society spent all of yesterday placing exhibit tickets on the jams, scones, cakes, embroidery and the like. Fortunately the exhibition hall survived the fire. Word is that the blaze was started accidentally by a showman camped on the reserve. Fanned by hot winds, it spread quickly and almost consumed the buildings and animal pens. The local fire brigade arrived just as it threatened to leap the road and destroy the buttery opposite.

Lennie would usually be among the first down to the reserve. He and Ginger Mick are regular competitors in the horseriding events and they have a few blue ribbons to show for efforts around the district. Ginger Mick is well rested and ready for a bit of sport, but today something else is going on and he's not quite sure what to make of it as he shifts and twitches in the morning heat.

It's going to be a long day for the rural community. At sunset there's a special picture show in town with the 'handsome, debonair, charming' Edmund Low starring in *The Matrimonial Problem* at the Memorial Theatre. Later, a five-piece orchestra will take to the stage at the Memorial Hall for a good old knees-up.

The *Great Southern Star* says the dance will 'terminate one of the best entertainments seen locally for some time'.

There'll be bleary eyes in the milk shed tomorrow morning.

The paper, which is published every Tuesday, has been full of handy details, telling the women that hot water will be provided on the reserve so nobody need bother about boiling their own billy — which was probably how the showman started the fire. There's news that the Water Trust has imposed restrictions, banning the watering of gardens on Mondays, Wednesdays, Fridays and Sundays. Reading through the long columns as the day takes shape visitors learn that the Leongatha shoemaker has bought a mechanised stitching machine that will allow customers to have the soles of their boots re-stitched while they wait. There's news from New South Wales too, where the Premier, Mr Lang, has been denied a £500,000 loan from the federal government after the Loan Council also rejected his requests. That will get them talking. The whole of Australia is watching the controversial Labor leader who has defied calls to pull in his belt. At a time when debt, public or private, is considered almost sinful, Lang is the most sordid of characters. The Leongatha council is wrestling with the vexed problem of feeding the unemployed. It gnaws at the capitalist heart to hand out welfare to the needy, a practice which degrades the human spirit according to some civic and religious leaders. Australia is as uncomfortable with borrowing money as it is with feeding the unemployed and today the paper has printed Section 9 of the *Unemployment Relief Amendment Act 1931* which details the sort of work that can be demanded of the jobless and homeless who wander into districts, eyes downcast and hands out.

These wandering armies of shamed men can be made to maintain parks, repair fences and municipal properties, destroy weeds, dig ditches or carry out foreshore improvements. The trades union movement strongly objects to the unemployed being forced to work. It takes precious jobs from the employed and in most Labor-dominated areas 'susso' is handed out without such demands.

The Depression has not bitten so hard in the country, but in some parts of the cities, particularly Sydney, 40 per cent of the men are out of work. Every day thousands queue from the early hours of the morning in the hope of getting a bit of work here or there. Those with jobs have had their days cut to share the labour around and one employed man or woman can often be found supporting the families of his immediate family.

At least today, with the show on, Leongatha can think about something else.

And Lennie?

Well, buried in the Personal Column of the local paper, below a story about James Jarvis who suffered internal injuries after his horse stood on him in town last Friday, is a passing mention of the local lad and his restless pony:

> Feats of endurance in men are often quoted, but a feat by a lad of 9 years of age is about to be made. We refer to Lennie Gwyther, son of Captain Leo Gwyther and Mrs Gwyther, of

The Lone Rider: Lennie Gwyther and his pony, Ginger Mick, about to set off from the Victorian town of Leongatha for the opening of the bridge. February 1932.

Leongatha South. This youth has been invited to spend a holiday with friends in Sydney, and he intends to make the journey on the pony he has used to ride to school daily. His idea is to be present at the opening ceremony of the world's largest bridge in March. The friends of the parents will wish Lennie every success in his undertaking.

Rural Australia in the 1930s might have been another country, but even then the idea that a nine-year-old boy could ride alone on his horse 600 miles to a distant city raised an eyebrow or two.

THE BRIDGE

Not least because it was Sydney he was headed.

Sydney was a strange concept to rural folk; they'd a sense of mistrust about any city, but Sydney was a special case. In 1932, it hadn't been that long ago that the plague had broken out among its prostitutes and sly grog shops. There was a sense it had never lost its convict stain and now its socialist Premier, Lang, was always in the news, as were its soup queues, militia groups and sinister urban crime. The almost-finished Sydney Harbour Bridge was the only positive news they ever heard from up that way. Even the old farmers were impressed by the stories and pictures that made it into the Victorian papers.

The bridge was assuming its own significance in the early moments of the Australian historical narrative. If men like Lennie's father, a decorated soldier, had proved themselves the equal of anybody at killing and dying on foreign shores, the bridge spoke of a different pride and competency in the adolescent nation. The biggest bridge in the world. Built by Australians. Our engineers are as good as any, the papers said. Our workmen brave and industrious. Our future bright. Our Bridge.

At last this threadbare antipodean population was starting to make its mark and there could be nothing more permanent or impressive than this engineering masterpiece of the machine age that would carry more trains and trams and buses and cars than any built in the more civilised parts of the globe.

The Sydney Harbour Bridge was already seeping into the consciousness, it was something to be compared to the Eiffel Tower, the Pyramids of Egypt and the Great Wall of China. It was a celebrity marriage of the symbolic and the functional.

To be alive during the construction of such a structure was an honour and it was difficult not to be caught up in the excitement.

And the Captain's son was making his way to Sydney to see the Sydney Harbour Bridge and that was something too. Even as the Leongatha locals wondered about the sense of it they couldn't help but be quietly impressed by the determined little boy and his pony.

'It is the first occasion known to this paper where a Gippslander has made the trip to Sydney in the saddle. So the Leongatha lad must be regarded in the light of an overland pioneer,' the *Journal* ('The Paper with a Punch') told local readers on the following Monday. The Captain's chest swelled with pride at these reports and in the coming months he became a reliable source of information to journalists who took up his son's story. Lennie was a chip off the old block. A little soldier and man in the making.

In the days that followed he was celebrated in extraordinary terms. 'A typical bush lad,' they said in the *Cooma Express*, 'unassuming and casual, and tremendously interested in machines and engines.' 'A real Aussie with that inborn pluck, prepared to tackle anything,' they sighed in Queanbeyan. 'The good pioneering spirit which has always sent men out regardless of the dangers ahead is very much alive in this sturdy Australian boy,' the *Goulburn Evening Penny Post* opined, while a letter writer in the *Sydney Morning Herald* saw in Lennie the 'spirit needed ... to make a nation'.

Poor Lennie had no idea as he sat upon Ginger Mick in his Sunday best, swatting a lazy hand at the flies that were gaining energy as the day heated up, he wanted little more than to see how engineers could suspend all those tonnes of steel over such a wide space. He was fascinated by engines and engineering. A potentially skilled draughtsmen, he could have made a career out of that, but a few years later, when his parents scraped up money for a drawing teacher, the man ran away with the cash before Lennie received a lesson. When they did get machinery on the farm Lennie understood it better than he understood himself. Later, after his journey, he left Gippsland and took up a job as an engineer in an automobile factory in Melbourne.

It was hot the day Lennie set off, but the previous winter, the winter of 1931, had loomed cold and miserable for Lennie, the Captain and the rest of the Gwythers on their farm which snuggled in land below the road that ran out of town.

The family had known plenty of hard times since the first Gwythers cut a path through the virgin bush to the district in the 1870s. Over the years they had set about clearing the giant blue gums and thick forests, opening up the red volcanic soil of the rolling hills until the area began to resemble the old countries. When the railway came through the family farm earned its own siding, which meant the men could load their hessian sacks of potatoes straight onto the trains and not carry them along the 7 km of rutted track that led into Leongatha proper.

Lennie was the eldest son of Leo Tennyson Gwyther, war hero and farmer. His father was known, and insisted upon being known, as the Captain. He was a strange fish, the locals said, an officious and aloof man, shaped by a terrible war and two generations of hard farming. The Captain served with the first battery of the field artillery at the Somme and Gallipoli. In November 1916 at Flers, France, his battery came under heavy fire and a shell hit the ammunition pit, which began to burn and threatened to explode. Gwyther ordered his men to evacuate, but one man was buried in a dugout and could not escape. Just the day before Gwyther, too, had been buried in a dugout by enemy fire which had killed the two officers with him. Despite the shelling and obvious danger, he could not leave the injured soldier and began digging. For fifteen agonising minutes he pawed at the French mud, shells falling around him, the burning munitions set to explode at any time. Eventually, with the help of another soldier, he freed the man and the trio escaped to safety.

The advent of the aeroplane meant artillery positions were extraordinarily vulnerable in World War I. The enemy planes would spot the positions and relay locations to their own guns. In July 1917, near Zillebeke Lake, Belgium, Gwyther's outfit were again bombed while digging in, again the munition dump caught fire and again it was Gwyther who braved the flames and imminent explosion to put out the blaze, receiving severe burns to both hands in the process.

For his bravery he was called to Buckingham Palace and presented with the Military Cross and bar by the King of England.

The Captain came home proudly decorated but with the sounds of enemy bombardment ringing in his ears, his skin scarred and his lungs burned by mustard gas, his legs so badly ulcerated that one was eventually amputated — but not before causing him years of agony. Despite the injuries he rode his horse and buggy about town straight-backed and dignified. When it rained the paddocks and roads around Leongatha became boggy and impassable. It reminded him of those times when he and his men showed their real mettle. After the war he married Clara Amelia Simon, the daughter of another pioneering Leongatha farm family. The Captain wore his uniform, his riding jodhpurs tucked into high polished boots, the medals of bravery pinned to his chest. He took his wife back to farm a part of the family property he dubbed Flers after that terrible place on the Somme where he first earned a Military Cross.

In 1932 the Captain was only 40 years old but already an old man who had seen the King in his English palace and a muddy hell in what had been the farmlands of Europe. He would only live another seventeen years.

Lennie was achingly proud of his father; after all, the Memorial Hall and Memorial Theatre at the top of town were built to honour men like him. He was probably too young in 1932 to understand the psychological damage the war inflicted on people like his father. In Australia the war's cost was not measured in the damage to cities and borders, but by the damage to the men who did not return and those that did. Many carried crippling physical and mental scars which took their toll on their families and the country for decades to come.

Up in Sydney, Norm McAlpine, another soldier's son, did it tough. His father, too, had fought in the war.

'He was released in 1918, or 1919 and then he went around the country quite a lot,' Norm recalled. 'I remember seeing him on the tram when he went away. He left me with about two shillings I think. He put two shillings in my hand when he got on the tram.' Norm would sometimes see his father around town. 'He was the kindest and most gentlemanly man, but he drank. Of course he used to turn up at all sorts of places... he never lifted a hand to me.' Norm left school early to care for his sick mother, and the landlord of their Darlinghurst flat found him a job in the workshops for the

Sydney Harbour Bridge unloading steel plates that came on ships from Newcastle and England.

Many returned soldiers had trouble settling back down to life. Others slowly rotted on the ill-fated soldier settlements, unworkable portions of land, divided from bigger farms and handed out to the ex-diggers to remove them from the cities where there was no work. Few of the men knew about farming and even if they did the land was often so barren nothing could be grown or grazed on it. They were encouraged to borrow to survive and then driven from the districts when they could not meet the payments.

The soldiers, despite policies that encouraged their employment ahead of other men, again found themselves marching in small armies from town to hostile town.

The Captain was among the lucky ones. He returned home to the farm, started his family and quietly dealt with his demons, but his health was not good. To make matters worse, in 1931 the Captain fell and broke his leg and was taken to hospital in Melbourne. His pain was compounded by the knowledge that the fields needed to be prepared for planting and if it wasn't done there would be serious difficulties ahead.

With nobody else around to help, Lennie harnessed a four-horse team and set about ploughing 24 acres of the rich, dark soil to prepare it for sowing. It is back-breaking work for a grown man, let alone a pre-pubescent boy. Day after day he worked behind the horses, determined to fulfil his role as the man of the family. Somehow, he managed to harrow and smodge (smooth) the fields and the crops were eventually planted.

When the Captain returned from hospital he proposed a reward for the boy.

Lennie knew exactly what he would do. He had sat at the kitchen table in the farm poring over pictures and descriptions of the Sydney Harbour Bridge for most of his life. With the combustion stove crackling in the dark kitchen he announced that he would like to ride his horse to the New South Wales capital that summer and arrive in time for the opening ceremony.

He would be alone on the road, but not in his quest. While they did not leave as early as Lennie, thousands had booked special trains from Adelaide and Melbourne to be on hand for the celebrations. The opening of the Sydney Harbour Bridge was a bigger event in Australian history than the Sydney Olympics 68 years later and almost everything else that happened in between.

The Captain decided the boy could go and his mother swallowed her concerns as she set about manipulating the family's thin budget to buy him a new suit for the ride.

And, on that summer morning in February 1932, the time had come for him to leave. It was almost 1000 km to Sydney and estimates said that it should take him 35-odd days to get there. The opening ceremony was scheduled for 19 March which meant there was no rush, but Lennie was keen to get going.

The boy was up early and put on his suit — a woollen jacket and short trousers — rolled his spare clothes inside an oilskin swag that sat across the front of the saddle and slung a sugar bag of rudimentary supplies over his shoulder. He had a special sou'wester-style hat for the ride with a brim that turned up at the front and hung low behind to protect his neck from the sun. After saddling up Ginger Mick he and the family rode into town early as the Shire President, Bob McIndoe Jr, had arranged to see him off from the showgrounds.

His three younger siblings gathered around their mother's skirt, as unsure about the fuss as she was about letting her determined nine-year-old ride away. His mother worried as much about the journey as the destination; the roads and rural towns were crowded with hungry men, but the Captain was sure his eldest was up to it. It would make a man of him.

Lennie would celebrate his tenth birthday on the road and would not be back until summer had passed and winter set in. The plan was for him to ride to Sydney and then to book a berth on a ship once he had finished with the bridge and the Easter show.

Lennie, at nine already an accomplished horseman, had grown up with Ginger Mick, a dark chestnut horse that stood 12.2 hands high who was the same age as him and was a present from his maternal grandfather. A horse is no indulgence for a country boy when he lives 7 km from school. When the work was done they competed at the Leongatha, Forster and Yarram shows in the schoolboy events and often won prizes.

Lennie loved his horse. He would tell a newspaper man: 'He is quiet, and does not mind double dinkey in the least, has a few tricks, and is easy to catch and lovely to ride, game as they are made and can carry twelve stone without effort. A real keen stock pony, that can stick like a leech to a beast; you almost want some glue on the saddle to stick to him when he screws and twists after an animal.'

Ginger Mick had been spelled for six weeks before setting out and the toes of his shoes were inlet with a piece of motor spring steel which would be good for at least six weeks. While most of the journey would be on dirt, some roads near the cities were sealed and hard on the horse's feet.

With a small crowd looking on, councillor McIndoe made a short speech to Lennie, presented him with a letter of introduction to the Lord Mayor of Sydney and it was time to go.

The nine-year-old said goodbye to his family and set off. A photograph shows the boy and Ginger Mick on the main street, Lennie in short trousers, a woollen coat and the odd hat. Nobody else is in frame. The family have dug deep to clothe him properly for the trip and he looks suitably respectable. Ginger Mick, ears pricked, is turning from the camera, apparently eager to get on the road.

'Leaving the South Gippsland capital with the benediction of his parents ringing in his ears, the lad turned in the saddle, and looking back on Leongatha, commenced the climb to Mirboo,' reported the *Journal* on the following Monday.

Lennie and Ginger Mick climbed north-east from Leongatha, the sounds of the show fading in the background as they rode away. It was a steep, winding road and while there was at least 1000 km ahead of them, Lennie knew that it all had to be done with patience. Ginger Mick needed to be rested often if they were both to make it.

After a steady day they stopped and camped at Mirboo North, about 25 km from home and barely twenty minutes in a modern car, but a fair day's ride for a boy on a horse. The next morning they were on their way early, continuing along the winding road, through Boolara and Yinnar, then dropping down into the dairy farms of the Latrobe Valley. They rested at Morwell, before pushing on and it was almost nightfall by the time they reached the outskirts of Traralgon, but they were still earlier than expected.

The Gwythers' family friend Sam Phillips, a local horse trainer and Vacuum Oil Company man, was supposed to greet them on the road, but Lennie arrived in town early and knocked on the door of George Sparke, who steered him in the right direction. Traralgon was the biggest town in the area but still small enough for everybody to know everybody else. After Ginger Mick was watered and bedded down for the night, Lennie was fed by the Phillipses. Later, an exhausted little boy climbed into bed for the night. Meeting the Phillipses was fortuitous; Vacuum Oil had representatives in almost every major centre from Traralgon to Sydney. The company had been importing bulk oil shipments for almost a decade to cope with the increasing demands of the motor vehicle, and later would be better known as Mobil. Lennie might have been on a horse, but the Vacuum Oil men were sent a message to be on the lookout for the little fellow and to extend him every courtesy.

Even in 1932, the boy and his horse represented an era that was fast passing. Perhaps that was why the quiet soldier's son received so much attention. Lennie and his horse appeared to have materialised from the bush folklore of Banjo Paterson and the devil-may-care characters of C. J. Dennis. In fact, Ginger Mick's name was taken from one of Dennis's larrikin inventions — Mick was a knockabout Melbourne type who fought and died at Gallipoli.

The Traralgon press was certainly impressed by the young visitor and the following Monday the *Journal* published an article under the banner: A STURDY LEONGATHA BOY WILL RIDE TO SYDNEY ON PONY TO HARBOUR BRIDGE OPENING. A smaller heading noted: Nine Years Old — But Can Plow as Well. The journalist was clearly more impressed with the boy's efforts than those on his home town paper.

The article began: 'A little lad, on a stocky pony, parked in front of "the Journal" early on Friday morning ...' It detailed Lennie's journey so far, the reasons he was on the way and finished with an encouraging two-word flourish: 'Atta boy!'

Friday was only Lennie's third day on the road, but it could easily have been his last. He set off from Traralgon early, but by mid-morning a terrible hot northerly was blowing gusts of smothering wind into the valley, filling the air with dust and then, more worryingly, smoke. In no time the pair were lost in a thick, choking cloud, blown down from the hills to the north as a fire raced through the heavily timbered hills. At midday it was pitch-black, the sun completely eclipsed by the smoke. There was another large grass fire raging ahead, around the Bairnsdale area. Lennie and an agitated Ginger Mick rode blind, not sure if the fire front was about to leap out and consume them, and aware only of a deep burning red on the horizon to the north, east and west. It was a terrifying day for everybody in the area, but particularly for the boy alone on the road.

The blaze to the north burnt through the milling towns of Erica, Gilderoy, Warragul and Noojee. O'Shea's sawmill, 6 km from Knotts Siding, was right in the path of a fierce blaze. Local schoolteacher, Mr Vague, rode out to warn the workers. The mill was surrounded by firebreaks and had a modern sprinkler system to protect the buildings and men from just such an incident, but a falling tree cut the water supply and the workers had to run for their lives. Some made it to a nearby river, remaining partially submerged until the front had passed, but nine were killed, including the schoolteacher Mr Vague.

After a 20-km ride through the black smoke, Lennie and Ginger Mick were relieved to arrive at the home of relatives at Kilmany, near Rosedale.

Lennie saw to his horse and then washed the soot from his face and eyes. He was lucky to be alive, homesick and reconsidering the whole adventure as he fell to sleep. Saturday, however, arrived clear and fresh. The north wind had died and Lennie needed his oilskin before the day was over as rains brought relief from the fires and the heat. That night he veered off the road to stay with Mr and Mrs Rash at Munro and by Sunday he had arrived at the large rural centre of Bairnsdale, where he stayed the night with his mother's best friend from her school days, Mrs Furnier. The family operated the Main Hotel, where he was given a room for the night.

On the front page of the *Bairnsdale Advertiser* readers were informed that 'Lennie Gwyther, to give him his full title, has more than the usual quota of self assurance for a lad of his years, and has absolutely no fears for his future … the lad weighs five stone and the saddle is only 10lb more so Ginger Mick's load is not a heavy one … the youngster proposes to complete the journey to Lang's capital alone.'

Back in Leongatha, Tuesday passed but there were no reports in the *Great Southern Star*, which seemed to share some of the town's cynicism about his adventure, but other papers, including Traralgon's *Journal* picked up the story and stuck with it. Lennie was suffering a prophet's lack of recognition in his home town, but couldn't have cared less. He and Ginger Mick had fallen into an easy rhythm and were enjoying the journey along the less populated eastern extremity of the state. An independent boy, Lennie didn't want for company, falling in with people on the road and stopping regularly to water the horse and rest at convenient home-steads.

Still skirting the ranges to the north, the pair continued along the long straight plains heading due east towards Sale and then made it to Cann River, 400 km from home and almost halfway to Sydney. From there the Bombala road veered directly and steeply north.

Captain Gwyther had planned to drive the family jinker to meet his boy at the town in the far east of the state, but accepted a lift in a neighbour's Model A Ford and the pair were reunited in Cann River. Along the way the Captain dropped into Traralgon's *Journal* to inform it of the 'courageous little lad's' progress:

'It is quite possible,' said the Captain, 'that if I were to go right on to Sydney with my son, it would take much of the glamour off his enterprise, and it is therefore more than likely that I shall turn back after I see him safely through Bombala.'

'The game lad is in excellent fettle, the captain told us, and the pony looks as though he had not travelled more than a few miles,' the paper in turn told its readers.

The Captain escorted the boy from Cann River along the first sections of the Monaro Road, a trail that wound up into the lower reaches of the South Coast Range before joining the Great Dividing Range. While not an easy route, his father hoped it would at least avoid the extremes of the coastal climate.

Father and son made it to Bombala on Friday 19 February, almost three weeks after leaving home. The pair were greeted by the local mayor, Alderman Charles Warne, and Lennie was then taken to the schoolhouse where the children were given rides around the oval on the patient pony before Lennie found lodgings at the Globe Hotel.

Captain Gwyther took his 5-stone son to the local GP to see how he was holding up to the rigours of the relentless dusty road and occasional civic receptions. The doctor proclaimed Lennie 'as sound as a bell, and in buoyant spirits'.

By now his journey was starting to gain attention in Sydney, where everybody was eagerly preparing for the following month's bridge celebrations. The *Sydney Morning Herald* reported on his ride on 20 February 1932.

Above the item were details about a police case against Eric Campbell, leader of a right-wing militia group based in Sydney called the New Guard. Campbell was facing charges of using insulting language toward the Premier of the state. Lennie and one of Campbell's horsemen would cross paths in the following weeks and share more newspaper space.

On his return journey from Bombala the Captain dropped in to the *Journal* office to update them on the *Game Little Chap* — as the paper had dubbed its *Leongatha Boy*.

Lennie and Ginger Mick were travelling without incident but Lennie's father almost came undone on the journey home, running the Model A off the road and losing a mudguard in the process.

Lennie and Ginger Mick continued along the Monaro Highway, spending Sunday night at Bobingah Station and stopping for lunch at Rock Flat. They were greeted at Nimmitabel by a party of men and boys who rode along the road and escorted them into Cooma on Monday 22 February, and Lennie was invited to stay with the Rolfes, who owned the Prince of Wales Hotel.

While it might have been hard on the road, Lennie was spending his nights like a little prince, fêted by civic leaders, fed in hotel dining rooms and sleeping in hotel suites. It was a far cry from the anonymous, hard life on the little farm back in Leongatha and must have seemed like a fairytale to the little boy. No school, no curfews, no chores and nothing but a ribbon of dusty road ahead.

They respected a horseman up that way and 'the lad was given a great welcome when he arrived, particularly by the many local lads who envied him his adventure, and admired his staunch little pony, very aptly named "Ginger Mick"', the *Cooma Express* reported. Lennie was taken to the hotel before heading into Centennial Park for a 'romp' with some of the locals. Later there was a community singing around the piano at the Rolfes'. The boy had a *bonza* time before setting out again the next morning escorted by Tom Stroud and the Body brothers, John and Edmund. 'It was characteristic that when Mrs Rolfe asked him what he would like in the lunch she was making up for him to take with him he asked her not to worry about him but to put in an apple for his pony.' Then, according to the *Cooma Express*, it was on to the Quarmbys' at Bredbo and the Kellys' at The Creek, Michelago.

By Friday 26 February Lennie was approaching Canberra and on the downhill run toward Sydney. While at Bombala he had received a telegram from the headmaster of the Canberra Grammar School offering him accommodation on the campus, but before bedding down, Lennie had some official duties to attend to:

Charles James Gwyther, 9, rode his chestnut pony up to the steps of Parliament House this afternoon and paid a courtesy call on the deputy leader of the United Country party (Mr Paterson) who is the member for Gippsland, in which his parents have a farm at Leongatha ... Mr Paterson was extremely proud of his guest, and introduced him to nearly every member of Parliament. It was not surprising that the boy was overwhelmed and bewildered. Then Charles was entertained at afternoon tea in the refreshment rooms reserved for 'members only'.

He has a diary recording the towns at which he has spent the night and the names of his hosts. Only once, he said, had he been refused shelter. That was at a town near Sale, Victoria. There one resident refused to take him in. The occupant of another house was absent, but he received a warm welcome at the next house at which he called.

Charles Gwyther said that he intended to write a book of his adventure on his return home ...

Local Hero: Lennie Gwyther and Ginger Mick were celebrated in every town they passed through and invited to join the bridge's opening ceremony in Sydney. March 1932.

Canberra is a proper place and the paper used the boy's real name, although he was known to all as Lennie. Canberra also found him 'overwhelmed and bewildered', a theme the Sydney newspapers would return to and a fair indication that the taciturn young man was less than comfortable with all the attention, especially in the larger cities. His private journey had become confrontingly public. Lennie obviously did not lack confidence in his ability to ride the distance but the real fears of the skinny farm boy were to do with town halls and sitting rooms, not open roads and country towns. His reported intention to return by steamer was later abandoned as the nine-year-old had fallen in love with the rhythms and sights of his journey and was beginning to form a plan to return home via Melbourne.

The visit to Canberra made news in Sydney and the towns he had been to previously and even sparked the *Great Southern Star* into the first mention of the local lad since he had left town a month before. On 1 March it reported in the Personal Column:

> Captain Leo T. Gwyther received a telegram from the Hon T. Paterson, M.H.R. on Friday last stating that his son Lennie arrived safely that day at Canberra, looking well, and the pony in good condition. He was to stay two days at the Grammar School and then leave for Sydney. Lennie Gwyther, aged 9, left the Leongatha show ground on February 3rd, on his pony, for Sydney, and should shortly arrive at his destination.

With Canberra behind them, the pair now had Sydney in their sights. On the way to Queanbeyan Lennie was presented with a boomerang at Station Hill by a Mr Jolly — another souvenir for the sugar bag that was later said to also include a cricket bat autographed by cricketing legend Don Bradman.

In Queanbeyan he was again welcomed by civic dignitaries including the deputy mayor and a councillor, then taken home by Sergeant Ruffles and fed dinner. The *Queanbeyan Age* was impressed. 'It is questionable whether there is another lad of

Lennie's age, who can boast the attempting of such a big journey all alone. Everybody who meets young Gwyther and 'Ginger Mick' will wish the pair the best of luck. A real Aussie, with that inborn pluck, prepared to tackle anything.'

On Saturday 5 March Lennie trotted into Moss Vale on Sydney's outskirts. By now the *Great Southern Star* was showing a little more interest in the story, reporting:

> A message from Sydney states that Lennie Gwyther, who set off for Sydney from the recent Leongatha show, for the purpose of viewing the opening of the harbour bridge, rode on to the Moss Vale show ground unannounced on Saturday last, and entered in the class for boy riders under the age of 10 years. He won second prize and was awarded a special ribbon from the society. He afterwards continued on his journey to the capital. Lennie is the son of Capt. and Mrs Leo Gwyther and his friends will be pleased to hear of his successful progress.

Clearly, Ginger Mick was still in fine fettle. Lennie reached the outskirts of Sydney, stopping to rest at Liverpool that Saturday where accommodation had been arranged by the Royal Agricultural Society. He woke early the next morning, keen to get into town and see the Sydney Harbour Bridge, but as he groomed Ginger Mick in preparation he was set upon by a film crew from 'the talkies' keen to record an interview. Two escorts arrived from the Royal Agricultural Society. Finishing the interview, Lennie could wait no longer. 'Now let me see your bridge — quick as you can,' he told his guides.

Finally, on 8 March 1932, 33 days after leaving Leongatha, Lennie and Ginger Mick rode through suburb after endless suburb, toward the city.

As they approached Martin Place, where one last civic reception stood between him and the bridge, Lennie's heart must have fallen slightly, for a large, pressing crowd had spilled into the streets despite the best efforts of two dozen policemen.

The child from Leongatha was received like a returned explorer from an earlier century but was sick of ceremonies. The pair picked their way through the surging city crowd, then Lennie alighted from Ginger Mick and finally set his country boots down on the paved streets of Sydney.

'Oh what a bonza town!' he exclaimed to the waiting dignitaries, his eyes darting from one grand building to the next. He had never seen so many people in one place and you can imagine the sight of the city buildings to a boy who had never seen anything bigger than a gum tree or a grain silo. It was all a little overwhelming.

The event was recorded by the *Sydney Morning Herald* and the next day it ran a report with a photograph of Lennie and Ginger Mick. Sydney, it seems, had fallen for the pair, although another report told how souvenir hunters pulled hairs out of the pony's tail, no doubt confirming to Victorians some of their mistrust about Mr Lang's capital and its inhabitants. Most Sydneysiders, though, seemed genuinely moved by the anachronistic sight of the little farm boy who was drawn to their city and bridge. Three days after Lennie arrived in Martin Place another article appeared in the *Sydney Morning Heral*, apparently written by the young horseman, although it was more likely concocted by a reporter after discussions with the monosyllabic traveller. Still, it's an insight into Lennie's world.

… I know that I have bitten off rather a big chew, as sailors say, but education is what I want, and it's one of the main objects of my trip. Amongst the many things I have is a letter from the president of our local shire to the Lord Mayor of Sydney, as I am desirous of seeing the opening ceremony of the bridge, and would be glad to see also the Sydney Show and the yearling sales of thoroughbreds … Do not think that I want to be adventurous. Not so. I am contented, but I did want to see the biggest bridge in Australia and the greatest ocean-going liners that call at Sydney's beautiful harbour. I visited Melbourne when the Hood was here, and was on her at Port Melbourne. One sailor wanted to put me down a big gun muzzle, but I was quite off being cannon fodder; not that I would mind, perhaps, when I am older, since for over five generations there have been soldiers in the family. A photograph of the painting of the Scotch Greys [the 2nd (Royal North British) Dragoons, so called because they are mounted on grey horses] is my very special fancy, for I love horses and a gallop. My father, of whom I am very proud, is a captain, and won the Military Cross and a bar, and was twice decorated at Buckingham Palace by the King …

Lennie was a hero in Sydney, one letter writer seeing in him values that made the humble colony the equal of any nation.

Sir, — Just such an example as provided by a child of nine summers, Lennie Gwyther, was, and is, needed to raise the spirit of our people and to fire our youth and others to do things — not to talk only. The sturdy pioneer spirit is not

No Mummy's Boy: Lennie Gwyther is greeted by his mother and a sibling more interested in her bag of lollies on his return to Leongatha. 1932.

dead, the spirit that explored and settled this country and is now operating in Central Australia.

The patriotic writer, using the nom de plume 'Gum Tips', invoked the names of the conservative Prime Minister and Colonel Lindburgh ('who I feel safe in saying could easily be beaten by at least a score of Australians, and possibly equalled by 100') and ended with a swipe at those on the dole.

A reporter from Melbourne's *Age* was also moved by the reception at Martin Place.

> If he had been a royal prince he could not have got a better reception. Thousands awaited his arrival in Martin Place, the scene of great receptions. They were not all Victorians. There were some who showed themselves proud of the State that could produce such a youthful adventurer. But the majority of those who shouted a welcome to the boy did so because he was an Australian and to be an Australian in getting a first and foremost place in our estimate of things. Perhaps the welcome given the boy was not unexpected for children and youth seem to be playing an important part in bringing about a better understanding between the various States.

He might be a Victorian and an Australian but he was also a Leongatha boy and the next edition of the *Great Southern Star* carried the item from the *Age*.

Lennie was in for a further surprise in Sydney. He was invited to join the official celebrations for the opening of the Sydney Harbour Bridge on 19 March, the biggest event ever seen in the city. Lennie would ride Ginger Mick ahead of a group of Aboriginals gathered from near Botany Bay who would be daubed in white paint.

Sometime the following week the fares for crossing the bridge were published in the Sydney papers. While Lennie could cross the structure for free on the opening day, any subsequent trips would set him back threepence, although a herd of horse or cattle was cheaper at twopence and sheep or pigs could cross for one penny.

The Australian horseman was not dead just yet. The opening ceremony of the Sydney Harbour Bridge gave one in particular the chance to almost steal the show — but it wasn't Lennie Gwyther.

12

LANG ROBS THE BANK ...
DE GROOT STEALS THE SHOW

Will the Premier of New South Wales get away with
robbing the banks? Can he really tell the King that
he is not wanted at the opening ceremony and what
will the conservatives do about it if he does? Enter
another horse and rider keen to make the opening
ceremony.

Late on the morning of Saturday 12 March 1932, seven days before a strange little man on a borrowed horse rides his way into history, two long, well-appointed cars come to a halt, one outside the Commercial Banking Company of Sydney, the other nearby at the Bank of New South Wales in Sydney's Martin Place.

A brazen heist is in progress. Within hours the state's coffers will be drained. Not a single penny will be left in the New South Wales savings account and the world will be none the wiser until Monday morning. Dark forces are afoot in the city and people are spooked; the State Bank has already closed after a run on funds; militia groups, organised labour, the New South Wales police and the army are involved in a tense stand-off. The poor are hungry and agitated, the rich are watchful and the government is stuck somewhere between the two. Against this background the cars pull up outside the bank. As tellers prepare to balance the day's takings, nervous pairs of suited men step out of the vehicles and hurry inside. Each carries an empty suitcase and is accompanied by a pair of armed police officers who study every face and observe every movement.

At the Bank of New South Wales the manager is summoned and presented with a cheque for withdrawal of £750,000, while at the Commonwealth Bank the manager is asked for £400,000. The men inform the swooning bankers that they want cash, small denominations and they want it immediately. The managers instruct staff to open the safes. White-shirted tellers tear their eyes from the clock and their thoughts from Saturday afternoon and quietly begin to count the money into piles. Their disappointment at being kept late at the end of the week is countered by their curiosity. Rarely have they seen so much cash leave the building at one time, but some remember something in the newspapers about a new act passed in Canberra the day before. They keep their eyes and voices down.

Eventually the money is ready, counted and recounted, the front doors of the two banks are unlocked, the police check that there are no threats lurking outside and the men walk back to the cars and drive away with £1.15 million.

Were an accountant to have checked the bank balance for the State of New South Wales on the afternoon of 12 March they would have found that its balance read £0-0-0. There was not a penny left, every pound, shilling and pence had been withdrawn.

The Labor Premier, Jack Lang, had drained the coffers and pulled off a cunning move that displayed a belligerent political precision but was in reality the last shot of a man cornered in a desperate political situation.

As the clock struck noon that day, while the money was being counted into tidy piles, new federal legislation took effect. The Saturday papers carried news that the Senate in Canberra had given final approval for the Financial Agreements Enforcement Bill by a vote of 45 to eight, the minority being referred to as 'the Lang group'.

The federal government had bailed New South Wales out when it failed to meet its interest commitments to British bondholders in April 1931, but the Labor party had lost the intervening federal election and the conservative Joe Lyons was now Prime Minister. Lyons set out to destroy Lang, and the introduction of the new Bill was a declaration that the battle had begun.

In the months prior to the passing of the Bill, Prime Minister

Joe Lyons's conservative federal government had become so aggrieved with New South Wales's refusal to pay interest rates to bondholders it had drafted legislation which allowed the federal treasurer to seize the state's money and send it off to the English whether Lang agreed or not. The Bill was now law but the minute it had become so there was no money left to seize, at least not without the use of force.

Formidable Foe: Premier Jack Lang was a determined man who clashed with the monarchists who demanded the King or Governor General open the bridge.

Lang had beaten Lyons to the punch.

The left-wing Premier was not seeing the last of his government's money disappear on a steamer bound for the old country. Hell, no. This was the sort of stuff that got his working-class blood boiling and the words flying in a spray of indignant spittle. Not when his poor were already hungry, homeless and desperate. Not when his state was on its knees. The Big Fella, as they called him, would not be intimidated. He would not bow to the demands of the

conservatives in Canberra, the State's howling opposition or the puff-chested fascists bellowing in town halls about God, Empire and fiscal honour. When the anthem sounded, the former paper boy stuck his hat back on his balding head and his bum back on the seat.

Jack Lang was sitting this one out.

And, just for good measure, there was no way he was going to allow any of those people to open the Sydney Harbour Bridge the following Saturday. Jack Lang was going to do it himself, the Governors, Governors-General and colonial loyalists could pull on their top hats and military uniforms and stand by and watch while he did it. It will save money, he told them, his strident Australian accent laced with mischief. The conservatives were always on about saving money.

The decision by Lang to open the bridge himself was another red rag to the right, an act of defiance that led to a much-celebrated counterpunch the following Saturday. However, on that particular weekend, seven days before the opening, Captain Francis de Groot was an anonymous member of the right-wing New Guard movement and not even he had any idea of the act that would write his name into history the following Saturday. If the truth be known, the group that had publicly declared it would not let Lang open the bridge had no idea what it would do about it on Saturday 12 March. In fact, it was a cartoon published in *Smith's Weekly* during the coming week which would plant the seeds. Fortunately for all sides in the battle, the New Guard's fighting words resulted only in a comic act of defiance which, rather than inflaming, deflated a potentially violent and dangerous situation.

Lang ordered all the state's money to be stored in vaults at the Treasury that Saturday morning. He even organised for unemployed workers to form a guard on the building, just in case the conservatives tried to come knocking. Lyons's Financial Agreements Enforcement Bill had also legislated to grab state taxes that flowed into the government's bank accounts, but Lang was ahead of them on that front too. When the New South Wales income tax officials arrived at work at the Taxation Department in Hamilton Street the following Monday, they found the locks had either been changed or damaged. Most employees were sent home on immediate annual leave. Nobody could grab taxes that weren't collected, but just to make sure, Lang ordered people not to pay bills to the state government's accounts.

From that Monday, government departments were run on a strictly cash basis. When pay day came, officials lined up at Treasury's door and money was loaded into calico bags. In small bills.

Lyons and the conservatives were incandescent with rage when they heard what Lang had done and swore revenge. The New Guard could barely contain itself from direct action and the Governor, Sir Philip Game, sat dismayed in Government House with its views of the harbour and its completed bridge. He had already been told in no uncertain terms of His Majesty's displeasure about not being invited to open the bridge and was not looking forward to word from home when they learned about Lang's latest trick. Game was under enormous pressure to sack the Premier but resisted at every turn.

By 1932 the tension cables supporting the bridge had long since been slackened, but the strains had shifted into the sandstone bedrock of Sydney and threatened every foundation. Newspapers and political leaders sensed the state of New South Wales, like much of the world, was at a fork in the road. With unemployment at 30 per cent, soup queues on corners and shantytowns ringing Sydney, capitalism was facing its greatest crisis. Wall Street had crashed in October 1929 and with it faith in the markets. Hitler and his obnoxious anti-communism were on the rise in Germany. In Europe and Australia the establishment were unsure whether to jeer or cheer. Many chose the latter. The world was tearing itself apart along ideological lines, communists stared down fascists, moderates attempting a middle path were denounced as appeasers or fools. War was seven years away; at the time it appeared much closer, although the enemy was not so apparent.

Sydney itself was seething with paranoia and menace. Lang was at loggerheads with the establishment. Right- and left-wing groups and even the police practised military manoeuvres in the streets, each determined to intimidate the other. Student reservists were armed and told to prepare to back the police should fighting break out in the streets. The RAAF mounted machine guns on its vehicles in preparation for an uprising and the city, in fact most of the country, held its breath.

If the public could forget its woes on 19 March, when the bridge was to be opened, the dignitaries and politicians invited to sit on the dais could not. It was indeed the best of times and the worst. Despite the persistent heat, many felt a frigid sweat beneath their fine suits and hats as the ceremonies progressed.

On the Friday that Canberra passed the legislation to seize New South Wales's money, members of the New Guard marched on the Governor and presented a petition for the King demanding Lang's sacking and an end to his 'Communist agenda'. All 'decent citizens were alarmed and disgusted' by the government's actions, the petition read and '100,000 responsible men, law-abiding and of good repute, whose feelings are stirred to the very depths' were ready to act. And this was before they knew about the banks.

On the Monday morning the front page of Sydney's *Daily Telegraph* revealed the news about Lang's withdrawals, right next to a report about Germans going to the polls to choose between Herr Hitler with his 'cinema star appearance and tactics' and President von Hindenburg.

It had been a long, hot and tense summer. Temperatures hovered in the high to mid-forties in the west of New South Wales, locust and thrip plagues besieged the south and numerous bushfires, including a 90-mile wide fire front stretching from Cobar to Wilcannia, flared across the state. In the hysteria of the time, the Old Guard, another right-wing movement, warned that the communists had set fires to distract the good country folk from an uprising in the city. Alert and prepared for action, the New Guard set off to fight the fires in January, but it took three days to get to

Wilcannia because their buses broke down. The militia members arrived with the wrong equipment and by the time that arrived from Sydney the fire had abated. If the Right saw the fires as a metaphor for the political situation, its hapless attempts to quell them could be read as metaphors for their own quixotic quest.

Insult was added to injury when the country folk made noises about running these crazed city types out of town. That sort of help they could do without.

Jack Lang was a man of his times and one of the era's most enduring political symbols. His surname became shorthand for a practical Australian socialist agenda that was mixed with a republican disdain for the Empire and its ceremonies. Unaccustomed to compromise or challenge, he decided to meet the establishment head on and irritant splinter groups like the New Guard could look forward to plenty of broken heads should they try to challenge order.

At 193 cm and 100 kg, Lang was a formidable man and great hater. His father had taken sick when he was still a boy and the family had fallen on hard times. He learned to despise poverty almost as much as he despised those who crossed him. He was also persuasive, a hypnotic orator who could sway men to his side with his passion and logic. In fact Governor Game said he used to look down and play with his dog to guard against falling under the Premier's spell during their often fraught meetings.

Interest payments were due to England's bondholders, but New South Wales did not have the money or the will to pay them. Lang argued that his choice was either to feed the people of New South Wales or pay interest to those who oppress them. To him there was no choice.

In a book published two years after the opening of the bridge, titled *Why I Fight* by John T. Lang, he raged about the Depression and the burden the poor were expected to carry.

Enthroned in our society is a hierarchy of financial anarchists playing with a world of men and women for sheer personal gain, putting them to work under the whips of hunger, throwing them into idleness to keep them in discipline, massing them for war, dividing them in peace — and from every activity into which it deploys them drawing toll in gold, counted over and over in human tears and blood.

If England and its loyal servants were to add to the misery of New South Wales, Lang would make sure he created a little misery and anxiety for them too.

As it was, he gave them quite a fight and quite a fright.

In 1930 Lang had inherited a state which was 'virtually bankrupt' and things appeared to get worse at every turn. A whispering campaign during the election turned ugly, with the Nationalists taking out newspaper advertisements that warned people Lang would 'seize their savings'. This led to a run on the State Bank and a suspension of trading. The Premier called it 'the most tragic chapter' in New South Wales's political history. The right blamed Lang for the bank's failing.

A few months before Lang's landslide win the Bank of England advised Australia to cut back its public spending in the face of a worldwide depression. The English bankers were keen that money owed them not be spent on the people of Australia. Such instructions from abroad were slavishly adopted by all except the Labor Premier, who promised more public works to counter unemployment and doubled payments to couples on the birth of their first child.

By mid-1931 the other state premiers pressured him to join a plan to reduce all government expenditure, including wages, by 20 per cent. Lang reluctantly agreed, but turned around the moment they were all gone and announced he would make the saving by capping the amount paid to all government officers to £500, which meant the rich would pay while public works and the lowly public servant would go untouched.

Lang did not have a conciliatory bone in his body and baited the conservatives at every opportunity.

In October 1931 he announced at the Sydney Eight Hour Day dinner that the 'revolution had come'. The statement sent the right into a terrible flap. While Lang added that the revolution had come by 'Act of Parliament' such qualification was ignored by his ideological enemies.

He then precipitated a constitutional crisis by trying to load an obstructive upper house with appointees to give his party the numbers to pass legislation enabling the state to raise money to meet its debts. He pressed the Governor to appoint 25 new members of the upper house, all of them trade union officials or unionists. Two were women and thirteen were Catholics at a time when the Catholics were viewed with almost as much suspicion as women who wanted to join the democratic process.

Fortunately Game was a shrewd man and despite his position as the King's representative he was a quiet admirer of Lang's determination and sense of social justice. While he was lobbied heavily to sack the government and under constant pressure from his peers, Game moved with caution and restraint.

The Governor voluntarily refunded 25 per cent of his salary to Lang when the Premier proposed that high-ranking public servants bear the brunt of cost-cutting measures, and he infuriated the conservatives by giving in to Lang's demands to load the upper house with appointees.

Game thought that by giving Lang his way it would defuse tension and he had no great objections to the Government being able to operate without obstruction.

The Governor and his wife were active in charity works, visiting the unemployment camps around the city and supporting schemes to relieve the suffering. In 1930 the Church of England decided it should look to some way to set up a charity group to aid the poor along the lines of the Catholic St Vincent de Paul society. Game sent a cheque to the organisers before they could hold their first meeting. This was at a time when charity, or at least the receiving of it, was viewed with suspicion.

Lang's announcement in January 1932 that he would not pay

British bondholders was to begin the Premier's endgame. He told the people of New South Wales at the time it was a choice between 'your children … or those overseas creditors of Australia'.

Lang told parliament that if the federal government wanted war 'they will get it'. The *Labor Daily* warned its readers that civil war was at hand. Few doubted it would happen, but they underestimated the Premier.

When the federal government discovered what had happened to the state's coffers over the weekend of 12–13 March it was apoplectic and no doubt regretted overturning an amendment to the bill which proposed penalties of life imprisonment for obstructing its intent. What would this Lang do next? they asked themselves. He was a loose cannon and totally unpredictable.

Lyons may well have feared that Lang would scatter the money from the Sydney Harbour Bridge the following Saturday just to spite him.

The real danger of violence spilling into the street at the time should not be underestimated. In July 1931 the army handed over to the New South Wales state police 10,000 cartridges and a job lot of steel helmets. Forty years later former Air Commodore Ewart told a newspaper that in early 1932 senior service commanders had been called into an emergency meeting with representatives of the Prime Minister, who was concerned about a civil war. 'The belief was that Commonwealth instrumentalities in Sydney might easily become targets for unruly mobs,' he said. The RAAF was put on alert and Wing Commander W. D. Bostock cancelled all leave. Extra security was placed around the Richmond air base and the canvas hoods on the units' lorries were stripped and replaced with wire mesh 'to protect crews from sticks, stones, bottles, etc, and on each vehicle a machine-gun was mounted with live ammunition'.

At Belmore on 13 February 1932, 700 Guardsmen turned out for military training. Zone inspections of up to 1500 men were held every Saturday and noses of unionists, the unemployed and communists were bloodied by police or anonymous thugs at every opportunity.

The issue of who would cut the ribbon at the Sydney Harbour

Bridge opening became symbolic of the times.

The troubled days leading up to 19 March were thick with dignitaries and egos, but this little play centred around three central characters: Lang; a pugnacious and ambitious Glaswegian policeman, Superintendent W. J. Mackay; and a supercilious 43-year-old Dubliner in a camphor-balled uniform.

And so it is time for Francis Edward de Groot to mount his borrowed, pot-bellied steed and ride into the history of the bridge.

In 1932 the Irishman Francis Edward de Groot was in early retirement at Pittwater with his wife. Born in Dublin in 1879, he had served in World War I and reached the rank of captain during the occupation of Germany. In 1920 he sailed to Australia and set up a business in antique furniture and fine arts, but by 1930 the economy was so bad he and his wife had left Sydney for Pittwater.

'I had come to the conclusion that we might as well take life easy and let the clouds roll by, so we just fished and enjoyed our life,' de Groot wrote in a rather self-serving autobiography two decades later. De Groot complained that the Depression was a 'dull period' marked by 'unemployment, doles, track rations and general misery … a feeling of growing tension'.

As a businessman and a retired member of His Majesty's forces he was a natural enemy of Lang. While de Groot was clearly wealthy enough to ride out the tough years at his country property, he apparently could not resist the siren call of class war. After two years of watching the sun set over the gum trees and water he began to fear that it may well be setting over the Empire too.

'I was splendidly fit, and in no mood to let either Mr Lang or the communist arrange my life for me,' he wrote. He was determined that 'Russian Communism', which he said he had witnessed at first hand in Europe, would not come to New South Wales. He worried that the left-wing soapbox orators, not to mention the unions and the Labor government, were taking advantage of the economic situation to promote the introduction of communism and he worried over what action should be taken.

In 1931 he heard of the New Guard, led by the loud-mouthed quasi-fascist Eric Campbell, a politically incompetent but financially successful solicitor who managed to alienate both the left and right with his brash and inflammatory rhetoric.

Campbell was well connected and wealthy. He had fallen in with a secretive military group that had formed in the 1920s. The Old Guard (they were given this name only after the New was formed) was determined to act as a counter-revolutionary force should the communists get their way in Australia. The establishment group had connections to the military, rural and industrial elite and was mirrored by similar organisations in other states. It was democratic at heart and bided its time in the wings, waiting for the call of capitalism in crisis and acting with the utmost discretion and reserve.

Vain Glory: Captain de Groot poses on horseback for photographers after he gained himself a degree of infamy by his actions at the bridge opening. 1932.

Lang's election in 1931 spooked the more hysterical elements of the Old Guard, including Campbell, who believed it was his duty to take revolutionary action against the socialist government. However, the more conservative members rejected his stance, counselling caution. The solicitor became shrill, demanding the group out itself and take on Lang. He set out to recruit sympathetic members to his cause.

Annoyed by his volume and aggression, the Old Guard asked Campbell to resign. The solicitor reacted by gathering together like-minded radicals at the Imperial Service Club. After a vigorous and beery discussion about the evils of Lang and communism the men formed the New Guard.

News of the new group began to spread, but its gala public debut did not occur until July when 3000 men turned up to the Sydney Town Hall to find out what this movement was all about. De Groot was in there that night and heard Campbell's rallying cry that the communists' 'deadly pestilence' should be stamped out 'ruthlessly and without mercy'. Photographs at the time show the hall packed with well-dressed men in orderly rows before the dais, on which the hierarchy are assembled below a large Union Jack. It is difficult to detect the frayed cotton edges or stretched faces of the unemployed in this assembly.

Inspired, de Groot applied for membership to the city locality, as he was about to return to Sydney. He wrote that the men of that division were 200 chaps 'of highest character' and most 'inspirational'. None of your sallow-faced unionists here, these were returned soldiers and businessmen, fine figures one and all. These were the people who had something left to lose should economic conditions worsen or the political paradigm shift toward the left.

Impressed by his military record, the leadership appointed de Groot as a local commander and he swore a pledge of loyalty to the throne, the Empire, 'honourable' government, suppression of disloyal and immoral elements, the abolition of 'machine politics' and maintenance of 'liberty'.

After a decade of peace and two years of relatively comfortable retirement, this former soldier, like many others, had found a calling.

'We were convinced that ruin was being brought upon the State and upon ourselves by the Labor Government and the Communist Party,' de Groot wrote, and he worried that their opponents wanted to make New South Wales 'the first Communist State in the British Empire'. Every day de Groot would cut clippings from a wide range of publications, both left- and right-leaning, that related to the simmering class war.

Within months of the first public meeting the New Guard had opened hundreds of local divisions across Sydney, and Campbell's outrageous rhetoric and threats were gaining plenty of column inches for de Groot to paste into his scrapbooks.

Campbell and his New Guard were convinced that the federal government, police and army should be on their side. The police and military organisations had close links to the Old Guard and appeared to be natural enemies of organised labour. There is some evidence that the New South Wales police force was initially sympathetic, but it is a mark of how poor a political player Campbell was that he managed to alienate all these groups and other conservative forces and turn the heat back on himself.

The New Guard may well have had an easier passage in 1930s Sydney were it not for a no-nonsense Glaswegian copper, who, like many who followed in the rest of the century, realised that the best way to advance yourself in New South Wales was to do your masters' bidding. Superintendent of the Criminal Investigation Branch, W. J. 'Wee Willie' Mackay forged a reputation for cracking the heads of striking workers under conservative governments. A loyal servant of Macquarie Street, he sniffed the changing political winds and promotional opportunity and fell in line with Lang on his election.

Campbell by contrast was a hothead who went so far he managed to become the one thing that Lang and the establishment could agree on. Neither could stand him; where the Old Guard recognised that violence might be a last resort, he appeared to threaten it as a first move, so unfortunately for these defenders of the right, they not only had the police and the government offside, they also had forced a split among those with similar political views.

De Groot said that it was at the Lane Cove Picture Theatre on 11 January 1932 that the seed was planted for his most famous moment. Reading this in 1957 Mrs Campbell said it was at a meeting in Chatswood. She was right on this point and Eric Campbell later published her account in his autobiography.

Campbell recalled the event:

> A day or so before this meeting Mr Lang had stated that he personally would open the Bridge. In view of the deep dissatisfaction with the State government and Mr Lang's personal unpopularity with so many, his decision was not well received. After I had finished speaking there was the usual string of questions, one of which was, 'Who did the New Guard think should open the Bridge?' I replied to the effect that the Bridge was above party politics and should be opened by the Governor, the Governor General, or if possible a member of the Royal Family.

It was a throwaway line but one that gained traction among royalists and Lang's various enemies and raised real concerns for Mackay, who had to head off any such shenanigans.

One of Mackay's policemen in the audience at the Chatswood meeting heard Campbell refer to Lang as 'a nasty tyrant and a scandal' during the address. Campbell was charged with slander — a move that made it clear to the movement and de Groot that the formerly sympathetic police had 'turned completely in the opposite direction'. The New Guard complained that 'Communist speakers would insult the King in the foulest terms'.

It was a favoured practice of the Guardsmen to show up at communist or unionist meetings and loudly sing the national anthem while knocking the hats from left-wing heads. In fact, its habit of turning up at public meetings to interrupt labour movement speakers saw the group pilloried in some papers as The Boo Guard. Lang, however, was not laughing and leant on Mackay to put the right-wing army in its place. The old-fashioned copper believed cracking heads was the best means of cracking cases and set about his job with relish, breaking up New Guard meetings with the same violence he had used to break up strikes under a conservative government.

A little concerned at being on the wrong side of law and order, de Groot sought a private meeting with Mackay. The Irishman gives a colourful and unverifiable account of the meeting in his memoirs. 'I had the most distinct impression that he had been threatened in some way, either with the loss of his job, or in some way, certainly he was a very frightened man that day, and in view of the close approach of the Bridge opening, I am afraid I took advantage of the chance to see what made him tick,' de Groot wrote with an unconvincing smugness.

Mackay allegedly told de Groot, in a 'broad Glaswegian accent', 'if ma ideals were there, an' ma' bread an' butter there, ma' ideals could go to b—y'.

'I knew that as an opponent he was negligible. I had nothing but contempt for his outlook and thought him undeserving of any consideration should his self interest clash with my "b—y ideals," ' de Groot wrote.

De Groot's version of events has to be treated with some cynicism — long after Lang was deposed and Mackay retired, the captain still wished to have the upper hand over his old enemies and as such is a self-serving witness to history.

The New Guard decided that it should try a peaceful approach and called for the overthrow of the government via the petition mentioned earlier, but it found Sir Philip reluctant to become involved or even meet them.

Eventually the Governor decided to indulge the group, which had gone to the trouble of illuminating and colouring its petition on vellum and presenting it in a leather case the size of a golf bag.

They met him eight days before the bridge opening ceremony and the day before Lang drained the state accounts.

The New Guard had approached Government House in a large mob, but only twelve were allowed in. De Groot wrote that they were photographed by 'MacKay's CIB men en route' and 'I acquired two shadows from that day'. He also got his name in the paper for the first time.

De Groot noted that Game 'did not appear overjoyed during the interview'.

The petition read: 'All decent citizens have been alarmed and disgusted by recent revelations, and by the open alliance of the Premier and certain ministers with the revolutionary socialists.' It was handed to Game, who duly placed it beside another petition calling on the governor to outlaw the right-wing militia organisations. The Governor had little sympathy for extremists on either side of politics and resented these self-important radicals taking up his time. And while the federal government was clearly agitated about the bridge opening, the Prime Minister took time out from pushing his anti-Lang Financial Agreements Enforcement Bill through parliament to announce he would not tolerate militia groups and called for calm.

'The government cannot, and will not, countenance or permit unauthorised military formations in any part of Australia,' Lyons told the country via written statement. 'I would appeal, therefore, to all law-abiding citizens clearly to recognise the position as set out in this statement, and to co-operate in every way with constituted authority for the maintenance of the peace of the community.'

Although he did not name the New Guard, Lyons's timing — on the day the organisation petitioned the Governor — was pointed.

The group's public demands for the sacking of Lang also created a terrible headache for Game, literally and figuratively. A letter written by Lady Game to her aunt on 11 February 1932, shows just how angry Lang had made the loyalists.

Philip is having dreadful worries over the bridge opening but The King is obviously intensely annoyed at the Premier opening it instead of Philip. There are all sorts of complications, but I persuaded Philip into trying to get it arranged that he does it after all. I hope I am right. I simply hate to interfere, but it seems disastrous to let His Majesty be so angry … which apparently is the case. Now we are on tenterhooks as to what will happen, and I will really dread the next few days.

Reading de Groot's account of the visit to Government House, it's easy to believe he had become paranoid about the police and the government, but Lady Game reveals that they were indeed being watched. In a letter to her mother on 13 March 1932, six days before the opening of the bridge, she wrote:

> He [Philip] is in constant anxiety about it now [the opening], and the strain of being surrounded by envy, hatred and malice and all uncharitableness continually is very great … The bridge opening has brought out all these jealousies and schisms like a searchlight on a dark night. You will see by the enclosed cutting that the 'New Guard' presented their petition to the King to Philip the other day, and of course he has to forward it. He received it with great dignity and tact, I believe, and he had the garage full of hidden policeman [it is close to the gate] who very firmly prevented the mob of a hundred or so coming in with the twelve who were allowed. It is the 'New Guard' who under the guise of loyalty have really made things so extremely difficult about the bridge … I believe, but without them it was possible that Philip could have opened the bridge after all. Having made all this trouble and threatened force, it was quite impossible to let them think that they had won.

Lady Game's revelation is remarkable but apparently sensible. If Lang had not been cornered by the conservatives he may well have let Game open the bridge, but once it became a matter of ideology and honour this was impossible. The Big Fella had too much pride to bow to his opposition.

Campbell argued that if the Governor or the Prime Minister were unwilling to stop Lang from destroying the state he would do it himself. If Lang opened the bridge, he told the newspapers, there would be a 'gladiatorial tournament'.

Campbell had also created a headache for himself; his assertion that Lang not open the bridge had created a groundswell of support and loud debate. Unfortunately for him, people expected the New Guard not just to talk but to act. In the paranoid climate, many strange plans were suggested and occasionally overheard.

The government views seriously threats which have been made recently that Mr Lang will not be permitted to open the Harbour Bridge.

Following a cable received by the Chief Secretary (Mr Gosling) today, from the Agent-General in London (Mr Willis), the police will take even greater precautions to prevent any disturbance on Saturday.

The cablegram reads:

In the House of Commons on Tuesday evening, a section of the members interested in Australian affairs, held a secret meeting to discuss the Sydney bridge opening. It was stated at the meeting that a movement led by Campbell, intended seizing the Premier and throwing him into the river, I most strongly urge that you take every precaution to protect the Premier and to save the State from this disgraceful act.

Canberra Times 18 March 1932

The same story was reported in *The Times* of London. It was only a minor matter that the bridge spanned a harbour and not a river but it was interesting that the conservative forces were so horrified by the New Guard proposals that they now wanted Lang protected.

As locality commander, de Groot was charged with protecting the south side of the harbour, an area that included Watsons Bay, Coogee and the eastern suburbs. He claimed 'that placed the actual spot where the ribbon was afterwards to be cut, within what I considered to be my sphere of responsibility'. De Groot recalled later, with a hint of bombast, his role in hosing down some of the more radical elements of the New Guard.

> As the big day drew near, and a number of the young hotheads were not satisfied with vague promises and I commenced to hear all kinds of hare-brained schemes, such as plots to kidnap Mr Lang and some of the boys were quite capable of it too, also I would not have given much for his chances of survival if they had laid hands on him.
>
> One youngster whom I will call by his first name John, and who was especially pressing to be let do something drastic, and whom I had trouble in quieting down, some years later in the AIF, when his evacuation transport looked like being captured by the Germans, jumped onto the wharf in Crete with a Machine Gun, set it up on the wharf, and did such execution that his ship was able to get away, unfortunately without him, after capture, he burst his way through the roof of a cattle truck, and after many adventures, found his way back to Australia, only to be killed by Japs in New Guinea. Lads like him had faith in me, and I felt I had to keep faith with them.

Eric Campbell wrote later that he had 'Planned three alternative schemes and selected the requisite men for each. I scrapped two and put my faith in one involving an ambulance that I was convinced could not fail.' This apparently involved causing a diversion, abducting Lang from the parade and dumping him at Centennial Park. Other plans included overthrowing a country jail where members of the government could be held while the New Guard set about restoring order.

With just a week to go to the opening it seemed the New Guard did have plans to abduct the Premier and was ready to go through with them. Had this occurred, things may well have taken a much

Moving Image: A Cinesound cameraman caught footage of Captain de Groot. It played to packed movie houses until Premier Lang's government seized the film. 1932.

less peaceful path. Both sides of this battle were on edge and it could have been the incident which led to further violent confrontations; however, Mackay's CIB were tailing the New Guard leadership and making things difficult for the group.

The New Guard's decision to abandon the abduction plans and cut the ribbon itself came from a most unlikely source.

Just days before the bridge opened, the cartoonist Joe Jonsson sat at his desk at *Smith's Weekly* and began to think about the controversy. A fine draughtsman, he drew all the New South Wales dignitaries gathered before the ribbon: Lang knock-kneed and instantly identifiable from his trademark scowling mouth that echoed the Harbour Bridge arch; Sir Philip Game in his fancy plumed hat; Bradfield, short and plump; schoolchildren with British flags and behind them a swarming mass.

In the picture the crowd is recoiling in horror as an unidentified man slashes the ribbon.

Jonsson wrote the words 'THE MAN WHO BEAT LANG TO THE TAPE ' beneath his picture which was published on Thursday, two days before the opening of the bridge.

The cartoonist had cracked a joke and unwittingly drawn Lang's enemies a map, outlining for them a plan of attack. Fortunately it was indeed a cartoon act, a cream pie instead of a bullet, at a time of tinder-box tension. Life was about to imitate art in the most spectacular way. A court jester was set to defuse the situation.

De Groot came across Jonsson's cartoon and the plan was hatched.

The whole idea was one of those 'brain waves' where the entire picture presents itself. Borrow a horse, dress up in uniform, sharpen a sword, wait until the ribbon is stretched taut, charge it at a gallop, cut the ribbon before Lang, and declare the Bridge open on behalf of the decent and respectable citizens of NSW. Hang the expense, and let Lang cut it again on behalf of the others if he gets any pleasure out of it. Keep the Captain's promise, prevent the NG disintegrating, and while showing Lang and his mob that they cannot push us around, let the sharp sword be a hint to the Communists that the revolution here would not be a one-sided affair. So many of us had spent the best years of our lives and lost so many of our friends while defending what is now called 'our way of life' that we had no intention of handing over Australia to the tender mercies of the rubbishy kind of people who aspired to rule us, and by this, I don't only mean Communists, we thought there was very little difference between them and revolutionary socialists.

Within 30 minutes de Groot had run to Campbell waving the copy of *Smith's Weekly* under his nose.

' "This is it," he said with a gleam in his eye and a brogue that he reserved for moments of intensity,' Campbell recalled.

De Groot loved the plan and explained that the horse held added benefits. 'From earliest days the mounted man has had a moral ascendancy over another on his flat feet and this particular citizen, aged 43, 5ft 8in high, and weighing less than 10 stone, certainly needed some reinforcement,' he wrote later.

They swung into action. Campbell could not do the job because he would be recognised, but the relatively anonymous de Groot with his background in the Hussars and Light Infantry was perfect, if only he could shake off the two CIB detectives who shadowed his every move.

De Groot had a uniform, a sword, a plan and the only thing this tin soldier needed, like Shakespeare's Richard III, was a horse. It was a mark of the changing times that horses were not readily available. Lennie Gwyther and Ginger Mick were somewhere in town, but having come so far it is unlikely the boy from Leongatha was about to give up his steed, although Lennie later expressed some admiration for the right-wing movements.

It was too late that Thursday to find an animal so that evening de Groot fished out his old uniform which 'fitted all right' and polished the buttons, while a friend put an edge on his thrusting sword, close to the hilt 'where I thought it could do no damage to anyone or anything except the unfortunate ribbon, designed for slaughter anyway, and so to bed and a rather restless night'.

According to de Groot, while lying in bed, he worked out a way to give his detectives the slip in the morning. He awoke before they arrived and moved his car three blocks away. When the police pulled up at his home they panicked, thinking they had missed him and in desperation rang his home phone to see where he was. The Irishman could not help but gloat in his retelling of the incident: 'My idea was to try and induce one of my braves to ask me a question, to which I would reply by telling the simple truth. Working on the assumption that a policeman and especially a Detective has a peculiar and restrictive attitude to the truth.'

De Groot said the detective asked him about the opening of the bridge and a conversation along these lines followed.

'Have you not heard yet? I am going to open it myself.'

'Are you going to be disguised?'

'Of course, I will be dressed up as Ned Kelly on a horse.'

The policeman apparently told de Groot that he could get good odds against Lang opening the bridge and the New Guard's man advised him to take them.

'I was not followed that day,' he wrote.

He spent Friday searching for a horse. Claiming to have spied a young girl on a likely steed, he followed her home and convinced her father, who turned out to be anti-Lang, to lend him the animal for the plans afoot.

Not so, cried Mrs Nancy Campbell from her corner of history. The wife of Australia's would-be Mussolini thought de Groot might have been trying to protect her with his account of obtaining a horse.

'You're always wanting to do something, see if you can find a horse,' Eric Campbell told her that Thursday night.

Mrs Campbell said she stumbled upon a horse ridden by a young girl, Margot Reichard of Telegraph Road, Pymble, on the Friday and that with de Groot she negotiated with the girl's father, a Mr Reichard, who was a French trade representative.

De Groot said the plans almost came unstuck again when, having obtained permission to borrow the animal, Margot came in to announce it had thrown a shoe. A farrier was duly located; unfortunately he was a Langite and had to be spun some story, but he did shoe the horse.

The next morning, Mrs Campbell said, the horse was taken across the harbour on the horse punt to meet de Groot at Fort Macquarie. Perhaps it was the last animal to ever use the service, as its return journey, some days later, would be across the bridge.

However, upon picking up the horse he began to doubt that the plan would work.

'I was not overly pleased with his turn out, here was I in the

Field Dress of my old Hussar Regiment, every detail correct, but the same could not be said for the horse, the grooming was only fair, no bit and bridoon [bridle], only a light ring snaffle with a thin pair of reins,' he recalled.

There wasn't even a place for the sword so he stuck it in his Sam Browne belt and proceeded to ride up Macquarie Street.

> I doubt if anyone noticed me at all. It was from there that the procession was to start, floats were arriving, and being given the last touches, no one seemed to have any spare time to worry about anyone else's affairs apart from their own. Just before the entrance to Government House, and near to the Conservatorium of Music, the 'Old Time Show' without which no big procession in Sydney was ever complete, was also collecting itself, the Hansom Cab., the Cobb & Co.'s Coach complete with passengers, the Penny Farthing Bicycle, all the fun of the Fair.

Forced to kill time, de Groot became nervous when he was approached by the hansom cab driver, but was relieved when the man asked him if he was 'part of the show'. Later a group of army officers emerged from the Automobile Club and seemed to give him the once-over.

De Groot then claimed to have had a fantastic encounter. 'A magnificent maroon-coloured saloon car passed within feet of me, and inside reclining on the back seat, giving a perfect rendering of a profiteer, was no one else but the State Premier, John Thomas Lang. I could have poked a hole in him through the window had that been my intention.'

De Groot was still wondering how he would slip through the streets and onto the bridge when a troop of New South Wales Lancers arrived to escort the Governor-General. They had come all the way from Parramatta and were running late. De Groot and the old horse struggled to keep up and he nearly fell when the horse slipped on a tram track.

He arrived at the bridge before 10 am and pulled from his glove a copy of the running order he had clipped from the paper. Lang was due to deliver his speech and cut the ribbon at 10.05 am. The area was crawling with police. 'I could see them regarding every pedestrian walking about loose with great suspicion, very few raised their eyes enough to look at me, and if one did, I scratched my nose with the thumb of a fur-lined glove, until he looked elsewhere.'

De Groot nervously found a place for himself toward the northernmost end of the ceremonies, which were held at the southern edge of the bridge. He claimed one senior officer brushed his boot and apologised. When the Governor-General arrived, de Groot took his sword from the belt and saluted him and then held it in a prone position.

The New Guardsman was about 100 metres from the official dais and was trying to locate the area where the ribbon would be cut when a Cinesound cameraman (de Groot says it was Ken Hall, but other records indicate it may have been a man named Stan Cross) asked him how long he intended waiting there.

De Groot asked why he wanted to know.

'Because you are right in the way of my camera when the ribbon is being cut,' he apparently answered.

De Groot told him he would not be there 'when the ribbon is cut' and said that the cameraman suspected what he was up to and climbed down from the roof of his van with his camera.

The Irishman claimed a last-minute attack of self-doubt.

It was a perfect March day, even for Sydney. I wondered, should I do anything about it, or just sit there and enjoy the show, later going home quietly.

From where I sat, with the added elevation of my 17 hand horse I had a wonderful view, that every Sydneysider had waited seven years to see, the opening of the bridge we had all watched creep across the Harbour from each side, and now soon we could walk over it if we cared to, and drive instead of taking that old Horse Punt, or 'going around by the bridges'.

Looking down the Harbour it seemed that every sailing craft that would float was out, so were the motor and rowing boats, and I knew the procession that was getting ready to pass under the Bridge as soon as the maroons gave the signal led by the pilot steamer Captain Cook, and followed by the biggest Liners in Port.

In spite of my strong feelings against Mr Lang's regime I might have let him get away with it only for one factor that had quite decided me. A few minutes before when the Governor General had arrived, the RAA Band had played the National anthem and those included [sic] most if not all of the visiting Governors from other States, Generals and Admirals, while loyal citizens bared their heads.

But not the Premier of the State, Mr Lang, he remained covered, and, taking their cue from him, the majority of the men in the stands nearest to me, not only kept their hats on, but laughed and jeered at those who did uncover.

I no longer had any doubts.

De Groot then heard the 'unmistakable' working-class Australian voice of the Premier over the speakers and watched as workmen began to unroll the grey-blue ribbon across the roadway.

De Groot said he then became concerned for his own safety, recalling a conversation he allegedly had had with the CIB detective the morning before when the policeman said he would be at the opening 'with a gun in each pocket'.

The New Guardsman was close enough to touch the ribbon, which was flanked by police, but took a deep breath and moved his horse toward the centre of the road, applying both spurs to cut a path through the officers. The Cinesound cameraman followed the strange-looking rider. He was about to film one of the most famous incidents in Australian history, a short sequence that would be briefly celebrated and then banned.

De Groot intended to burst through the tape, slashing at it at the same time, and made his move. 'I applied both spurs, shaking up my poor old horse in a way he had probably not experienced for years, and then, nearly dashing the cup from my lip, he taught me something I did not previously know.'

De Groot was sitting on a racehorse, animals which were trained not to break ribbons but stand behind them in the days before starting gates. It reared up high and indignant. De Groot had it on a short rein and made an attempt to slash the ribbon by drawing the sword from underneath while still in the air. 'Though gashed, it was not severed.' The police fell back in fear of the rearing animal and de Groot let go of the reins, grabbed the ribbon and 'it, simply burst into tatters for about a yard of its length'.

Harry Peach from Bradfield's office later recalled the incident:

> … my mother, my wife and I were there. Bill Lush had the job of putting the ribbons in position. There was a joke about this because there would be several ribbons used, one on the north

Led Away: The horse that Captain de Groot borrowed from a Pymble girl for the opening ceremony is led away by a policeman after the rider's arrest. 1932.

side, one in the middle and one down the south side. There were one or two spare ribbons, in anticipation of trouble later on … It was well known that there was going to be trouble. There was a chance that somebody, and there was a good deal of the New Guard particularly, was likely to create some difficulty. So as far as we were concerned we did what we could. We had chaps at the ribbons whose job it was, once the ribbon had been cut open, to return with the ribbons that they were looking after. They had to bring all the full lengths of ribbon back.

As a matter of fact I had the job of designing the trestling, which was used on the southern side of the bridge just south of the toll gate, to accommodate the official guests. The seating was just immediately south of the bridge to be used by the Premier in the opening of the bridge. I was fortunate in being able to arrange quite good seats for the opening. My wife, my mother and I had the three top corner seats overlooking the ribbon itself, with the strict instruction that if anything happened when the ribbon was being cut, then Bill Lush and I would go down into the toll gate and get the spare ribbon and run it across in place of the one that may have been damaged. Whilst this was all going on de Groot, whom we saw and noticed on the horse and wondered who he was, started to disturb his horse and the horse was tramping around. We heard somebody say, 'In the name of . . .' something or other and De Groot then with an upward stroke cut the ribbon. He was quickly apprehended by possies of detectives who were all over the place. He was only a little man and they got him under his arms and his feet were about six inches off the ground, and they carried him across the roadway down into the toll gates.

The electrical people had also been asked to design a device so that, in the event of the ribbon having been cut, nothing else would happen. Associated with the cutting of the ribbon aeroplanes were to fly around, there was to be a pro-

THE BRIDGE

cession, some parade on the harbour, flags were to fly and all this sort of business. The actual cutting of the ribbon operated all this at once. A chap called Hadley, he was watching the ribbon and he could only throw the final switch just the moment before the ribbon was cut. Fortunately the precautions operated quite well and nothing happened.

Over at the official dais some heard a small commotion, but apart from those in the immediate vicinity the act passed unnoticed. The dais was too far away from the ribbon and only a handful of policemen, it seems, were aware of what took place. The dignitaries, VIPs and general public were blissfully ignorant of de Groot's defining moment. Again the shrewd organisational hand of Bradfield had managed to navigate a path through a potential political disaster.

The cutting of the ribbon was set to trigger a signal that would see planes dive from the sky in salute — one of which was piloted by the aforementioned Air Commodore Ewart — and a 21-gun salute sound from the shore, but when de Groot severed the ribbon nothing happened. Bradfield had foreseen the possibility of sabotage and disconnected the electrical link. He was always a step ahead.

Unaware of this, de Groot raised his sword and declared the bridge open in the name of the decent and respectable citizens of New South Wales.

Incensed, Mackay, who had rushed to the scene, grabbed de Groot and unceremoniously dragged him from the saddle. The Irishman's foot stuck in the stirrup and he fell awkwardly, his colleagues later complaining that he suffered a bruised back. De Groot would only admit to a minor thumb injury. He was never prepared to give his rival an inch, but claimed the policeman 'received great praise from the Communist speakers in the Domain next day, and promotion from Mr Lang in due course' for pulling him down.

Tempers soon simmered down, my foot was released from the stirrup, and I was hurried into the toll house, where I remained for about an hour, while Lang, his Cabinet and

Cops debated what best to do with me. And a very entertaining hour it was for me.

De Groot wrote that the look on Lang and Mackay's faces made the effort worthwhile.

Lang for his part maintained that he doubted that de Groot actually cut the ribbon. Some 40 years later he told an interviewer he did not see the incident.

I don't know whether de Groot cut the ribbon because I didn't see it.

I was about 600 yards away on the official platform with hundreds of people around me.

There were enough police there to look after anything. Anyway, it's all of no consequence. All I know is that I cut the ribbon again later and opened the Bridge.

The subsequent court case heard of angry exchanges in the tollhouse between Mackay, Police Commissioner Childs and de Groot. The police decided that they would not hold the Irishman in one of their cells before charging him as he would have been released on bail by the end of the day. Instead they dragged him off to the Reception House, a holding place for the insane, where he would remain until a hearing could be held the following Monday.

De Groot claimed to have enjoyed the peace and quiet of the Reception House and that Sunday received hundreds of visitors. He was a hero of the right and his exploits made his name famous around the country.

On his release de Groot went to Nutcote, home of New Guard supporter Mr J. O. Kelly and famed children's author May Gibbs. He apparently took telephone calls from around the world. Australian newspapers certainly reported that there had been inquiries from London about his identity.

The aftermath of the de Groot ribbon-cutting fiasco continued for months. The Cinesound movie of the event was advertised widely and screened to packed houses. This infuriated Lang, who had it summarily banned and sent 300 police officers to raid the 100-odd cinemas showing the offensive scenes. Newspapers reported that the government asked them to omit all news of de Groot from their accounts of the opening ceremony. There was little chance of that and the incident was reported in newspapers across the world.

De Groot later claimed that on being informed of the news the King slapped his thigh with delight. Two years later Sir Philip and Lady Game attended a garden party for His Majesty where he told the Governor how annoyed he was that Lang wore a homburg hat and lounge suit to the bridge opening when a loyal subject would have worn top hat and tails.

However, the Games told friends that the King was most annoyed by the New Guard's comic rebellion. Even the ex-servicemen's association decried the act in the local newspapers.

Mackay, who was promoted to acting metropolitan superintendent at the end of March, and de Groot met again at the court case a few months later. The New South Wales police showed just how upset they still were over the bridge incident and set upon the New Guardsmen who gathered outside the courthouse, giving some a fearful beating.

The police had taken to military drills themselves in city parks and gardens, an ostentatious show of force aimed squarely at the New Guard.

Less than a month after the bridge opening, Lang was finally dismissed by the governor over the bonds issue. When Lang received the news he went without a fight, telling a reporter who was on hand at the time, 'Well, I must be going. I am no longer Premier, but a free man. I have attempted to do my duty.'

De Groot, too, bowed out of the New Guard, following a sensational court case when members of the organisation were found to have beaten a local alderman. A police raid, led by Mackay, found Ku Klux Klan type clothing in the organisation's possession, which further damaged its public reputation.

The bridge, however, was only just getting into stride.

Lady Game wrote to her mother about the ceremony:

It really was far better done than we expected, quite dignified and well arranged … As we waited for the GG to arrive, Mr Lang said to me in a cross childish voice: 'That's the only thing I'm afraid of — the Governor-General coming in — it's *our* show, not *his*. It's a State thing.' … speeches were made, most of them dull, and far longer than necessary. The sun was broiling, and I felt quite anxious for Mr Kitson, who has come out from home for the ceremony, to represent the firm who built the bridge, and is such a nice man, and who is very bald, so that the sun struck on his bare head with *fury* as he read his speech, which was a particularly charming one.

Well, just as the first speeches began after Philip's, there was a violent commotion a little way up the road, and one's heart rather jumped in one's throat as one thought of the 'New Guard' and we saw a riderless horse and a struggle in the crowd, and a moment later the news came through that one of the escort had cut the ribbon … A little later still we heard that it was *not* one of the escort, but a man dressed very like one, who had joined in with them unnoticed, and was one of the members of the 'New Guard' who had presented the petition to Philip the other day, called de Groot, an Irishman. The police arrested him at once, and got him away and the merciful thing was that owing to the real foresight of Dr Bradfield, the electric charge which was to connect the ribbon with the bomb that went off and gave the signal to the 21 guns to be fired, was not connected. So nothing happened beyond a slight fuss and when the moment came for Mr Lang to cut it, it was joined again and connected by electricity and the guns fired, and the bridge was opened. I don't think anyone could pay much attention to such a silly incident, and most people think it will finish the 'NG'.

Indeed, it did. Within a few months the New Guard began to disintegrate; de Groot took his sword and returned to Ireland. Almost 75 years later the sword was rediscovered and brought back to Australia.

> Even on the eve of celebrations marking the consummation of a truly great enterprise the significance of the occasion is somewhat distorted by excessive attention to gnome-like figures that lit across the stage. Yet it is salutary to contrast the permanence of the Bridge and all it symbolises with the ephemerality of issues and conditions that to some extent subdue the festive spirit. The Bridge was commenced in one financial era and finished in another. It spans, as it were, that chasm between the prosperity of yesterday and the depression of today. Part of its symbolism is that it reaches the other side. So too, will Sydney and the rest of Australia find safe conduct over the Bay of Despond on the Bridge of Faith, whose concrete is the inflexible will of the people and whose steel is reinforced with the national courage. What, in the history of such a bridge, is one depression.
>
> *The Age* Friday 18 March 1932

13

THE PEOPLE'S BRIDGE

They might have been hungry but there was no way
anybody in Sydney would miss the greatest show
the city had ever seen. An incredible exodus of
people leaves the suburbs deserted as an estimated
one million people flock to see the bridge opening.
They even get to see little Lennie.

Nor is there any strong sense of realisation that the vampire city, of which this Bridge is so complete a symbol, is sucking the lifeblood out of the suffering country. We have not learned our lesson, many of us, because we will not. The easy money on which we lived riotously has gone; yet we want to go on living riotously. Our hundreds of thousands of unemployed are proof that, without this easy money, our natural wealth and national income are insufficient to maintain the old standards.

The Bulletin 16 March 1932

Today North Sydney and the city will join hands across the harbour. The dreams of fifty years will be fulfilled. The bridge is a triumph of engineering. Science is at an apotheosis in a work such as this. A world of scientific knowledge has been poured into it.

Sydney Morning Herald 19 March 1932

Rigger Tom Evans had watched the crowds grow at Circular Quay from his privileged position above the harbour. He asked workmates

what the down-hearted men were doing and was told they were collecting the dole or unemployment payments. He had never heard of such a thing and could barely contemplate what it meant to be unemployed, having worked on the bridge since construction began — back when the economy was robust and everybody had jobs.

By March 1932 Evans and the last of his fellow workers had downed tools and finished their work and on the nineteenth they marched in proud formation before hundreds of thousands of spectators during the opening celebrations, their years of effort finally complete and the spectacular result towering above them. Australians, however, have a particularly black sense of humour and there was one refrain that rose above the cheers.

'I remember many girls singing out while we were walking in the procession, "You'll soon be on the dole mate." Little did I ever realise I would be on it. It was the most meanest thing ever I thought of, that dole,' Evans said later.

Second Chance: After Captain de Groot's act the ribbon was repaired so Premier Jack Lang could officially cut it and announce the bridge open. 1932.

Within months the former bridge builder was taking a sugar sack from shop to shop begging for food to feed his children. When a doctor recommended his malnourished baby be fed three bottles of milk a week he had to create a scene at the rations office because the regulations said children could only get coupons for one bottle. To make matters worse his landlord dragged him to court for not paying the rent. Granted three months' grace because of his situation, he bided his time before fleeing in the middle of the night, the rent unpaid and the future uncertain.

Singing in the Rain: The children of Sydney were invited to take part in their own opening ceremony three days before the official event. March 1932.

The opening celebrations for the greatest and most costly engineering achievement in the history of modern Australia could not have been more badly timed, falling as they did in the blackest moment of a crippling depression. To some it seemed as inappropriate as dancing at a funeral.

Church leaders denounced the planned public holiday as obscene. Mealy-mouthed editorialists took the opportunity to point out that the bridge was the perfect example of what damage the

THE BRIDGE

'vampire city' and its profligate ways had done to the country; the bridge to them was an expensive piece of cosmetic surgery wasted on a chronically ill man. And, of course, federal and opposition politicians heaped scorn upon the government and people of New South Wales for daring to celebrate their achievement, particularly if they planned to celebrate it without inviting them or their king.

The histrionics of the New Guard, Premier Jack Lang and the establishment obsessed some in the early months of 1932, but they were, in effect, distractions from a more serious state of affairs for the citizens of New South Wales. Lang's government was reeling from a series of blows and was on its last legs. Sydney accounted for over half of the state's unemployed, businesses went bankrupt at an alarming rate, construction had slowed from 100 building approvals in 1930 to just six in 1932. In Brighton Le Sands, Rockdale, Long Bay, La Perouse and Clontarf thousands of unemployed and homeless families lived in shantytowns, fed by the churches who lured the poor to religious services with the promise of clothes and food. Almost half the male population of Redfern and Alexandria had no work. That year the New South Wales government would spend £7 million on food relief but still many were forced to beg.

Things were so tough even the banks showed some heart, allowing a moratorium on mortgage repayments and even assisting some customers with the payment of rates. The real estate market was so flat the bankers would have been unable to realise their debt by the seizure and sale of homes.

These were desperate times. Some who attended the opening of the Sydney Harbour Bridge had a door to pull closed behind them, a job to attend on Monday and food in their ice chest, but at least one family in every three had no wage to look forward to, many no doubt listened to the bands and speeches with stomachs rumbling from hunger, and thousands returned to homes that were little more than a few pieces of tin and timber.

Somebody dubbed the bridge the Iron Lung because its continued construction at least gave people a job. In the later years those who worked paid an unemployment tax to help those who could not and as things grew worse hours were reduced so that more men could be employed on the one task.

Norm Schofield, a plasterer who put the finishing touches to the approaches, remembers the system:

> It was Depression time and jobs weren't easy. All the plasterers used to go down to the union rooms and put their names on the roster. As the roster moved, barometer like, they took you on when your name came to the top. That is how I got involved with the Main Roads Department. Well on our section there were … between ten and fourteen. We worked three weeks and then we stood down for a week while somebody else took our place. That is how they spread the job out for more plasterers to get a job out of it. My wages in those days were four pounds six shillings a week and we paid a shilling in the pound wages tax, or unemployed tax. It was a tax that Mr Lang had put on, doing his best to keep everybody employed and that was it.

While some of the final bridge workers were included in the opening ceremony, the thousands who had worked on it over the years had spread far and wide in search of employment. Charles Brown wasn't on the bridge that day, but he was under one.

> Well at the end of 1931 we were in the depth of the Depression. I finished up there with my last week's pay. I think also because I was about three months short of the five years that I was indentured to I got, as I remember, about fifty pounds. That is what I had. My father was unemployed, he had been thrown out of employment, he was a victim of the Depression at that time. I being a fully-fledged tradesman then, full of hope, went around a few of the steel fabrication shops at the time. I remember going to Sydney Steel looking for a job and they chased me out of the bloody place. There was no hope at all of getting a job.

Rather than stop home under the conditions that existed then, I took to the bush. My first stop was Albury. From there, with a cousin of mine, we travelled through to Victoria and other parts carrying our swag. In fact on the day that the bridge was opened, 19 March 1932, I was camped under another much smaller bridge. It was the bridge over the Campaspe River at Elmore in Victoria.

As I say I finished up on the bridge without too much fuss, without too much glory. With a great future behind me and a wide open road in front of me.

In 1982, on the fiftieth anniversary of the bridge, a caller to a Sydney radio station recalled attending the children's day celebrations.

We were poor, but my parents weren't going to let me miss children's day. We set off at 6.30 in the morning to walk the eight miles to town — me to march with the children and mum and dad to watch.

I was barefooted and mum had a small parcel under her arm. When we got to the assembly point she opened the parcel and out came a brand new pair of sandshoes — I was so proud and so grateful. To me the bridge will always mean my first pair of sandshoes bought with sacrifice.

In March 1932 the Iron Lung had breathed its last gasp, but nothing was going to stop Lang, Bradfield or Sydney celebrating the great achievement.

For at least one day in that bleak year the cloying humidity of the depression lifted and a fresh breeze blew across the city. Moods brightened. The heavy emotional weight eased, pulses quickened and despite the hunger in many stomachs life was good again.

The people found their best clothes, they turned out from the shantytowns, the working-class inner city suburbs, the mansions and the hovels. They marched, as one, in bustling armies toward the harbour, taking up any vantage point possible. The rest of Sydney was a ghost town.

The central business district had never seen such a gathering. One *Sydney Morning Herald* reporter hired a light plane to view the celebrations above. He was struck by the contrast between the deserted suburbs he called the 'streets of the dead', where 'no pedestrian, no motorist is to be seen. Streets and houses and backyards, devoid of life' and the incredible crush flowing back from the bridge and into the city.

No matter how tough times were, Sydney and much of Australia was intent on celebrating its bridge.

It is hard to imagine a public event, before or since, which has attracted such interest and almost unanimous involvement. The whole town gathered around the harbour for the 'greatest pageant in Sydney's history'. Anybody of that age will tell you they were there; in fact it would be quite a unique boast to say you were healthy and in town on 19 March 1932 and did not attend the Sydney Harbour Bridge celebrations.

> A great surging human tide from early morning onward swept the city streets … Rapidly increasing in density as the morning wore on, the crowds thronged into every niche and corner that could give them a viewpoint for the procession. The whole of the route was lined with cheering and applauding people, packed into all available areas — a vast good-natured, happily expectant throng. Some places, notably along College-street, which gave a good view of the approach of the pageant before it turned into park-street were dense masses of perspiring humanity.
>
> *Sydney Morning Herald*

Similar scenes were repeated on either side of the bridge. A combination of the heat and the crowds caused a nightmare for ambulance staff, who treated over 1000 people. At times the sick were passed over the heads of the crowd so they could get medical treatment.

Authorities estimate that when the ribbons were cut and the carriageway thrown open one million people crossed the bridge by foot, tram, train and, later, motor vehicle.

Lennie Gwyther had long planned his visit, but he wasn't the only interstate visitor to Sydney that day.

The *Argus* of 15 March 1932 reported that 'eight special trains will leave Spencer street for Sydney today and tomorrow carrying about 3,500 Victorian visitors who will attend the opening of the harbour bridge. In addition a special train from Adelaide will pass through Melbourne today, carrying 230 South Australians to Sydney … The trains will leave from the platforms opposite the Bourke St entrance to Spencer St.'

Big Times: Almost the entire population of Sydney, huge numbers from around New South Wales and thousands from interstate came to town for the opening ceremony. March 1932.

In another letter to the same paper:

Sir—The Association of Victorians has taken rooms on the first floor, 230 Pitt street, Sydney, between Market and Park streets, where visitors will be made at home. … light meals, Melbourne papers, writing materials, information on tours … Several entertainments will be held by the association, mainly the Victorian's first annual dance at Ciro's café, 174 King Street, Sydney, on Tuesday March 22, proceeds of which will go towards making the association's room a permanent address. No space at the official opening of the bridge has been granted for Victorians. Yours &c.

    A McWhinney Hon. Sec. Sydney. March 12

As the big day approached, Melbourne newspapers even carried reports which claimed the local police had nothing to do. The *Argus* noted that:

For two days there has been a surprising lull in the activities of criminals in Melbourne. This was attributed by one officer of the police force yesterday to the migration of criminals to Sydney for the opening of the bridge. Such an occasion provides particular opportunities for pickpockets, confidence men and other types of criminal. For 30 hours the wireless patrols were not required to investigate a complaint, and there was no parade of criminals at the city watch house yesterday morning … an unusually small number of accidents also has occurred in the city and suburbs this week.

The southern state could later boast that the first person arrested on the bridge was a Victorian pickpocket who had tried to relieve an elderly man of his wallet.

It must have been with some sense of mischief that the *Bombala Times* reported that 'trips to the Harbour Bridge opening are being postponed by residents wishing to see the steer riding at the

Bombala Show on the 10th March'. The claim could perhaps be taken as seriously as the warning from Archdeacon Hirst at the town's St Matthias' Church the week before when he told his flock:

> The plain facts are these: it cost too much; it is not and has never been indispensable; in its gigantic proportions it is a fitting symbol of the extravagance which has been the undoing of this State; and we propose to hold it up as an object of veneration at a time when outside our shores the guns of war resound with menace for Australia, and within the border hungry men are tramping everywhere in search of the means of subsistence.

The mean-spirited were abroad and alive to the symbolism of the bridge, whose budget blow-out made it an easy target. These early economic rationalists viewed public works as a symbol of the dangers of state enterprise. The *Bulletin* noted that the privately owned ferry services had done an adequate job but the forces of state wished to consolidate and control.

Lang's decision to proclaim Friday a holiday — on the eve of the Easter break — caused outrage among church and civic leaders. The *Bulletin's* leader three days before the opening of the bridge was extraordinarily negative and pessimistic.

> Had we been self-contained, had we established great manufacturing industries, the accumulation of half, and in some cases more than half, the population of an entire State in its capital city would not have been such a crime against commonsense. Instead of deploring this movement and taking measures to counteract it, we gloried in it; in our folly we regarded this disproportionate growth of largely-parasitic cities not as a sign of weakness but of strength. And in a pride which we had no reason to feel we made mammoth plans to match the mammoth bloat. The Bridge was one of them; the

still more costly underground railway another. To-day these things stand as monuments not so much to our enterprise as to our improvidence and other folly.

If we had learned our lesson, with three holidays coming within a fortnight, we should not have proclaimed still another for the opening of the bridge. But instead [it is] a reminder to us that we have lived riotously for years, so deeply mortgaging our patrimony that we can only pay our debts.

The pettiness of politicians can never be underestimated and even with the question of who would open the bridge left to one side for a moment the opening celebrations had been the focal point of pathetic jealousies and complaints for some months.

R. T. Ball, the former minister for public works, refused to attend because he was invited to the B seats. Naturally the Premier, Mr Lang, was not keen to invite the federal government. In Canberra the MPs huffed and puffed, Western Australia's Senator Lynch protesting against what he termed 'a lack of courtesy' in a motion one week before the opening. 'Even if I was invited, I doubt if I would go to see a bridge that has not been paid for,' Lynch told the house. The Premier of Adelaide mocked the celebrations, stating 'the opening of the Sydney bridge resembles the worship of the golden calf by the Israelites of old'.

Money was so tight and the New South Wales government being watched with such a hawk eye that the whole show was done on the cheap by cutting a deal with the Royal Agricultural Society using money set aside for the unemployed.

An opening celebration committee took £30,000 from the Unemployment Relief Fund and gave it to the RAS to construct a building at the showgrounds in return for the show society to provide an exhibition of floats for the opening ceremony and to tie its celebrations in with the event. Some money was raised by selling off the cinematic rights to Cinesound, who recouped their outlay by getting exclusive film of the de Groot incident. More money was raised by selling seats on the first train to cross the bridge.

The celebrations were given a broad stage by including in the official program the Royal Easter Show, the interstate cricket match at the SCG, bowls championships, special church services, horse racing, yachting regattas and even a night surf carnival at Coogee. In the end the Programme of the Official Opening and Celebrations was packed with apparently unrelated events which began on 19 March with the official ceremony and concluded 1 April with the Artists Ball in aid of Distressed Artists at the Town Hall.

Lang believed the opening of what he called the 'people's bridge' should be a public affair and not a chance for the powerful to promenade, and when Bradfield suggested the Wednesday before the official ceremony that the children of New South Wales be allowed to have their own opening ceremony he agreed immediately.

Children's day on the bridge was wet but by no stretch of the imagination miserable. An estimated 100,000 (estimates vary from 50,000 to 100,000) schoolchildren, specially chosen for the occasion, caught trains into the city and congregated at special meeting points before marching across the structure, which until that time had borne the weight of steam trains but not the restless energy of so many young people. The *Daily Telegraph* anticipated the event with some humour:

If we are any judge, the Harbour Bridge is in great danger today. Between 10am and 3pm, 50,000 school children will cross in an almost continuous stream.

Having in mind our own school days, if there is anything left of the Bridge after that it doesn't matter who opens it.

On each girder will be inscribed things like 'Skinny, the Tell-tale', 'Our Teacher is a Big Mug' and 'Fatty Lee couldn't hurt a flea'.

And there will be cries:—

'Please sir — Freddy Johnson is cutting his initials in the pylon.'

'Now! Now! Hughie! You mustn't pull the planking up off the roadway. That's very naughty of you.'

'But I want it!'

'Miss! Do little girls who fall off bridges always come up for the third time — because Mavis Anderson didn't.'

'Marshall! Put that down! Stay in after school and write, three hundred times, "I must not bend the railway lines".'

'Please, teacher, may I leave the Bridge …?'

Of course, things may have altered since we were a boy.

Despite the inclement weather and a rumour that the children had been asked not to march in time as the vibrations might cause the bridge to fall, children's day was a sparkling memory for all who took part.

There was no rain on Opening Day, 19 March 1932, just an endless and almost flawless popular celebration which began in the morning and continued well into the night on and around the gleaming, freshly painted structure.

In keeping with Lang's disdain for officialdom and ceremony, the VIPs were squeezed onto a small stage and only a few given access to the microphone.

The official speeches kicked off at 10 am, but Bradfield arrived at 7.45 am to make sure everything ran smoothly. The Prime Minister, Mr Lyons, was booed by some members of the audience as he drove to his position on the deck, but the crowd showed it had no particular political bias by also booing Lang. It was noticed that the Labor Premier arrived without a top hat and at one stage Lady Game reached across the political divide and shielded his head from the hot sun.

Lang's speech was brief but optimistic, claiming 'the achievement of this bridge is symbolic of the things Australians strive for but have not yet obtained. The bridge itself unites people who have similar aims and ideals but are divided by geographic boundaries.'

A message was read from the King, Sir Philip Game made a short speech then pushed a button which magically unveiled tablets naming the structure The Sydney Harbour Bridge and the road the Bradfield Highway. Lang unveiled the tablet which contained the compromised words about who built and designed the bridge.

Paying the Price: The first cars line up at the toll gates for the honour of crossing the bridge on the night of the opening ceremony. March 1932.

When it came Bradfield's turn he took the chance to lobby for another project.

> The bridge will make it possible for upwards of a million people to reside in the Northern Suburbs, and when I visualise the future I feel that I was born some 30 years too soon, because the achievement of today will be but a stepping stone for greater engineering feats, a bridge across the Heads maybe, and other traffic facilities necessary for the development of this great city, one day to be the Queen City of the Empire.

Bradfield thanked his family, concluding:

> My wife and children freed me from home cares, and for the past twenty years the aim of my life has been to bring to fruition the function of today. There is something within the hearts and minds of any people which kindle with pride at some great national achievement, and Sydney's bridge is, I think, something to be proud of.

His engineering nemesis, Ralph Freeman, was curiously absent from the Dorman, Long deputation, but Lawrence Ennis spoke with pride and a hint of mischief:

> I have watched its construction from the base of its great foundations to the top of its graceful and beautiful arch and I can assure you the structure is as sound and as strong as it is beautiful. The workers, my staff and myself feel that we have placed the Union Jack and the Australian ensign at the apex of bridge building of the world. We expect future British designers and bridge builders to keep them there.

The speeches were broadcast across the bridge by loudspeaker and the country by radio waves.

Immediately after Lang had cut the retied ribbon, the official party moved to the northern end of the bridge where they were met by the mayors of the northern suburbs. Alderman Primrose, the Mayor of North Sydney, cut the second ribbon and the signal was given to begin a huge air, sea and processional celebration. A cavalcade of gaudy floats representing the historical progress of the country since the landing of Captain Cook stretched for over a mile and took more than an hour to pass. Beneath the bridge ocean liners, ferries and sailing boats sounded their sirens as they passed underneath while aeroplanes swooped in salute from the skies. Hubert Opperman led more than a thousand bike riders. Lennie Gwyther and Ginger Mick led a bedraggled Aboriginal tribe dressed for modesty's sake in kangaroo skins. There were brass bands, jugglers, walkers on stilts, motor vehicles and horsedrawn coaches.

After Cook and the other floats had passed, the public were allowed up and onto the deck of their bridge for the first time and a continuous stream of people crossed, climbed and gawked until late in the night.

People lined up to buy special tickets to be the first to cross on the trains and 632 paid a special fare of 10 shillings to make the first trip. A few days later two confused clergymen confessed they had been the first citizens to cross the bridge after mistakenly catching a train on the Friday which was making a practice run across the harbour.

As the sun set a brilliant light display began across the harbour and then at 7.50 pm the Sydney Harbour Bridge was host to the first of what would be many spectacular fireworks displays.

After midnight automobile traffic was allowed on for the first time. The following day a Model A Ford pulled up with four people on board. It was Bradfield and family. The engineer produced his fare and drove into the city on a highway bearing the family name. His immense pride and sense of satisfaction can only be imagined.

Some years later his son Keith (Bill) Bradfield revealed that the family had driven the car across the bridge a few nights before.

The papers reported three fatalities from opening day.

Electrician Fred Watson, 20, jumped from the back of a lorry in the city but slipped under its wheels and was crushed; Murramia farmer Alexander McArthur, 63, dropped dead at Circular Quay and an unidentified man dropped dead in Belmore Park.

The bridge opening inspired poets and leader-writers, painters and philosophers. It marked a new age for the city of Sydney; while three days before the opening the list of tolls had included horse and rider, cattle, sheep and sulkies, the modern steel structure was a towering symbol of the end of that era and the beginning of a new age. It represented a future where the factory and the ingenuity of urban man conquered the landscape and redefined the relationship to a hitherto hostile continent.

The *Sunday Times* in London announced that Australia had come of age: 'Standing where the first settlers erected their huts in 1788, it is both a superb achievement and symbol of another superb achievement — the making of a nation.'

Bridge Week celebrations continued during the week and included many events directly and indirectly related to the great structure over the harbour. On Thursday, Friday and the following Monday hundreds of select cattle were led onto the showgrounds and arranged in a Sydney Harbour Bridge pattern drawn by the head of construction, Ennis, while on the following Thursday 4500 schoolchildren formed a tableau to commemorate the bridge opening, with the students from Newcastle, Rozelle and Redfern in the foundations, and the Orange Grove scholars awarded the honour of forming the apex of the arch. On the same a day Mr Kunosoki, chef on the *Kitano Maru* ocean liner, baked an elaborate Sydney Harbour Bridge cake complete with approach spans and nearby buildings for the Benevolent Society dance on the ship that night.

The bridge which had once been barely imaginable was now a reality.

14

BRIDGE LIVES

So, now you've got a harbour bridge what are you going to do with it? Well, you could jump from it, climb it, make love on top, protest on the road, knit a crochet pattern or buy a wonderful Coathanger coathanger from a souvenir shop.

To get on in Australia, you must make two observations. Say, 'You have the most beautiful bridge in the world' and 'They tell me you trounced England again in the cricket.' The first statement will be a lie. Sydney Bridge is big, utilitarian and the symbol of Australia, like the Statue of Liberty or the Eiffel Tower. But it is very ugly. No Australian will admit this.

James Michener, *Return to Paradise* (1951)

Before the towers fell, indeed before they were even complete, workers putting the finishing touches to the World Trade Center towers in New York came across a curious piece of graffiti in a stairwell near the top of the southern tower. In black felt pen somebody had sketched three buildings: the Notre Dame Cathedral, the Sydney Harbour Bridge and the towers themselves. The first two were dated 26 June 1971 and 3 June 1973, while the WTC had only a question mark beneath the illustration.

The drawing showed a stick figure walking on a tightrope between the cathedral spires, the bridge pylons and the towers and was signed Philippe Petit.

Some weeks later, without permission, Petit spent 45 minutes

performing on a narrow cable between the two WTC towers and has been celebrated ever since for his artistic daring. One year earlier he had made the front pages of Australian newspapers for a traffic-stopping walk between the Sydney Harbour Bridge pylons. The New York wire walk was six years in the planning. He came up with the idea of walking across the Sydney Harbour Bridge in the taxi on the way from the airport.

Petit had asked the driver which were the country's most famous structures and was told the Opera House and the Harbour Bridge. A few nights later he and a few friends painted themselves black, snuck inside the northern pylons and strung a wire between the pair. At 10 am he began a small performance which included juggling and lying down on the single strand as if he were asleep.

The New South Wales police halted the trains and traffic and when Petit refused demands to stop his performance they decided to give the Frenchman the same treatment they gave Francis de Groot, cutting the guide ropes which kept the cable stable.

The tightrope walker had to run back to safety and was promptly arrested for his efforts. He told local journalists: 'I just can't resist doing this sort of thing, mountains are made to be conquered.'

He wasn't fussed about being arrested either. 'This happens wherever I go. The police come and stop me. When I was juggling in Moscow's Red Square they stopped me and on Saturday in Martin Place, Sydney, when I strung up a low rope and was juggling on it, again they came and told me not to do it.'

With the builders gone the Sydney Harbour Bridge became a public space. The public embraced and engaged with the structure in ways both legal and illegal, ways that Bradfield and its other creators could never have imagined. It became something so much more than a just a vehicle carriageway and entwined itself into the life of the city. It became a place to dream and a place to die, a place to protest and a place to profit. It was, as so many discovered, a magnificent stage for statements big and small. Poets penned tributes good and grating, painters traced its arch across their canvas, revellers launched their pyrotechnic hysteria from its beams and every day cars and trains and trams and bikes and people went this way and that, spirited from north to south and back again on one of the world's most scenic urban transport routes.

In its first six months of operations almost 1,966,508 motor cars crossed the bridge and 716 head of loose stock were herded across its broad expanse of tarmac. What they were and where they were headed is not recorded. In 1932 times were changing but had not changed completely. The death of two traffic policemen and the tendency for drivers distracted by the structure above to wander across the road and collide with other vehicles drew complaints from the police, and the authorities decided to paint a line in the middle of the road to indicate the general division between north and southbound traffic. Until the mid to late 1940s more people crossed on trams, buses and trains than in private motor vehicles. In fact vehicle traffic on the bridge declined alarmingly from 1940 to 1945, dropping below 10,000 a day — the lowest levels ever as fuel rationing made an impact on private travel.

By 1959 usage had increased from an average of 11,000 vehicles a day to 66,000, and the two tram tracks on the bridge were converted to car lanes as car usage rose and public authorities decided to eliminate the trams from Sydney. The next greatest change on the bridge was the building of the Warringah Expressway in 1978 which saw the northern approaches radically altered.

By this time the bridge, despite Bradfield's far-sightedness, had reached traffic saturation point and had become a nightmare of traffic jams and accidents, and eventually a subway, as proposed by many early in the century, was built under the harbour to take pressure off the bridge. The Sydney Harbour Tunnel was opening in August 1992. Today some 160,000-odd vehicles and thousands of pedestrians walk across the bridge every day and in more recent times thousands climb the great steel beams.

Long before it opened, the Sydney Harbour Bridge had weaved its way into the physical and iconic imagery of Sydney and the entire country. For 150 years Australia had represented itself internationally with images of its natural curiosities. Tourist posters, maps and tea towels featured the uniquely identifiable images of the kangaroo and emu or Aboriginal curios in the form of boomerangs and didgeridoos.

In the bridge the recently appropriated continent found a symbol of its new civilisation. The international scale of the engineering triumph gave white Australia something of scale it could hold up to the Empire, Europe and the emerging engineering greatness of the United States of America, which had announced itself with a number of massive projects and was in the process of building the Hoover Dam.

Up until 1932 Australians had shown they could die on foreign soils like the best in the world — and would again before the decade was out — but through the bridge the country spoke of an equally vigorous creativity and industry. In a country with few great works of construction, the arch became an instantly recognisable symbol of Sydney and Australia, something grandly functional and at the same time inspirational, and, of course, something that could be embossed on a tea towel or set in a snow dome. Certainly the decorative and architecturally fascinating Opera House, which opened some 30 years later, is a more unique structure and rivals the Sydney Harbour Bridge as a symbol of the city of Sydney and the country itself, but many who live and visit the city never once set foot inside its shells while few, if any, who live in or come to town fail to cross the bridge, which has remained an essential part of the traffic infrastructure. Of course Australians are not allowed to get too carried away with their pride and soon knew their beloved icon by the derogatory nickname: The Coathanger.

In 1998 the bridge raised its tourist profile when BridgeClimb made it possible for people to go where only workers, trespassers, camera crews and VIPs had been before. Since then almost two million people have donned the grey suits, clipped onto the safety line and emerged from Dawes Point to make the spectacular trip. It is now the number one tourist attraction in the country and the experience rates alongside visiting the natural wonders of Uluru and the

Great Barrier Reef for a vast majority of visitors to the country. Almost 1000 people have proposed marriage while making the climb, many presumably took wedding photographs with the bridge as backdrop as so many do from different vantage points on the harbour each weekend.

In 1987 a model of the bridge was incorporated into the celebrations for the rugby league grand final at the SCG and later transported to a Sydney car yard, which now uses it as its logo. There are probably more kitsch representations of the bridge than any other Australian construction. These days it is possible to buy shirts, socks, ties, key chains and the like. Life finally imitated art when one manufacturer developed a Coathanger coathanger.

The bridge has developed its own stories. Myths abound; many people will tell you that it is painted in a continuous cycle. It isn't. There is a story about a man who disappeared and presumably fell into a concrete pour during construction. There are no records of such an incident and many major structures have a similarly apocryphal story attached. In the 1990s a mockumentary was made about a woman who beat both Lang and de Groot to the ribbon and cut it herself. Perhaps it was the appearance of actual historians that convinced some the short film depicted actual events and many to this day are still convinced a woman opened the bridge. In truth the stories of the bridge are as wonderful as its fictions.

Toward the end of its construction the bridge was known as the Iron Lung because it was seen as the only thing breathing life into a comatose economy in the early 1930s. It lived up to the name on another level by saving a life on the day of the opening celebrations in March 1932.

Dot Dowsell woke on the southern side of the recently unified city that day with a terrible pain in her stomach. It soon became apparent she would not make it to the opening ceremony and, as the morning wore on, that something was seriously wrong. An ambulance was summoned to transfer her to a local hospital.

According to a newspaper report the following day, no beds could be found on that side of the city and a decision was made to cut a swathe through the crowds and carry the girl across the Harbour Bridge to the Royal North Shore Hospital, where she received apparently life-saving treatment.

Twenty-five years later another ambulance came to a halt on the bridge deck on the eve of its anniversary celebrations. The lone ambulance officer climbed into the back to help deliver Pauline Stephenson into the world. As you would expect, there were many jokes about naming the baby Bridgette or Archie were it a boy.

The bridge has always loomed large in the consciousness of Sydney. It is a focal point for celebrations and demonstrations and for many decades was a rite of passage for a tribe who announced themselves to the city from the top of its arch before scuttling away inside the chords when the police arrived.

Like a mountain, the great height of the bridge challenged some to take it on.

For almost six decades small groups of youths would take a route up the steelwork on the city side above the railway line and then up the steep arch where they would clamber into the crows nest with its airport navigation light or simply enjoy the view.

Needless to say many were drunk or similarly affected. Some still go white as they recount the hijinks of themselves or friends. One night in 1979 five men dressed in dinner suits took a portable fridge filled with beer to the top of the arch and held a small party beneath the airline navigation light. Sex on the bridge was not uncommon and the Sydney Harbour Bridge club is the city's version of the mile-high club. One young female reporter was horrified to not only be caught in the act but to read about her risqué behaviour in a rival publication the next day.

The Magistrate's Court on a Monday morning was often packed with cases of primarily young men caught climbing the bridge over the weekend. One, now older and slightly wiser, recalls sitting on the wooden benches one morning after he and his friend were caught on the arch and listening while a long list of similar offences was read out. Everybody but one person on the list had been arrested climbing down from the bridge; the exception was caught allegedly having sex with a pet, which caused some hilarity among the climbers and threw their crime into light relief.

The commercialisation of bridge climbing was a masterstroke of enterprise and tourism, driven by Paul Cave, whose fascination with the bridge was sparked by a ticket his father-in-law had kept for the first train ride across. Cave's company spent years getting permissions and routing a climb over the bridge which did not interfere with maintenance work and did not risk the lives of climbers or those travelling below them. (One of the great newspaper headlines read BRIDGE HITS TAXI — the story was about a taxi hit by a bolt which shattered its rear window as it crossed the bridge).

The ability to legally interact with the structure gave another dimension to its iconic status. No longer satisfied just to photograph it or buy a tea towel embroidered with its image, the modern visitor takes home what many actually rate as the experience of a lifetime.

At least one person mourns the opening of the space above the harbour and he is perhaps its most famous son. Australian actor Paul Hogan found fame in Hollywood with his *Crocodile Dundee* movies; decades earlier he had dreamt of fame while working as a painter on the bridge. He has no desire to return on a safety line.

No. I've been offered it a few times but I can't imagine going up there and being tied to it. I don't know how the guys could work up there anymore with all the gawkers going over. When we were up there, the pylon [lookout] used to be open, you'd see a few tourists up there and you'd start to walk across the top a little bit more casually and sing out to try and freak them out, but now that they're up there with you I don't know how that would work.

It'd be really weird to go there now and the idea of attaching yourself to a cable, climbing around with a group of people, is a bit weird.

We used to get up there in about 20 minutes to get to the top, when you're going to work, maybe half an hour to the top from the base of the pylon, but we used to get down in eight minutes from the top, 'cos you were knocking off. You'd run down the arch, run down the stairs, 'cos the lift was too slow because that was what you did.

You couldn't work if you were tied on.

Hogan says he was never scared working at such heights and said that if you can walk backwards across a beam at 4 feet you can do the same at 100 metres.

Unless it's windy. You can't wire yourself on. And once you have it in your mind that you're not going to fall, you don't.

I chased the high rise [work] because the money's no good 'til you get up to about 30 floors and then you get height money or danger money. You'd go to a building when it got past the 30th floor and you'd stay on that and then go to another one when it got to that stage. No one wanted to work on the low stuff. That's how I ended up on the Harbour Bridge between gigs and stayed there for eight years. Because it's stable.

BridgeClimb was not the bridge's first commercial venture. The south-west pylon has a long and strange history; once a post office where people celebrating the opening of the bridge could purchase souvenir postcards or send commemorative telegrams, in 1933 Archer Whitford was granted permission to open a fun fair in its upper reaches, which he rather predictably hailed as The Greatest Show on Earth. The exhibits included a rooster with an 18-foot tail, penny peep shows and a series of funny mirrors.

Whitford's business was moved aside in 1942 when the army took control of the pylons and mounted machine guns there to protect the harbour during World War II.

Six years later Melbourne woman Mrs Yvonne Rentoul shifted to Sydney with her husband and took up the lease on the pylon with the intention of recreating the experience she had had in it before the war. Somewhat eccentric, she introduced her white cats to the rooftop. The animals clearly enjoyed the romantic harbour views and soon 60 of the distinctive creatures climbed around the structure and featured in the miniature wind-driven carousel. Ms Rentoul installed electric binoculars for visitors and a range of attractions including a replica of the crown jewels and a wishing well. She also sold kittens.

Mrs Rentoul's lease on the lookout was terminated in 1971 as the Department of Main Roads hatched plans to establish its own lookout, which it duly did some eleven years later. It remains open until this day.

The commercial bridge climbing operation combined with a heightened sense of anxiety about terrorism since the destruction of the WTC towers in 2001 has seen illegal climbing almost halted — but not completely. Another Frenchman, Alain Robert, probably did not know what was happening on the ground, but when he decided to make an illegal climb of the Harbour Bridge as a publicity stunt in November 2003 his timing was unfortunate for local authorities. The Assistant Police Commissioner was in the middle of a press conference expressing his faith in the tight anti-terrorist security surrounding the forthcoming Rugby World Cup when news crews filming the event spotted the bare-chested stuntman clambering up the outside of the structure.

Foreigners aren't the only people who have raised hairs on the long necks of authority.

Australian pilot Flight Lieutenant Peter Isaacson flew Lancaster bombers for Pathfinder Command over Europe in World War II and had a number of close escapes. In March 1943 he pulled *Q for Queenie* out of a terrifying nosedive above Germany and nursed the badly damaged plane home through a hail of anti-aircraft fire. For an extended time the Australian pilot was blinded by searchlights and was directed through the danger by his bomb aimer.

Isaacson received the Distinguished Flying Cross and elevation from pilot officer to the acting rank of flight lieutenant for his efforts that night. His citation read:

One night in March 1943, Pilot Officer Isaacson was detailed for an attack on Berlin. Following the attack, and while still over the target area, the aircraft was hit by anti-aircraft fire and severely damaged. The middle upper turret frame was twisted, the Perspex and two engine cowlings blown off, the aileron controls damaged and the aircraft was forced down to 4000 feet. On the return journey, the aircraft was driven off route and held in a cone of searchlights for 15 minutes during which further loss of height down to 900 feet occurred. In the face of a perilous situation, Pilot Officer Isaacson, showing coolness, resolution and skilful airmanship, succeeded in flying his aircraft back to the base. The officer is an outstanding captain of aircraft who has a fine record of many successful operational sorties.

In May Isaacson and his Australian crew were detailed to fly a new Lancaster, *Queenie VI* to Australia, where it would be used to complement the local air force. They almost didn't make it back, losing power in all four engines when struck by lightning outside Honolulu, but the heroic airman put the plane into a controlled dive and managed to restart the engines and regain control.

After Europe, Australia must have seemed rather dull to Isaacson, especially as he was instructed to fly from city to city using the Lancaster to raise money for War Bonds. In October 1943 the wartime pilot, who was basically left to his own devices, took off from Mascot airport with most of his usual crew and some guests to do some sightseeing. *Queenie VI* flew low over Sydney and then Isaacson took the plane down to 30 metres above the harbour. The crew had no idea what he was doing but realised something was on as the plane hurtled toward the Sydney Harbour Bridge which loomed high and large on the horizon. There is no record of what went through the minds of those manning machine guns in the pylons.

Sixty years later Isaacson, who went on to be a successful independent newspaper proprietor, was laconic in his memories of the event.

You know, there's plenty of room, you've just got to make sure that you use the room that there is properly and don't try to do anything silly like going too close to the water or too close to the bridge.

The size of the aeroplane doesn't matter, there's a pretty wide span and a pretty reasonable height from the water to the roadway. I took a look to make sure that there wasn't anything to impede my trip. I was very comfortable.

Isaacson said he had not told the crew but he had been thinking about flying under the bridge for some time and was waiting for the conditions to be right.

After successfully negotiating the large plane under the bridge, he then flew the Lancaster over to Manly where they buzzed the hotel of a crew member on honeymoon before turning south to Wollongong where they did the same thing to the man's family home.

Smaller planes had flown under the bridge before but nothing as big as the Lancaster, and although there were noises about court-martialling Isaacson, nothing came of it.

'My only regret is that I didn't do it both ways at the time,' he said 60 years later.

Isaacson's flight received barely a mention in newspapers the next day. They were very different times.

That same year 24 Wirraways were led under the bridge by Flying Officer Geoffrey Stevenson after a leaflet-drop over the city. Twenty-three of the planes made it without difficulty but legend has it that one pilot lost his nerve and pulled out at the last moment, only just managing to clear the top of the bridge.

In May 2004 a Queensland woman who claimed to be ignorant of local flying regulations which prohibit such navigation flew her ultralight Skyfox Gazelle plane beneath the bridge.

In June 1952 the tragic news of the bridge's collapse reached Melbourne. The urban myth swept across the southern city with breathless accounts, all of which involved hundreds of deaths and either the pylon crumbling or the middle section falling into the harbour. Sadly, Melbourne suffered its own bridge collapse during the construction of the West Gate Bridge on 15 October 1970, killing 35. Freeman Fox, the firm founded by Ralph Freeman, designed the Melbourne bridge and wore much of the blame for the disaster.

Speculation and rumour about the collapse of the bridge have often played themselves out in the years since the cynics of the 1930s confidently predicted the same fate. In August 1957 the *Truth* newspaper published a doomsday graphic of cars, trains and trams being flung in a fiery heap from the collapsing bridge into the harbour. THIS CAN HAPPEN! the headline screamed and the following article began: 'Take a good look at this graphic illustration by Virgil of the Harbour Bridge being smashed to smithereens by an enemy bomb. Exaggerated you think? It could happen!'

The report followed admissions by the Minister for Air, Mr F. M. Osborne, that during a mock air raid on Sydney enemy planes had reached the bridge, allowing it to be potentially 'wiped out'. The paper used the defence exercise as an excuse to agitate for the construction of a tunnel crossing. Twenty-three years later, in November, 1980 the *Sunday Telegraph* featured a similar graphic of a train spearing off the bridge and into the harbour. The headline? THIS COULD HAPPEN! And it began, 'DESPITE official denials, this catastrophe depicted here COULD happen'. The report fretted about the speed a runaway train could pick up coming down the hill from the north shore, guessing that it could jump the tracks on the bridge and fall into the harbour. Somebody should have told the artist, who had drawn a north-bound train.

A few months before the *Truth* article, the *Daily Mail* ran a story from Brian Nicholson, a former military engineer, who claimed he was ordered to plan the destruction of the bridge in World War II. 'We were given the broad outlines for a master plan to destroy communications and supply lines throughout NSW. If needed to stem Japanese drives on Sydney and Newcastle. I was not told under which circumstances the Harbour Bridge would be destroyed, I'm glad the decision was not mine to make,' Nicholson said.

·According to the former soldier the plans involved protecting an area north of the harbour.

> I spent a day crawling around the Bridge, inside the chords and over the arch picking the spots in which to place the cutting charges. I estimated that six men could plant explosive charges at eight points on the great arch in less than a day. The charge could be swiftly wired to an electric detonator near Miller's Point. Firing of the eight charges would have cut free a fairly large section of the arch in the southern half of the bridge. With this section cut away from the rest, both remaining sections would have collapsed into the Harbour. Probably the pylons would have remained intact because the bridge is hinged at each end on massive bolts. The two sections would have swung downwards into the water.

Mr Nicholson told the paper he had experimented with underwater explosives to remove the debris that would have blocked shipping when the bridge fell.

Today, like most functional icons, the bridge is considered a terrorism risk. It is guarded 24 hours a day and engineering plans have been withdrawn from public access by paranoid authorities. Along with the Opera House it is the most recognisable man-made symbol in Australia and attacking the bridge would cause major loss of life and have a disruptive impact on the transport infrastructure. A local anti-Islamic web site established in the post-2001 hysteria contains a fictional story of a Muslim truck driver who blows up his vehicle on the bridge while the Prime Minister sleeps unaware in his nearby home, hearing aid switched off. Structural engineers believe that such an act may damage the roadway but would not compromise the arch.

The bridge, unfortunately, has been a popular suicide place from the day it opened and by October of 1932 eleven people had leapt into the harbour from the pedestrian footpath. Toward the end of 1933 the state government proposed to build suicide-proof barriers along the bridge. The move was announced the same day that Brian Angell, an Indian tea plantation manager, scholar and nephew of Sir Arthur Conan Doyle, became the thirty-eighth suicide.

The fence reduced the number of suicides from the deck of the bridge but forced many to commit the same act from the pylons and approach spans.

Psychiatrists believe that suicides and daredevils are drawn to the bridge to make public statements. To overdose at home is to pass away without recognition; to jump from the bridge is to go out with a bang and may even attract newspaper attention. Certainly there was a period when bridge suicides were common headline fodder for the Sydney papers, which featured front-page stories about such incidents.

In May 1939 Irene Nola Jenkinson, 28, of Brisbane attracted headlines when her suicide attempt went wrong. The lonely young woman had been in Sydney only eight months and had just left her job as a domestic help when she climbed up over the suicide-proof fence and leaped to an almost certain death.

Ms Jenkinson was saved because her voluminous skirt acted as a parachute, slowing the fall, cushioning her impact with the water and floating her back to the top. Her brother said she had only visited him twice since coming to town, the second time just days before she jumped when she said she was returning to their parents' home in Ascot. Her mother was contacted in Brisbane and reported that Nola was in the best of health when she left home but subject to occasional fainting fits.

Over the years the odd person has bungee jumped from the bridge and in 1982, during the structure's fiftieth anniversary, three parachutists snuck among celebrating Sydneysiders and made an illegal jump. Unfortunately, for one the parachute failed to open properly and he was seriously injured in the fall.

If the bridge sated a desire for public statements in both illegal performers and suicides, it has done the same for politicians, civic leaders and protest groups over the years.

THE BRIDGE

In June 1946 the bridge was closed to traffic for the first time since its opening and 20,000 marched to celebrate Victory Day. The local motorists' association complained that drivers had not been warned and wasted precious rationed fuel when they were forced to detour via Fig Tree Bridge. A number even ran out of petrol.

In 1982 and 1992 the bridge was again thrown open to pedestrians for the fiftieth and sixtieth anniversary celebrations, the second event attracting 300,000 people and causing a pylon-to-pylon traffic jam. The half-century celebrations attracted a crowd that was variously estimated at between a quarter and a half a million.

Bradfield had suggested that the side of the bridge could be illuminated to represent the rising sun of the Australian military forces badge; over the years it has been used for many such political statements. In 1986 members of an environmental group suspended a 24-metre banner from the top of the arch which called for an end to nuclear testing. In 1999 Arthur Stace's trademark Eternity was lit large during the New Year's Eve celebrations, just as smiling faces, Olympic symbols and dreamtime symbols have also been illuminated or projected from the steel. The bridge was a natural focal point for the millennium celebrations. In May 2000, 150,000 protestors took part in a reconciliation march across the water and later the same year the Olympic marathon route crossed the bridge.

In Sydney the bridge as design icon sees it represented in various designs for plumbers, electricians, tourist operators and a thousand other businesses. It has been painted in every artistic style, sold on myriad T-shirts and rendered into endless forms to create souvenirs for visitors. In 1933 the *Women's Weekly* featured a Symphony of Steel crochet pattern which was apparently very popular.

News that his great steel dream had been turned into a crochet pattern would certainly have amused Bradfield but the great engineer had already moved on to other projects and had begun to plan his next moves before the bridge opened.

Bradfield retired from the New South Wales Public Works Department in August 1933 and set up his own office in Barrack Street with his son, Keith (Bill) Bradfield, the only family member to follow him into the engineering field. That same month he arrived in Brisbane where father and son took up the task as design engineer and construction supervisor of the Story Bridge. Bradfield lobbied to build a bridge across the Derwent River at Hobart and the Auckland Harbour in New Zealand but was not successful. In 1936 he began work on plans for a £30 million scheme to re-route a number of rivers into Lake Eyre for an irrigation scheme which stretched across four states and is still seriously debated in some circles. Never a man to rest on his laurels, he threw himself into all sorts of schemes and at the age of 76 he lay down in his Gordon home and died expressing frustration that there was still so much left to do.

Bradfield's monument remains virtually unchanged. The approaches have been altered and the tramways removed but the great arch known affectionately as the great grey coathanger stands impervious to fashion or fickle political whim.

As it approached its seventy-fifth anniversary a private consortium working with the bridge authorities began work on a proposal to strap a four lane deck below the existing roadway to ease traffic congestion in the city. Part of the plan included a roadway which utilised the unused tram/rail tunnel to Wynard station which the chief engineer had built all those years before.

The idea would have horrified Bradfield. It involved reducing the clearance for shipping and would have ruined the clean, utilitarian lines of the bridge's design. It was not, however, the first such plan.

Just before the bridge's completion the Premier of New South Wales, Jack Lang, was so desperate to raise a few extra shillings he had approached Bradfield with an idea to build a monorail over the top of the arch and charge tourists to take the scenic route across the harbour. Bradfield would not entertain the fanciful notion and chased the Premier away, just as he had chased away notions of tube trains, multiple tunnels, pontoons and a thousand other loony tunes. The monorail reared its head again in the 1960s when a local inventor got some publicity by taking his plans to the government and the newspapers. In the 1980s another 'inventor and self-taught engineer' was given space to air his plans for a mirror image harbour bridge and ten lane highway attached to the western side of the existing bridge. He believed that by duplicating the design of the original the city would save a lot of money.

Lennie Gwyther made it back to Leongatha after riding home via Melbourne. He lived much longer than Bradfield but he too died with some plans unfulfilled. The young man moved to the city and worked at one of the car manufacturing factories. When he died some 60 years after the trip to Sydney, relatives were left with the issue of a rather large aluminium boat that was taking shape in the backyard and could only be removed by crane. Lennie was planning another journey, this time south from his home across the waters to Tasmania. Ginger Mick was buried in a back paddock near the milking shed on the Leongatha farm.

The Sydney Harbour Bridge remains in service and engineers confidently predict it will do so for hundreds of years to come.

BRIDGE FACTS

Length of arch span: 503 metres

Height at top of arch: 134 metres above mean sea level

Height at top of aircraft beacon: 141 metres above mean sea level

Width of deck: 49 metres

Shipping clearance: 49 metres

Height of pylons: 89 metres above mean sea level

Pylon dimensions: 68 metres across and 48 metres long (two pylons rest on each abutment tower)

Total length of bridge: 1149 metres including approach spans

Size of bearing pins: 4.2 metres long and 368 millimetres in diameter

Thrust on bearings: 20,000 tonnes maximum load on each bearing

Number of rivets: Approximately 6,000,000

Largest rivet: Weighed 3.5 kilograms and was 395 millimetres long

Longest hanger: 58.8 metres

Shortest hanger: 7.3 metres

Total weight of steelworks: 52,800 tonnes including arch and mild steel approach spans

Weight of arch: 39,000 tonnes

Amount of rock excavated for foundations: 122,000 cubic metres

Amount of concrete used for bridge: 95,000 cubic metres

Amount of granite used for bridge approaches: 17,000 cubic metres

Allowance for deck expansion: 420 millimetres

Allowance for arch expansion: 18 centimetres (due to heating or cooling)

Number of panels in arch: 28, each 18.28 metres wide

Record tonnage erected in one day: 589 tonnes of steelwork (26 November 1929)

Amount of paint used: 272,000 litres (for the initial 3 coats)

MISCELLANY

First sod turned: 28 July 1923

Arch joined: 19 August 1930

Official opening: 19 March 1932

Tender price: £4,217,721 11s 10d

Total cost: £6,250,000

Tramtracks removed: 1959

Tramway approach northern side removed for Warringah Expressway: 1966

OTHER SIGNIFICANT STEEL ARCH BRIDGES

No.	Bridge	Span (metres)	Location	Country	Year built
1	Lupu	550	Shanghai	China	2003
2	New River Gorge	518	Fayetteville	USA	1977
3	Bayonne	504	New York	USA	1931
4	Sydney Harbour	503	Sydney	Australia	1932
5	Chenab	461	Katra	India	2007

ENDNOTES

The workers' recollections in this book are taken from Richard Raxworthy, 'Oral History of the Sydney Harbour Bridge', Mitchell Library, NSW, Oral History Collection unless otherwise stated.

1 Closing the arch

Weights and measures quoted in this chapter are sourced primarily from J.J.C. Bradfield's report to the Public Works Department for the Year ended 1931 and figures quoted by Lawrence Ennis in the Sydney Harbour Bridge Souvenir.

'Walked Plank', *The Sun*, 7 August 1930

'First Across', *Sydney Morning Herald*, 8 August 1930

'Arch Joined', *Sydney Morning Herald*, 20 August 1930

Richard Raxworthy, Oral History of the Sydney Harbour Bridge

'It's Gone', *The Sun*, 20 August, 1930

'Battle With Whale in Sydney Harbour', *The Sun*, 12 August, 1930

'Big Whale', *Sydney Morning Herald*, 13 August, 1930

'Whales Visit Ends', *Sydney Morning Herald*, 14 August , 1930

'The Battle on the Bridge', *Sydney Morning Herald*, 18 August 1945

'Wind Storm', *Sydney Morning Herald*, 14 August, 1930

'Hard Swim', *The Sun*, 14 August, 1930

'Perilous Climb Over Harbour Bridge to Cut Away a Blazing Rope', *The Sun*, 14 August 1930

Ennis, L., 'The Building of the Bridge', *Sydney Morning Herald supplement*, 19 March 1932

Neil Conran, interview in *Stanton Library Oral History Collection*, Sydney

Bradfield, J.J.C. *Public Work Department Sydney Harbour Bridge Branch annual reports*, authors collection.

2 A bridge too far

Flannery T., *The Birth of Sydney*, Text Publishing, Melbourne, 1999

Brodsky, I., *North Sydney 1788–1962* The Council of the Municipality of North Sydney, Sydney 1963

Bennett, D., *The Creation of Bridges*, Lothian Books, 1999

Raxworthy, R., *The Unreasonable Man: J.J.C. Bradfield*, Hale & Iremonger, 1989

The Sydney and North Shore Junction League Manifesto No. 1, 1906

Birmingham, J., *Leviathan*, Vintage, Sydney, 2000

3 BRADFIELD'S BIG PLANS

Much of the material on J.J.C. Bradfield's life comes from author interviews with his son Dr K.N.E. Bradfield, Sydney, 2003–05

Raxworthy, R., T*he Unreasonable Man: J.J.C. Bradfield*, Hale & Iremonger, 1989

Bradfield's Suburb, *Sunday News*, 26 July 1924

Bradfield, J.J.C., *Office Diaries* 1921–2, Family Collection

Bradfield, K.N.E., general papers, Family Collection

Darwin, E., *Visit of Hope to Sydney-Cove*, near Botany Bay, a poem

Blainey, G., *A Shorter History of Australia*, Vintage, Sydney, 1994

Paterson, B., *Evening News*, 19 March 1904

Yandell, L.V., *The Life and Works of Dr J.J.C.Bradfield*, PhD thesis, University of New South Wales, 1980

Bradfield, J.J.C., *Lecture to the Royal Historical* Society, Sydney, 29 July 1930

Spearritt, P. and Walker, D., *Australian Popular Culture*, George Allen & Unwin, Sydney, 1979

Bradfield, J.J.C., *The Sydney Harbour Bridge and Approaches*, Proceedings of the Institution of Civil Engineers, 1933–4

Bradfield, J.J.C., *The Influence of City Railway and Bridge on Scots Church Site lecture*, 1926

Bradfield, J.J.C., *The City and Suburban Electric Railways and the Sydney Harbour Bridge*, DScEng thesis, University of Sydney, 1923

Bradfield J.J.C., Linking Sydney with North Sydney, *The Australian Mining Standard*, 1913

Bradfield J.J.C., *Sydney of 1950 and Later*, Art in Australia Bridge Celebrations, 1932

Bradfield J.J.C., Address to Millions Club, 16 October 1933

'The North Shore Bridge and the Traffic Problem', *The Sydney Mail*, 18 August 1920

'The North Shore Bridge', *The Sydney Mail*, 5 October 1921

'Record of a Great Australian', *The Sydney Mail*, 8 March 1922

'When The Bridge is Built', Kathleen Butler, *The Sydney Mail*, 21 November 1923

'The City Railway', Kathleen Butler, *The Sydney Mail*, 20 February 1924

'Our Harbour Bridge', Kathleen Butler, *The Sydney Mail*, 26 March 1924

'Sydney Harbour Bridge', Kathleen Butler, *The Sydney Mail*, 7 May 1924

'Sydney of the Future', *The Sydney Mail*, 14 May 1924

'Making History', *The Sydney Mail*, 1 April 1925

Additional sources: *The Sydney Harbour Bridge Broadcasts of Dr J.J.C. Bradfield* transcripts, 1931

4 THE FIRST SOD

'At Last', *Sydney Sun*, 28 July 1923

Official Souvenir of the Ceremony of the Turning of the First Sod of the Northern Railway Approach at the Site of the North Sydney Station, Author's Collection, 1923

Cash, F., *Parables of the Sydney Harbour Bridge*, Sydney, 1930

The Sydney and North Shore Junction League pamphlet, Author's Collection, 1906

5 WORK STARTS

Cash, F., *Parables of the Sydney Harbour Bridge*, Sydney, 1930

Raxworthy, R., *The Unreasonable Man: J.J.C. Bradfield*, Hale & Iremonger, 1989

6 THE PRICE OF PROGRESS

Park, M., *Building a Bridge For Sydney*, North Sydney Council, 2000

Merle Coppell Oral History Collection, Stanton Library

Sharpe, A., *City of Sydney*, ATR Kingsclear Books, Australia, 1999

Warne, C., *Pictorial Memories Lower North Shore*, Kingsclear Books, Australia, 1999

'Bridge Approach', *Sydney Morning Herald*, 20 September 1923

'Rocks Area', *Sydney Morning Herald*, 2 June 1927

'Those Resumptions', *The Labor Daily*, 12 February 1925

'Doomed Houses', *The Sun*, 27 February 1925

Department of Public Works Correspondence, State Records New South Wales

Legge, J.W. and Gibson, F., *Victor Trikojus, Historical Records of Australian Science*, vol. 6, no. 4, 1987

Cash, F., *Parables of the Sydney Harbour Bridge*, Sydney, 1930

Bridge Supplement, *The Times*, 17 March 1932

7 Tenders

Freeman, R., *Sydney Harbour Bridge: Design of the Structure and Foundations*, Proceedings of the Institution of Civil Engineers, vol. 238, pt 2, 1933–4

Bradfield, J.J.C., *Chief Engineer's Visit Abroad to Interview Tenders Report*, 1923

Bradfield, J.J.C., *Report on Tenders*, 1924

8 Building the bridge

Bradfield, J.J.C., *The Influence of City Railway and Bridge on Scots Church Site* lecture, 1926

Lang, J., *I Remember*, McNamara Books, 1980

Bradfield J. J. C, *Personnel File*, Department of Railways

Sydney Harbour Bridge Branch annual reports 1926–31

Ennis, L., Special Supplement, *Sydney Morning Herald*, 19 March 1932

Ennis, L., *Bond of Empire*, Sydney Harbour Bridge Souvenir, 1932

Webberley, R., *Granitetown Memories*, Moruya & District Historical Society, Moruya, 2003

Stiskin, P. and Unwin, R., *Moruya The First 150 Years*, Moruya Historical Society, 1983

Colefax, B., *Moruya's Golden Years*, Moruya & District Historical Society, Moruya, 1997

Additional sources: *The Sydney Harbour Bridge Broadcasts of Dr J.J.C.*

Bradfield transcripts, 1931

Cash, F., *Parables of the Sydney Harbour Bridge*, Sydney, 1930

9 CHARACTERS AND CALAMITIES

Richard Raxworthy, Oral History of the Sydney Harbour Bridge

Harvey, P. M. and Solomon, B.J., 'Survival After Free Falls of 59 Metres into Water from the Sydney Harbour Bridge', *Medical Journal of Australia*, vol. 1, no. 11, May 1983

Richard Raxworthy's research notes

Interview and correspondence with Con Johnson by author 2003

Interview with Reg Moore by author 2003

'Bridge Accident', *Sydney Morning Herald*, 27 March 1929

'Miraculous Survivor', *Sydney Morning Herald*, 24 October 1930

Freeman, R. and Ennis, L., *Sydney Harbour Bridge: Manufacture of the Structural Steelwork and Erection of the Bridge*, Proceedings of the Institution of Civil Engineers, vol. 238, pt 2, 1933–4

10 DESIGN CONTROVERSY

Correspondence between Bradfield, Dorman Long, the NSW Government and Freeman, State Records NSW

Freeman, R. and Ennis, L., *Sydney Harbour Bridge: Manufacture of the Structural Steelwork and Erection of the Bridge*, Proceedings of the Institution of Civil Engineers, vol. 238, pt 2, 1933–4

SHB 50th Birthday Interviews, RTA NSW

Bradfield, J.J.C., *Office Diaries* 1921–2, Family Collection

'Bridge Designer's Story', *Sydney Morning Herald*, 11–13 March 1929

'Dr Bradfield's Reply', *Sydney Morning Herald*, 23 March 1929

'Mr Freeman's Reply', *Sydney Morning Herald*, 25 March 1929

'Dr Bradfield's Claim', *Sydney Morning Herald*, 28 March 1929

'Sydney Harbour Bridge', *Maitland Daily Mercury*, 26 March 1929

'Bridge Design', *Sydney Morning Herald*, 20 January 1932

'Mr Ball's Statement', *Sydney Morning Herald*, 29 July 1933

Bradfield, J.J.C., *Lecture to The Royal Historical Society*, 29 July 1930

11 LENNIE GWYTHER'S GREAT ADVENTURE

Love, D., *The Jaeschke Connection*, Lutheran Publishing House, 1987, provided a Gwyther family history.

'Leongatha Show', *The Great Southern Star*, 2 February 1932

Personal, *The Great Southern Star*, 1 March 1932

Personal, *The Great Southern Star*, 8 March 1932

'Lennie Gwyther in Sydney', *The Great Southern Star*, 22 March 1932

Personal, *The Great Southern Star*, 24 May 1932

Personal, *The Great Southern Star*, 3 June 1932

'Welcome to Lennie Gwyther', *The Great Southern Star*, 7 June 1932

'Vain Protest', *Goulburn Evening Post*, 26 February, 1932

'Sydney's Wonderful Carnival', *Queanbeyan Age*, February 26 1932

'Boy's Long Ride', *Canberra Times*, 26 February, 1932

'Boy's Adventure', *Sydney Morning Herald*, 27 February, 1932

'Lone Boy Rider', *Queanbeyan Age*, 1 March, 1932

'Dauntless Lad', *Goulburn Evening Post*, 12 March 1932

'Boy and Pony', 10 March 1932, *Sydney Morning Herald*

'The Boy with Pony', *Sydney Morning Herald*, 1932

'Lennie Gwyther's Example', *Sydney Morning Herald*, 18 March 1932

'Lennie Saw the Harbour Bridge', *The Journal*, 16 March 1932

'The Bridge and Gippsland 9 Year Old', *Great Southern Star*, 23 March 1932

'Dad's Here', *The Sun*, 19 March 1932

'Boy's Long Ride', *Morwell Advertiser and Gazette*, 3 June 1932

'Leongatha Lad Done 300 Miles', *The Journal*, 18 February 1932

'Leongatha Boy Gets Welcome Along Road', *The Journal*, 23 February 1932

'Lennie from Leongatha', *Bairnsdale Advertiser*, February 3 1932

'Lennie from Leongatha', *Bairnsdale Advertiser*, February 9 1932

'A Sturdy Leongatha Boy', *The Journal*, February 1932

'Tragic Bush Fires', *Morwell Advertiser and Gazette*, February 12 1932

'A Plucky Boy', *Morwell Advertiser and Gazette*, 19 February 1932

'A Young Traveller', *The Gippslander*, 25 February 1932

12 Lang robs the bank ... de Groot steals the show

Moore, A., *The Secret Army and the Premier*, University of Sydney, Sydney, 1989

Lang, J., *The Great Bust: The Depression of the Thirties*, Angus & Robertson, 1936

Lang, J., *Why I Fight*, Labor Daily Publishing, 1934

Clark, M., *A History of Australia*, Penguin Books, Melbourne, 1962

De Groot, F., *The Opening of the Sydney Harbour Bridge*, Mitchell Library NSW

Campbell, E., *The Rallying Point*, Melbourne University Press, 1965

Foott, B., *Dismissal of a Premier (The Philip Game Paper)*, Morgan Publications 1968

'Default Bill/New Guard', *Sydney Morning Herald*, 12 March 1932

'Mr Lang's Actions', *Sydney Morning Herald*, 14 March 1932

Community Song Sheet, New Guard Meeting, April 1932

'Ban Reimposed', *Sydney Morning Herald*, 24 March 1932

'Guardsman Severs Bridge Ribbon', *The Sun*, 19 March 1932

'Lang Withdraws £1,150,000', *Daily Telegraph*, 14 March 1932

'De Groot and that Horse', Nancy Campbell, *Sydney Morning Herald*, 1 March 1957

Article by Air Commodore Ewart, *Sydney Morning Herald*, 18 March 1932

'New Guard Plot to Throw Lang into Harbour', *Canberra Times*, 18 March 1932

'The Sydney Bridge Incident', *The Times*, 21 March, 1932

'The Country Lady Who Changed History', *Sun Herald*, 14 September 1986

'Ribbon Incident', *Sydney Morning Herald*, 23 March 1972

13 The people's bridge

Richard Raxworthy, Oral History of the Sydney Harbour Bridge

Spearitt P. and Walker, D., *Australian Popular Culture*, Allen & Unwin, Sydney, 1979

Programme of the Ceremony of the Official Opening of the Sydney Harbour Bridge, 1932

Programme of the Official Opening and Celebrations, 1932

Report of the Sydney Harbour Bridge (Official Opening) Advisory Committee, 1931

Bridge of Memories, by Richard Bush, *Sun*, 16 March 1982

'The Bridge', *The Age*, 18 March 1932

'Harbour Bridge Condemned', *Bombala Times*, 4 March 1932

'Premiers Caustic Comments', *Argus*, 18 March 1932

'Eight Special Trains', *Bombala Times*, 15 March 1932

'The Great Harbour Bridge Celebrations', *Cooma Express*, 26 February 1932

'The Truth About the Bridge', *Bulletin*, 16 March 1932

'Greetings from New York', *Argus*, 19 March 1932

'Children's Bridge Day', *Sydney Morning Herald*, 15 March 1932

'Lull in Crime', *Argus*, 18 March 1932

'Senators Protest', *Sydney Morning Herald*, 12 March 1932

'Opening Special', *Sydney Morning Herald*, 21 March 1932

Tableau to Commemorate Harbour Bridge Opening, 29 March 1932

'Over 1,000,000 Cross the People's Bridge', *Daily Telegraph*, 21 March 1932

'Simple Ritual Opens Bridge', *Sun*, 20 March 1932

'The Last Act of the Great Bridge Play', *Bulletin*, 23 March 1932

14 BRIDGE LIVES

Petit, P., *To Reach the Clouds*, North Point Press, New York, 2002

NSW Year Books 1932–1958, NSW Government Printer

'Bridge Closure Condemned', *Sydney Morning Herald*, 18 August 1945

'Coathanger Saved Dot's Life', *Sun*, 18 March 1982

'Happy Birthday to the girl who was nearly called Bridget', *Sun*, 19 March 1982

Interview with Paul Hogan by Michael Bodey, 2004

'Bridge Hits Taxi', *Daily Mirror*, 14 December 1953

Warner, D., *The Peter Isaacson Story in the Air – On the Ground*, Crown Content, Melbourne, 2002

Interview with Peter Isaacson by author, 2003

'There'll be no more Fun and Games at the Pylon', *Daily Telegraph*, 29 June 1947

'Catwalk in the Sky', *Sydney Morning Herald*, 19 March 2002

'Down to Earth for the Pylon Lady', *Sydney Morning Herald*, 27 June 1971

'Bridge Collapse Rumours in Melbourne', *Daily Telegraph*, 9 July 1952

'This Can Happen', *Truth*, 11 August 1957

'This Could Happen', *Sunday Telegraph*, 2 November 1980

'Blow Up Bridge', *Daily Mail*, 10 April 1957

'Death Roll of Bridge', *Sun*, 30 October 1932

'Harbour Bridge to be Made Suicide Proof', *Sydney Morning Herald*, 22 November 1933

'Bridge Jumpers Fined for Trespass', *Daily Telegraph*, 22 December 1987

'Brain Behind Bridge Highway', *Sun Herald*, 10 November 1985

Bridge specifications courtesy of Pylon Lookout™

Tables of longest bridge spans collected by Eur Ing-FEANI Juhani Virola

ILLUSTRATION CREDITS

Chapter 1: p13 courtesy of Lorna Bennetts; p14 author collection; p17 author collection; p23 State Records New South Wales, Sydney Harbour Bridge Photographic Albums (SRNSW): NRS 12685, [4/8730]; p24 SRNSW: NRS 12685, [4/8730]; **Chapter 2:** p32 David Earle Local Studies Collection, Stanton Library; p35 author collection; p36 author collection; **Chapter 3:** p45 SRNSW: NRS 12685, [4/8731]; p52 author collection; p58 author collection; p77 Mitchell Library, State Library of New South Wales; **Chapter 4:** p90 SRNSW: NRS 12685, [4/8722]; **Chapter 5:** p97 author collection; p98 SRNSW: NRS 12685, [4/8726]; p99(a) SRNSW: NRS 12685, [4/8727]; p99(b) SRNSW: NRS 12685, [4/8724]; **Chapter 6:** p103 SRNSW: NRS 12685, [4/8724]; p111 author collection; p115 SRNSW: NRS 12685, [4/8727]; **Chapter 7:** p133 author collection; p137 author collection; p140 author collection; p143 author collection; **Chapter 8:** p151 Department of Main Roads, NSW; p153 SRNSW: NRS 12685, [4/8729]; p154 SRNSW: NRS 12685, [4/8729]; p156 courtesy of Lorna Bennetts; p157 author collection; p159 SRNSW: NRS 12685, [4/8731]; p160 SRNSW: NRS 12685, [4/8733]; p163 SRNSW: NRS 12685, [4/8733]; p167 Mitchell Library, State Library of New South Wales; p168 Mitchell Library, State Library of New South Wales; p172 Mitchell Library, State Library of New South Wales; p173 SRNSW: NRS 12685, [4/8724]; p175 SRNSW: NRS 12685, [4/8732]; p179 SRNSW: NRS 12685, [4/8731]; p181 Mitchell Library, State Library of New South Wales; **Chapter 9:** p188 SRNSW: NRS 12685, [4/8731]; p193 Henri Mallard, Australian Centre for Photography; p196 Henri Mallard, Australian Centre for Photography; p200 author collection; p204 Henri Mallard, Australian Centre for Photography; p209 author collection; p212 Newspix; p219 Henri Mallard, Australian Centre for Photography; **Chapter 10:** p228 author collection; p235(a) artist: George Finey; p235(b) artist: George Finey; **Chapter 11:** p260 courtesy of Margaret Gwyther; p273 Mitchell Library, State Library of New South Wales; p277 courtesy of Shirley Gwyther; **Chapter 12:** p284 Newspix; p293 artist: Harold Cazneaux; p302 Newspix; p309 Mitchell Library, State Library of New South Wales; **Chapter 13:** p319 Mitchell Library, State Library of New South Wales; p320 author collection; p325 Mitchell Library, State Library of New South Wales; p328 Newspix; p331 Mitchell Library, State Library of New South Wales; **Chapter 14:** p339 Newspix.

Photograph of Richard Raxworthy: Julian Raxworthy

Chapter Opener photograph: Phil Campbell

Colour illustrations

In order of appearance in the book: **1** Newspix/Brad Newman; **2** Newspix/
Jason Busch; **3** Newspix/AFP; **4** Newspix/AFP

BIBLIOGRAPHY

Bradfield, J.J.C., *Office Diaries* 1921–2, Family Collection

Bradfield, J.J.C., *Lecture to the Royal Historical Society*, Sydney, 29 July 1930

Bradfield, J.J.C., *Sydney Harbour Bridge*, The Commonwealth Engineer, March 1932

Bradfield, J.J.C., *The Sydney Harbour Bridge and Approaches*, Proceedings of the Institution of Civil Engineers, 1933–4

Bradfield, J.J.C., *The Influence of City Railway and Bridge on Scots Church Site lecture*, 1926

Bradfield, J.J.C., *The City and Suburban Electric Railways and the Sydney Harbour Bridge*, DScEng thesis, University of Sydney, 1923

Bradfield J.J.C., *Linking Sydney with North Sydney*, The Australian Mining Standard, 1913

Bradfield J.J.C., *Sydney of 1950 and Later*, Art in Australia Bridge Celebrations 1932

Bradfield, J.J.C., *Chief Engineer's Visit Abroad to Interview Tenders Report*, 1923

Bradfield, J.J.C., *Report on Tenders*, 1924

Brodsky, I., *North Sydney 1788 – 1962* The Council of the Municipality of North Sydney, 1963

Bennett, D., *The Creation of Bridges*, Lothian, Melbourne 1999

Billington, R., *The Bridge*, Peribo, Sydney, 2000

Blainey, G., *A Shorter History of Australia*, Vintage, Sydney, 1994

Campbell, E., *The Rallying Point*, Melbourne University Press, 1965

Cash, F., *Parables of the Sydney Harbour Bridge*, Sydney, 1930

Clark, M., *A History of Australia*, Penguin Books, Melbourne, 1962

Colefax, B., *Moruya's Golden Years*, Moruya & District Historical Society, Moruya, 1997

De Groot, F., *The Opening of the Sydney Harbour Bridge*, Mitchell Library, NSW

Ellyard, D. & Wraxworthy, R., *The Story of the Sydney Harbour Bridge*, Bay Books, Sydney, 1982

Ennis, L., *Bond of Empire*, Sydney Harbour Bridge Souvenir, 1932

Flannery, T., *The Birth of Sydney*, Text Publishing, Melbourne, 2000

Foott, B., *Dismissal of a Premier* (The Philip Game Paper) Morgan Publications 1968

Greig, C., *Memorials in Granite*, 1993

Holder J. & Harris G., *Sydney Harbour Bridge Workers Honour Roll 1922–32*, Pylon Lookout, 2000

Lang, J., *The Great Bust: The Depression of the Thirties*, Angus & Robertson, 1936

Lang, J., *Why I Fight*, Labor Daily Publishing, 1934

Lang J., *I Remember*, McNamara Books, 1980

Legge, J.W. and Gibson, F., *Victor Trikojus, Historical Records of Australian Science*, vol. 6, no. 4, 1987

Love, D., *The Jaeschke Collection*, Lutheran Publishing House, Adelaide, 1987

Main Roads, Department of, The Story of the Sydney Harbour Bridge, (RTA)

Mallard, H., *Building the Sydney Harbour Bridge*, Sun Books, Melbourne, 1976

Moore, A., *The Secret Army and the Premier*, University of Sydney, Sydney, 1989

Moorehouse, G., *Sydney*, Allen & Unwin, Sydney, 1999

Nicholson, J., *Building the Sydney Harbour Bridge*, Allen & Unwin, Sydney 2000

Park, M., *Building a Bridge For Sydney*, North Sydney Council, 2000

Petit, P., *To Reach the Clouds*, North Point Press, New York, 2002

Raxworthy, R., *The Unreasonable Man: J.J.C. Bradfield*, Hale & Iremonger, Sydney, 1989

Russell, H., *The Proud Arch: Cleveland Bridge 125 Years of History*, Hemming Information Services, London, 2002

Sharpe, A., *City of Sydney*, ATR Kingsclear Books, Australia, 1999

Spearritt, P., *The Sydney Harbour Bridge: A Life*, George Allen & Unwin, Sydney, 1982

Spearritt, P., *Sydney's Century: A History*, University of New South Wales Press, Sydney, 2000

Spearitt P. and Walker, D., *Australian Popular Culture*, Allen & Unwin, Sydney, 1979

The Sydney and North Shore Junction League Manifesto No. 1, 1906

Stiskin, P. and Unwin, R., *Moruya The First 150 Years*, Moruya Historical Society, 1983

Warner, D., *The Peter Isaacson Story: In the Air – On the Ground*, Crown Content, Melbourne, 2002

Warne, C., *Pictorial Memories Lower North Shore*, Kingsclear Books, Australia, 1999

Webberley, R., *Granitetown Memories*, Moruya & District Historical Society, Moruya, 2003

White , R., *Inventing Australia*, George Allen & Unwin, Sydney, 1986

Yandell, L. V., *The Life and Works of Dr J.J.C.Bradfield*, PhD thesis, University of New South Wales, 1980

ACKNOWLEDGEMENTS

There are many who have helped compile this book, not least Lucy and Harry Lalor, who sacrificed many quality hours they could have spent playing computer games while the machine was put to use for lesser purposes.

At Allen & Unwin Sue Hines must wear some responsibility for the concept, and to Phil Campbell, Jenni Walker and Clare Emery. Karen Ward's wise editing translated the author's ramblings into English. Her advice and care were invaluable.

The Bradfield family, in particular Dr K. N. E. (Bill) Bradfield and his son Peter Bradfield showed remarkable patience and gave the author access to J. J. C.'s diaries and papers. Thank you.

The relatives of Lennie Gwyther were also a great help, in particular Beryl Ferrier, Clara Luxford, Margaret Gwyther and Shirley Gwyther.

Peter's attorney-at-football Ken Oldis took time from his own historical research to also help trace Lennie's tale. Thanks mate.

Vince Taranto at the Roads and Traffic Authority was a joy to discover and a great assistance.

Michael 'Showbiz' Bodey agreed to slip some bridge questions into an interview with Paul Hogan and provide the transcripts. A generous gesture for a Geelong boy.

Thanks to the many people who rang or wrote with their memories of the construction and opening.

Peter and Sue Lalor

INDEX